The Con

At the present point in the history of the world and in the biography of human evolution, we find ourselves at a very crucial turning point in the transition between two civilizations—actually two qualitatively different *states of consciousness*—the first dedicated to the conquest of matter and the achievement of a higher standard of living, and the second dedicated to the exploration of the inner worlds and the harnessing of the inner energies with the development of the psychospiritual faculties.

Truly this is the passing away of the Old (Piscean) Age and the birth of a New (Aquarian) Age.

What is really happening, in simple words, is that humanity is now being given, collectively and individually, during the last two decades of the 20th century, a very major "test" in the School of Life—a true and lived Initiation!

The Apocalypse refers to an inner process of purification and transformation, not to an outer one; to the opening up of the unconscious and the Superconscious, to being given "the keys of Hell and Heaven"—the revelation of one's true nature and destiny. Armageddon is the last great conflict between our lower and Higher Self in the arena of personality which will determine our capacity for receiving and reflecting the Light of pure God-consciousness. The Coming of the Antichrist is the conscious recognition of our own dark, unregenerated self and its final transmutation and integration by the Higher Self, the Christ within who will finally "rule" consciously in our personality and life, and regenerate our entire personal world—physical, psychological and spiritual.

What can we do *now* to prepare ourselves for this great test, for our "personal Apocalypse"? How can we recognize the true meaning and purpose of the trials that lie ahead? How can we respond to them to lend our hand in the accomplishment of the Great Plan behind the pages of history? How can we unfold a philosophy of living, a personal "Philosopher's Stone," that will enable us to meet these challenges with strength and vision?

This book offers a program for not only understanding the Challenges of Our Times, but for personal transformation and spiritual growth to fulfill the opportunity and potential of this New Age, *NOW!*

About the Author

Peter Roche de Coppens was born in Vevey, Switzerland. He has studied with Pitirim Sorokin of Harvard University and was trained in Psychosynthesis by Roberto Assagioli of Florence, Italy.

He practices psychotherapy using personal and transpersonal Psychosynthesis with a particular interest in existential crisis due to psychic and spiritual awakening. For the last 15 years he has been a Professor of Sociology and Anthropology at East Stroudsburg University, Pennsylvania.

In 1980 he was knighted "Knight Commander of Malta." He is a member of the Board of Directors of the International Institute of Integral Human Studies of Montreal, Canada, Vice-President of the U.S. branch, and a past Field Faculty member of the Humanistic Psychology Institute of San Francisco. He is a Fellow of the American Orthopsychiatric Association, and is listed in most standard directories. He is a member of the New York Academy of Sciences, a spiritual consultant at the UN in New York, and a lecturer at various universities and institutes of the USA, Canada, Italy, Switzerland, and France. He is a member of doctoral committees at several universities and travels to Europe three times a year, and gives regular lectures and workshops at the Sorbonne University, the French Institute of Psychosynthesis, and various other Centers.

A productive writer, for the last 30 years the Leitmotif of his life has been the study of spirituality and the investigation and development of spiritual consciousness. In these studies he has traveled widely to meet mystics, scholars and spiritually awakened people who have provided him with "living models" for his investigations. He belongs to and holds high offices in several esoteric and spiritual organizations, and considers this present work to embody the very best of his personal spiritual investigations and experiences.

To Write to the Author

We cannot guarantee that every letter written to the author can be answered, but all will be forwarded on to him. Both the author and the publisher appreciate hearing from readers, learning of your enjoyment and benefit from this book. Llewellyn also publishes a bi-monthly news magazine of New Age esoteric studies, and some readers' questions and comments may be answered through the *New Times'* columns if permission to do so is included in your original letter. The author participates in seminars and workshops and dates and places may be announced in *The Llewellyn New Times*. To write to the author, or to secure a few sample copies of the *New Times* write to:

Dr. Peter Roche de Coppens
c/o THE LLEWELLYN NEW TIMES
P.O. Box 64383-Dept. 677, St. Paul, MN 55164-0383, U.S.A.

Please enclose a self-addressed, stamped envelope for reply, or $1.00 to cover expenses.

About Llewellyn's Spiritual Sciences Series

SIMPLE, PRACTICAL, EFFECTIVE, COMPREHENSIVE, AUTHORITATIVE, INDIGENOUS TO OUR CULTURE

In a world and time that is becoming more complex, challenging and stressful, filled with "over choice" and "cognitive confusion," we are making available to you a unique series of books for self-exploration and growth that have the following distinctive features:

They are designed to be simple, cutting through abstraction, complexities and nuances that confuse and diffuse rather than enlighten, and focus your understanding of your life's purpose.

They are practical; theory always leading to practice to be crowned by devotion when followed through by you as the experimenter. You are the ultimate "laboratory" and "judge."

They are effective, for if you do the work, you will obtain results of psychospiritual transformation and expansion of consciousness.

They are comprehensive because they integrate the exoteric with the esoteric, the sacred traditions of the past with the best insights of modern science.

They are authoritative because they are all written by persons who have actually lived and experienced what they tell you about.

They are part of our Western Culture and philosophical and Mystery Traditions, which must be understood if the synthesis of the Eastern and Western spiritual traditions and Universal Brotherhood is to be realized.

This series will reconcile the fragmented aspirations of ourselves, synthesize religion and science to bring about that psychosynthesis which is the greatest need of our age and its highest aspiration.

Other Books by Peter Roche de Coppens

Ideal Man in Classical Sociology,
  Pennsylvania State University Press, 1976
Spiritual Man in the Modern World,
  University Press of America, 1976
The Nature and Use of Ritual,
  University Press of America, 1977, 1979
Spiritual Perspective,
  University Press of America, 1980
*Spiritual Perspectives II: The Spiritual Dimension and
  Implications of Love, Sex, and Marriage,*
  University Press of America, 1981
The Nature and Use of Ritual for Spiritual Attainment,
  Llewellyn Publications, 1985
The Invisible Temple,
  Llewellyn Publications, 1987

Forthcoming Books

Practical and Living Christianity,
  Amity House, 1988
The Sociological Adventure: A Holistic Perspective,
  William C. Brown, 1988
Alternation: The Sacred Dance of Life, with Dr. Jacques Pezé
  Amity House, 1988

Llewellyn's Spiritual Sciences Series

APOCALYPSE NOW
The Challenges of Our Times

Peter Roche de Coppens

1988
LLEWELLYN PUBLICATIONS
St. Paul, Minnesota, 55164-0383, U.S.A.

International Standard Book Number: 0-87542-677-8
Library of Congress Catalog Number: 87-45742

First Edition, 1988
First Printing, 1988
Second Printing, 1988

Library of Congress Cataloging-in-Publication Data
Roche de Coppens, Peter.
Apocalypse now.

(The Llewellyn's spiritual sciences series)
Bibliogrpahy: p.251
1. Spritual life.   2. New Age Movement.
I. Title.   II. Series.
BL624.R624   1988   299'.93   87-45742
ISBN 0-87542-677-8

Cover Painting: Martin Cannon

Produced by Llewellyn Publications
Typography and Art property of Chester-Kent, Inc.

Published by
LLEWELLYN PUBLICATIONS
A Division of Chester-Kent, Inc.
P.O. Box 64383
St. Paul, MN 55164-0383, U.S.A.

Printed in the United States of America

Acknowledgements

I wish to thank Dr. Jacques Pezé for his precious collaboration and the wonderful and creative moments we spent together in Paris, Carl Llewellyn Weschcke and his staff for publishing this manuscript, and the countless students and friends who have motivated its creation.

NOTE: Throughout this book, I have used the word "Man" to mean, of course, both men and women. For the sake of brevity, I have used the pronouns "his" and "him" implying also "her." In selected places, I have also used the form "he/she" and "him/her" to anchor and emphasize the former.

In dealing with the "Divine Spark," the "Lord," the "Holy Spirit" and various manifestations of the Divine, I have used the pronouns "He/Him" and "It/Its" implying also "She/Her." This I have done fully recognizing that the Divine Essence, or God, is Androgynous, above and implying all genders, masculine and feminine, personal and transpersonal, singular and plural.

CONTENTS

Personal Statement

The essence of Life is LOVE—of the Creator and Supreme Intelligence, and our fellow humans—which leads to the awakening of spiritual consciousness. The Art of Living revolves around someone to love, something to do which one enjoys, and hope in a better future. True wisdom is not "making mistakes," but never giving up and stopping to learn.

Foreword

Father John Rossner, S.T.M., Ph.D.

This timely book decodifies and demystifies those great archetypical myths and symbolic dramas of the Bible and of the subsequent Western prophetic tradition concerned with the themes of "Apocalypse" and "Armageddon."

Its author, Peter Roche de Coppens, is an expert in esoteric religious symbolism as well as a professor of sociology and anthropology at East Stroudsberg University in Pennsylvania. He is familiar both with ancient myths and with the adverse social and psychological reactions to them which can be created when they are misused by unlettered modern enthusiasts, whether Christian, Jewish, Moslem, or other.

In quite helpful Jungian and Transpersonal psychological terms, Roche de Coppens understands the "apocalyptic" passages in the Old and New Testaments as "mythmaps" which actually refer to the revelation of hidden but universal processes which will occur when the human race evolves spiritually to a higher, "Divinely-infused" consciousness.

In a consequence, he understands Armageddon, or the Great War between the Forces of Light and Darkness, and the Coming of the Anti-Christ as a symbolic depiction of a cosmic battle which occurs in the inner world of the psyche of persons when there is a ". . . conscious recognition of our own dark, unregenerate self" and of the need for ". . . its final transformation by the Higher Self," a codeword for the God [or in Christian terms—Christ] within.

Apocalypse Now thus interprets the otherwise fatalistic "outer plane" language of Apocalypse and Armageddon in the genteel allegorical and metaphorical fashion favored by the Pre-Nicean (before 325 A.D. Alexandrian school of Biblical egesis.

By so doing, although not mentioned by Roche de Coppens, the book redresses an "ancient" injustice, and defuses a modern political time-bomb.

The ancient injustice redressed is the rather simplistic—and unworthy conception of Deity—as a kind of "tribal war totem"—which frequently has been derived from Cyrus Ingerson Scofield's 19th century literalistic "Dispensationalist" interpretations of Biblical apocalyptic.

The modern political time-bomb defused is the dangerous error built upon that foundation of literalist misinterpretation by many contemporary 20th century Militant Evangelical Fundamentalists.

In Grace Halsell's *Prophecy & Politics:* Militant Evangelicals on the Road to Nuclear War (Westport, CT: Lawrence Hill & Co., 1985) one may discover what depressing things can happen in the real world when Christian Fundamentalists, ideologues and politicians team up to use the Bible ". . . as an almanac for predictions of a nuclear war."

By projecting one's personal and/or supposed national "enemies" into the "Anti-christ" to be destroyed, and by convincing oneself and one's flock that Armageddon refers to an inevitable thermonuclear contest between Russia and the United States to yield the holocaust required "before Christ can come again," we have all the necessary elements for a "Mad Hatter's Tea Party" like none other.

By contrast with that kind of all too familiar and illiterate note from the television airwaves of America, Peter Roche de Coppen's *Apocalypse Now* should be a revitalizing breath of sanity and fresh air for balanced Christians, sophisticated

Humanists, and intelligent New Agers alike.

The purpose of the book is to bring the focus of those from all traditions on a sincere spiritual quest back where it belongs: i.e., on the "inner process of purification and illumination" and away from the misapplication of ancient prophecies and visions from another context as if they implied a Divinely sanctioned destruction of civilization and the end of the human race.

The author views Armageddon as a symbol of ". . . the last great conflict between our lower and higher self in the arena of personality which will determine our capacity for receiving and reflecting the Light of pure God-consciousness.

That, indeed, is the "real" battle which all of us—whether we call ourselves Christians, Jews, Moslems, Hindus, Buddhists, Atheists or Agnostics—have already, or must one day, face.

Practical exercises are provided for remaining "balanced, centered and connected with the Light," while meeting this great, life-long challenge of "Everyman's Armageddon."

Personal challenges here and now are the "earth stations" at which this cosmic battle for the Light is fought every day. "Cognitive maps, tools and instruments" are described for those who want to recognize opportunities for winning victory in this "spiritual warfare" for Higher consciousness, transcendental values, and self-less service in the fulfillment of "God's Plan" for a "New Humanity."

This is portrayed as the true Armageddon which must precede the "Coming Again" of Christ, i.e. of the "Light of Christ" in every human heart. This is the true Apocalypse, or the final revelation of the "Sublime Light of Creative Intelligence and Love" which Roche de Coppens sees even now as awaiting to manifest "Itself" when we as a species are ready.

Certainly part of the task of our true preparation for the Apocalypse—in so refined and exalted a conception as that of Peter Roche de Coppen's *Apocalypse Now*—is our "rehumanization."

And when we are re-humanized, surely we must put aside the childish views of the many false prophets, would-be messiahs, and those television evangelists who would have us believe that the All Wise and Loving God in and behind the Universes expects of us a final "burnt-offering" on the altar of war.

Introduction

You and I, we are indeed blessed and privileged persons! Even though, most of the time, we might not be aware of this and, in fact, even think the opposite! But we are privileged, we are blessed, and we are fortunate* because we are living in extraordinary times. We are living in an epoch in which mystery, myth and magic, and thus marvels and wonders, are being discovered anew and re-experienced after having been declared gone forever by the Age of Reason . . . and in which *we can make it happen*, both in the world and in ourselves, through the conscious use of scientific *and* sacred technologies. We are living at a time when the "rewards" and the "penalties" for thinking, feeling, willing, and living "in a certain way" are being greatly intensified—*we are living at the dawn of a New Age!*

The paradoxes, contrasts, clashes and contradictions are everywhere, growing and exploding into consciousness both without and within ourselves. On the one hand, the psyche and society, people and the world, seem to be falling apart or to be on the verge of a major breakdown: nuclear holocaust, destruction of the ecosystems, pollution, slow personal psychosocial death caused by loneliness, or the lack of "Love Vitamins" (of the minimum vital human exchanges between people who genuinely care about each other and who can express altruistic love); violent swings

---

* I do not like this term in that good or bad "fortune" usually indicates the workings of "blind chance," "random occurrence" or an "arbitrary and capricious Power" whereas Life is so ordered by Cosmic Law that every "event" and development has its *causes* and *reasons* . . . that can be *experientially discovered* in a higher state of consciousness.

of the economic, social, and political systems; class conflict, intergenerational strife, personal and state terrorism; the waning away of the power of the great traditional institutions (family, church, state, education, medicine, justice, etc.) and of the traditional values and moral principles leading to the "me generation," unfettered experimentation with sex, new human relationships, and pills of all kinds, to exasperated individualism, hedonism, egoism, and nihilism—to the Kali Yuga of the Hindus. On the other hand, everywhere there are people who are waking up, who are seeking self-knowledge, self-mastery, self-integration, personal growth, right human relationships, and spiritual awakening. New organizations and countless groups are sprouting forth from the grassroots to study the Sacred Traditions, ancient ways of meditating and praying, to investigate traditional and natural remedies, and to explore new forms of human relationships; to synthesize in a simple, practical, and effective fashion the latest findings of modern natural and social science. Many amongst our youth are leaving drugs, sex, alcohol, and permissiveness behind to practice meditative, contemplative, and theurgic disciplines and to offer voluntary service to the elderly, the sick, those in prison or who are in a crisis situation. The Human Potential Movement appears, followed by the Occult Explosion and the Aquarian Conspiracy. People everywhere are feeling more deeply and passionately with exploding inner energies, and are *searching* and *experimenting* with new ways, many times not even knowing what they are really searching for!

A perceptive and relatively objective observer of the contemporary social and psychological scene cannot fail to realize that *"something* is really brewing in the air," that massive transformations and radical metamorphoses are taking place within human nature and human society under our very eyes, we being both spectators and actors in that ongoing psychospiritual drama. To John Naisbitt's *Megatrends* and Marilyn Ferguson's *Aquarian Conspiracy* we could well add a few more characteristic trends and traits of our times, namely the qualitative transformation or passage from:

1. Exoteric Religion, which saw and sought God in the World, to Esoteric Religion, which seeks God, the Ultimate Reality, in Human Nature, in the Self—with a rediscovery of Mysticism and Asceticism but in modern garb!

2. Analytic and Therapeutic Medicine to Preventive and Holistic Medicine.

3. Education seen as "instruction" (that is, filling the mind with external facts) to Education seen as "education" (that is, drawing out and actualizing innate potentials and faculties.)

4. The Family being based upon "blood" and "marriage" to the Family being rooted in "elective affinities" . . . the search for, and birth of, the Spiritual Family.

5. Looking for Heroes, Frames of Reference, and Authorities in the world to looking for them within oneself . . . in the Higher Self.

6. Love relationships based upon personal and social coercion and domination to love relationships based upon freedom and mutual respect or, if I may use a suggestive image, from being Empire-Colonies to being Sovereign States.

7. The Sculpture of plastic materials to produce statues to Personality and Soul Sculpture to produce character and integrity—an Awakened Human Being.

Underlying all of these trends and traits, however, I see one that is truly fundamental as it is connected with all the others, and that is:

The Passage From Unconscious to Conscious Living!

Our Age which has rightly been called the Age of Anxiety and Insecurity or the Psychological Age by some of our greatest social scientists could also be seen as the Age of Spiritual Awakening and the Age of Psychosocial Transformation or Metamorphosis. One thing both clear and certain is that we now stand at a truly vital crossroad of human evolution, at the Archimedean point where two states of consciousness face and confront each other: the past characterized by the conquest of matter and the search for personal power, and the future characterized by the exploration of the inner worlds, the mastery and harnessing of the bio-psychospiritual energies, and the unfoldment of the psychospiritual faculties—by the search for *love* and *right relations*. Here, the astronauts of today will become the psychonauts, or endonauts, of tomorrow as journeys in the outer Universe will be followed by journeys in the inner Universe, by explorations and voyages into the Unconscious (hell), the Subconscious (purgatory), and the Superconscious (heaven). The keynote of the education of the future will not be to prepare people to function in *one world*: the outer, physical and social world, but to function in *two worlds*: the outer and the inner, psychic and spiritual worlds. Thus, it will be *personal psychospiritual transformation*: the expansion, deepening and heightening of our consciousness and the slow but organic *metamorphosis of our being*. Here, we will be called to face God and the Devil, the Self and the Shadow, the Higher and the lower self, in the arena of *one's being* as well as *in the world*. And we will all have to become *artists* . . . the artists of our being, of our consciousness, of our character, and engage in personality and soul sculpture!

Up until the time of F. Hegel and of K. Marx, the basic injunction of philosophy was to *"know history* so as to *understand the unfoldment of events in the world,"* then it became to *"know history* so as to *change* and *make* the *events of the world,"* but today, it might well be to *"know oneself and history* so as to perfect and complete *the creation of the self and of the world."*

If the major characteristic of our times is, indeed, "the passage from unconscious to conscious living," let us then briefly put it under a microscope to see what it entails. It implies:

1. Knowing oneself and knowing the world so as to *integrate* and *synthesize* personal biography with world history, what happens and what we make happen in ourselves and in the world.

2. Acting in a responsible way, that is: realizing that we are responsible for what we think, what we feel, what we imagine, and what we want as well as for what we say and what we do; and that we are the *co-creators* of our being and destiny with God so that we indeed "reap what we sow," that there are causes and reasons for all that happens to us which can be found in a higher state of consciousness.

   Hence, that it is futile to blame our parents, society, fate, God, or whatever external agents we may think of, for what we *are* and how we *live*—that our being and our destiny can be affected and transformed by what we think, feel, will, imagine, say, and do—by conscious effort, voluntary suffering . . . and joyous being! This realization gives us both *hope* and the *knowledge* that we must go to work in a *constructive, balanced,* and *productive way* if we want to be better persons living in a better world.

3. Knowing and applying the laws of personal hygiene and of holistic health.

4. Being able to move up and down the elevator of our consciousness, toward the Superconscious as well as toward the Unconscious, to integrate *consciously* all of their materials and energies in our Field of Consciousness—to "find the keys of Heaven and Hell."

5. Bringing together and being able to synthesize the great polarities of:
   a. Individuality and Universality
   b. Egoism and Altruism
   c. Work and Relaxation
   d. Joy and Sorrow
   e. Extraversion and Introversion
   f. Supraversion and Infraversion
   g. Male and Female principles

6. The ability to work upon and regenerate our *Minds, Hearts,* and *Wills* with the Light, Fire, and Life of the Divine Spark, so as to truly know, dare, do, . . . and remain silent!

7. The ability to remain *balanced, centered,* and *connected* with the Light amidst all the trials, tests, and vicissitudes of Life, and of the great "exam" or "Initiation" of the end of this century.

In summary, it means to find and create a personal and effective philosophy of life and art of living—the legendary Philosopher's Stone—enabling us to face and cope with every possible situation that life might present us with, and to *accept* and *integrate,* consciously and productively, all the parts and aspects of our being and all the events and situations of life in the world. At the "micro" or personal level, it involves understanding and practicing what I call emotional purification, mental clarification, personal consecration, visionary unfoldment, and the opening of the intuition—*training and coordinating the "muscles of our consciousness."* At the "macro" or world level, it implies being able to understand and face what has traditionally, and symbolically, been called the Apocalypse, Armageddon, the coming of the Antichrist, and the Second Coming of Christ—*the great "passage," purification, or initiation of our times!*

The great challenge of our times can thus be stated succinctly as:

> *Developing our spiritual consciousness to rise to the next great stage of human evolution and thus consciously complete and perfect the creation of ourselves and of the world!*

The big question then is: How can one achieve this, answer this challenge, and be helped in this Great Work? Fundamental questions, of course, have many answers, but I shall briefly share my personal answer and the answer I hope you will share with us.

This is the third book that I have written for the *Llewellyn Spiritual Sciences Series*. These books, taken together, make up independent units as well as a sequential trilogy which are related to the other volumes of the series and to many other works that are being published today. Did you ever ask yourself why such a title was chosen, what it means in its essential sense, what it is designed to accomplish, and why it is coming out at the present time?

The word Llewellyn, in Gaelic, means "bringer of Light" and could well be compared to the Egyptian *Konx Om Pax* or "Light in Extension" and to the Indo-Aryan *Aor-Agni*, "Light-Fire," or "Wisdom-Love." Thus, I do not consider it chance or hazard (which do not really exist in the Cosmos and which are merely terms denoting little understood or as yet undiscovered laws and principles) that our publisher should be called Llewellyn. Rather, it seems to me to be the work of that uncanny synchronicity, as Jung would call it, or that "inner intermeshing of events," that brings the right people with the right objectives at the right time!

The words "Spiritual Sciences" come from the two previous books I wrote and published through the University Press of America, entitled *Spiritual Perspective I: Key Issues and Themes Interpreted from the Standpoint of Spiritual Consciousness,* and *Spiritual Perspective II: The Spiritual Dimension and Implications of Love, Sex, and Marriage.* These works point, very succinctly, to what I consider to be the major challenge of our times, the very *zeitgeist* or spirit of our Age: the development of a qualitatively higher state of consciousness than the ones (which are sensory, emotional, and mental consciousness) we are normally functioning in—Spiritual Consciousness.

The books of the *Llewellyn Spiritual Sciences Series** deal with *how* Spiritual Consciousness can be developed, with the inner technologies of Psychospiritual Transformation and human metamorphosis drawn from our own, indigenous, Western Spiritual Tradition. They deal with what can be expected from Spiritual Consciousness once it has born and activated in our consciousness and has taken roots in our lives and with the probable impact it will have on our world, our society, and our lifestyle.

This because I have become fully convinced, over the last 25 years through long studies, many direct personal experiences, and much experimentation with people from different cultures and backgrounds (as have, in fact, many other Brothers and Sisters in the Light) that, at this point, in

---

* Please bear in mind that the Series is an ongoing, open, and dynamic one with many volumes to come from different authors living and acting in different parts of the world.

human evolution, all valid solutions to our most pressing questions and problems can only come from a *transformation of our consciousness and a raising of our level of being.* In other words, there can be no personal or collective long-term and truly viable answers to our growing human problems without a qualitative jump upwards in our consciousness (the activation of our intuition, the connection with our Superconscious and with the Spiritual Self, or the Divine Spark within). This central thesis was, in fact, affirmed and reaffirmed many times by many traditions as well as by the greatest minds of our epoch. To cite just a few: "Seek ye first the Kingdom of Heaven (read: the unfoldment of Spiritual Consciousness) and all these things shall be added unto you." Sri Aurobindo and Pierre Teilhard de Chardin, the greatest contemporary visionaries and mystics of East and West respectively, stated clearly that: "the 21st century will be *spiritual* or will not be at all." Arnold Toynbee, Pitirim Sorokin, and Robert Assagioli came to exactly the same conclusion, as have Marilyn Ferguson, Shirley MacLaine, and many others.

If we focus our attention upon the image of the Sphinx which represented both human nature and human evolution, we can see that it entails three distinct phases: the *animal* (symbolized by the body of the lion or bull), the *human* (symbolized by the human torso and head) and the *spiritual* (symbolized by the wings of an eagle). In terms of human consciousness, these can be further correlated with the Unconscious, the Conscious, and the Superconscious. The Greeks, who were well aware of deeper meanings and implications of this symbol, deducted that human evolution is governed by three fundamental principles which they called *Physis* (Nature or the instincts), *Ethos* (Culture or reason), and *Logos* (Spirit or intuition). In practical terms, this means that human evolution is first *Unconscious*, when we are still ruled by Nature or the elements, then *Conscious*, when we have to forge and fashion ourselves by our own psychosocial powers, and finally *Superconscious* when we have succeeded in realigning our consciousness and will with those of the Self, of the Divine Spark within.

Today, we stand at the Archimedean point, or the crucial threshold where human evolution is becoming ever-more *Conscious* with ever greater flashes of *Superconscious* intuition breaking through. Moreover, if "Nature launched us on our way, but did not complete our being and destiny," we must *now*, individually and collectively, consciously take over this process of self-becoming and of realizing our destiny and our potential. To do this effectively, we need knowledge, love, and will, the awareness of what we are, what we want to be, and of how we can become what we want to be; the desire and yearning to consciously participate, not only as *spectators* but also as active *co-creators* of our consciousness and being; and the energies, resources, and life-force to actually do so.

The New Age is dawning, but it is dawning for us only to the extent that we *all* work, individually and collectively, to bring it about, and thus it is a reality for some (those who have done and are doing the work) but not for others (who have not or are not doing the work). At this historical juncture, therefore, the need is great for the Ageless Wisdom of the Sacred Traditions and for the latest insights of modern science to come together in a series of books that are, at the same time, *simple* and *comprehensive*, *practical* and *essential*, *safe* and *effective*, and based upon the direct experience of mature, dedicated, and responsible thinkers and searchers who have tested out, in their own flesh and blood, consciousness and being, and with many friends, students, and co-workers, what they are writing about and suggesting to others.

Thus it is that this series is being created and made available now through the visions, insights, and work of many dedicated persons. Its thrust is both *initiatory* and *practical*, and its contents are both *simple* and *essential*, but whether it will truly be *effective* and a living force in your consciousness and life depends upon *you* and what *you do* with its books, perspective, and exercises—how you apply them in your personal life.

Action, esoterically understood, is a *Cross* and a *Trinity*: it begins with awareness, knowledge, and understanding and it is realized and incarnated through the application of the right attitudes, tools, and techniques, but the vital link between these two components, at the very heart of the Cross, is *Love, Desire, Motivation*, which can only come from you, the reader and Candidate, from your Self and its energies (Light, Fire, and Life). We are making available the simple, practical, essential, and effective knowledge together with the practical exercises, tools, and instruments, but it is up to you to "stir up your being," to awaken your latent energies, and to train and coordinate your psychospiritual faculties—the "muscles of your consciousness"—to meet the great personal and collective challenge of our times . . . and to reap its tremendous and almost unimaginable benefits. Read this book, use its tools, and practice its exercises with this in mind!

Peter Roche de Coppens, Ph.D.
Milan, Italy
March 1986

Chapter One

THE SECRET OF OUR TIMES:
Its Nature, Law, and Challenges

———————

Every culture and nation, every historical period, and every generation have been faced with certain collective and personal existential crises which are really challenges to the human spirit, to a given nation and to its individual members. These challenges, or "tests," all have their dangers and opportunities, their failures and successes, with their ensuing consequences for the nation and for the individual that depend upon how they are faced, defined, and reacted to. Our nation and culture, our contemporary historical period and our present generation also face today their particular challenges, tests, dangers, and opportunities.

In the following series of articles, I plan to use the "Spiritual Perspective" and the philosophy of Christian mysticism to look at the nature, dangers, and opportunities of the challenges of our present time and to suggest positive personal responses to them—*to transform and redefine our way of perceiving and responding to these challenges* rather than

1

to attempt to *eliminate* these challenges. As for the collective or institutional responses to these challenges, I view them simply as a series of personal responses, as the spiritual perspective and spiritually awakened people do not advocate any particular form of politics, economics, or social reforms, viewing the transformation and regeneration of the human heart and human consciousness to be at the core of this enterprise and within the means of every individual.

True Christian Mysticism, also known as Rosicrucian Philosophy, is a practical compendium or applicable synthesis of the three royal roads into truth and reality: Religion, Philosophy, and Science, with a cognitive perspective which includes the spiritual dimension—a larger and higher perspective which looks at the slow evolution of human nature and actualization of human and spiritual potential over many lifetimes. It is the fruit and crystallization of the spiritual visions, experiences, and realizations of human beings who have achieved spiritual illumination or genuine Initiation. From this vantage point and state of consciousness, from their lived experience and perception of reality at a higher level and with a wider perspective, they left us this philosophy of life, or cognitive map, by which we can discover and make greater sense of our own experiences and existential vicissitudes, by which we can discover greater meaning and purpose in all the tests, trials, and experiences of our lives and by which we can, by degrees, live and incarnate this vision.

If we study the very best insights and conceptions of the present age, of its challenges and their meaning, drawn both from the perspective of the modern social sciences and from the sacred traditions of the past, we find certain basic themes and principles which beautifully describe and explain what is happening to us today and which can greatly increase our understanding of ourselves and of the world, as well as of what is going on in our inner and outer universe at the present time. In essence, these are:

1. *The law of polarization.* Today, it is becoming increasingly difficult, if not impossible, to remain lukewarm and uncommitted. Human beings, in other words, are being compelled to *make choices* and to *become committed* to one set of values, beliefs, and ethical principles or another, and to adopt a certain perspective or philosophy of life. Thus, good and evil, growth and decay, regeneration and degeneration are becoming more clear, more visible, and more alive as one is forced to choose, consciously or unconsciously, between Light and Darkness, between progression and retrogression, between greater life and consciousness or their opposite.

2. *The law of intensification.* As human consciousness grows and awareness increases, our sensations, our desires, our emotions, our thoughts, our imagination, our hopes and fears, needs and ideals, joys and sorrows become more alive, intense, and acute; as our consciousness unfolds and our energies rise, our inner and outer lives intensify and refine themselves. This means that a greater conscious effort is necessary to remain in control of our emotions and imagination, to remain balanced and properly integrated at the psychological and at the social levels.

3. *The law of acceleration.* As evolution moves forward and our consciousness develops, everything in our inner and outer lives not only polarizes, intensifies, but also accelerates its rhythm, happens faster and in a more concentrated and rapid fashion. At the inner level (physical, emotional, mental, and spiritual developments) and at the outer level (political, social, economic, and inter-personal events), things are taking place at a faster and faster rate which has

been called by a variety of names (e.g. future shock, social stress, cultural anomie, etc.). The working out of cause and effect, the relationship between what we sow and what we reap, or the consequences of our actions, words, thoughts, and aspirations have now been greatly accelerated, together with the world-wide diffusion of information and our collective and personal responses. What used to take years to happen now takes only a few weeks or even a few days!

4. *The law of etherealization.* More and more the "center of gravity" or the "focal point" of our consciousness and energies, and the thrust of the evolutionary forces are moving from the physical to the non-physical levels, from the outer to the inner dimensions, and from the material to the non-material, emotional, and mental levels. Thus, survival and the main tests of life which used to be anchored on the physical, biological level are now shifting more and more to the emotional-mental, or psychological level, and even to the spiritual level. Joys and sorrows, hopes and fears, aspirations and strivings, and the major battles of life are becoming ever more *inward consciousness experiences* rather than physical experiences in the material world. Even "wealth" and "success" are now becoming more and more a question of a certain state of consciousness, attitude, and perspective by which to look at ourselves and at life rather than being material possessions, social achievements, or external symbols.

5. *The law of the unfoldment of human consciousness and energization.* The whole thrust of human evolution lies with an ever greater expansion, deepening and heightening of human consciousness with a concomitant increase in vitality, in life-flow, or vital

energies. This is precisely what is now happening in a greater and more noticeable scale than ever before and which is really underpinning the other four laws. Our consciousness, both individually and collectively, is presently undergoing a major quantitative and qualitative expansion bringing a much greater sensitivity and receptivity, entirely new mental perspectives and frames of reference, and a true explosion of energy and vitality. This is why we have the law of polarization, intensification, acceleration, and etherealization now coming consciously into play and making us much more powerful beings for good or evil, for regeneration or degeneration, for light or for darkness.

At the present point in the history of the world and in the biography of human evolution, we find ourselves at a very crucial turning point or point of transition between two qualitatively different states of consciousness, two cultures, which are the articulation and expression of the collective state of consciousness, and two civilizations, the first dedicated to the conquest of matter and the raising of one's standard of living, the other dedicated to the *exploration of the inner worlds* and the *harnessing of the inner energies*, and the *development of psychospiritual faculties*. Hence we can truly say that "one world is dying and a new world is being born," that we are witnessing the end of one Age and the beginning of a New Age, or the passage between the Piscean and the Aquarian Age. What is really happening, in simple words, is that humanity is now being given, collectively and individually, during the last two decades of the 20th century, a very major "exam" or "test" in the school of life—a true and lived "Initiation." Various names have been given to this major test coming at the end of two millenia, and many prophecies have been made, in symbolic form, to tell us what we could expect at this time. This period has been called the Apocalypse (from the Greek *Apokalyptein*: the revelation of a hidden truth), Armageddon, or the Great War between the forces of Light and the forces of Darkness, and the coming of the Antichrist. Most people have interpreted these prophecies and visions as pertaining to the outer physical world and implying the end or destruction of our civilization, if not the end of mankind, and of the very world in which we live. While it is true that our outer physical world will be greatly affected and transformed by what will happen over the next two decades, it is my position and conclusion that it is the microcosm, the inner world of man, his consciousness, which will be directly affected by this great test and which will lead those who pass it successfully from the Fourth to the Fifth Kingdom, to the Kingdom of God, or genuine spiritual consciousness.

The Apocalypse, therefore, really refers to an *inner* process, purification, and transformation, not to *outer* ones; to the opening up of the unconscious and the superconscious, to being given the keys of Hell and Heaven—the revelation of one's true nature and destiny, both at the lower and at the higher end of the spectrum. Likewise, Armageddon implies the last great conflict between our lower and Higher Self in the arena of the personality and of the soul where all our deeds, tendencies, and yearnings will meet and confront each other, and raise or lower our vibrations and our capacity for receiving and reflecting the Light. The coming of the Antichrist will really be the facing of the "Guardian of the Threshold" of our "Shadow": the conscious recognition of our dark, lower, unregenerated self, its struggle to reaffirm itself and to regain control over our personality, consciousness, and lives, and its final transmutation and integration by the Higher Self, the Christ within, who will finally rule consciously in our personality and lives, and regenerate our entire nature—physical, psychological, and spiritual.

This tremendous event, test, or exam will, naturally, involve very profound and radical changes in our consciousness and in the world: dying to many parts of ourselves and of our former lives, giving up many of our desires, aims, and habits, taking many new risks, facing the unknown, taking the jump into the void, and great emotional and mental anguish. There will indeed be great sufferings, anguish, anxiety, gnashing of teeth, and the passing away, or "dying," of many parts of our old consciousness, being, and lives. But there will also be an increased sensitivity, the unfoldment of new perspectives and ways of looking at and interpreting the world and experiences therein, and many rebirths and resurrections.

Hence, the old prophecies and symbolic visions of Saints and Seers were, indeed, correct when they are properly understood and interpreted, but they can also very easily, as they have for many people, degenerate into *superstitions*— which are nothing but higher truths distorted, caricatured, and misinterpreted when their symbols are taken *literally* and applied to *external, physical events*. The central point here is that all these things do have a meaning and a purpose which are good and which are part of God's Plan for human evolution, and thus "allowed to happen by God Himself." When we are in the midst of them , on the line of fire as it were, we may be too emotionally involved in what is happening, too personally identified with these events, and too myopic to perceive their true long-range meaning and implication and their proper place and purpose in God's Plan. Thus, it is very important that we now watch and pray, and to keep in mind that in the midst of every great danger also lie great opportunities; that everything that happens is allowed by God to happen and thus is, ultimately, good, and that what is now happening is really a great test or exam to promote human beings who are ready to have a much more conscious, creative, and joyful way of life.

If one accepts the above premises, the central questions one will then want to ask are: what can we do now to prepare ourselves for this great test, for our personal Apocalypse, Armageddon, and the coming of the Antichrist? How can we recognize the true meaning and purpose of the tests and trials that lie ahead and which will be coming our way at an accelerated rate? And how can we respond to them so that they will work out for the best and so that we will be able to discern the ever-presence of God's hand, God's Love, and God's Light in all the turmoil that will descend upon the world, upon those around us, and upon us, and thus be able to remain *balanced, centered,* and *connected* with the Light in the very eye of the storm? How can we unfold a philosophy of life and an art of living that, together, will function as our Philosopher's Stone, which would enable us to face and cope with every possible test, experience, and situation that might present itself to us during this period of time?

How can we develop character, personal integrity and the faith and strength to face all of this, even more than we can presently imagine, without losing ourself, giving up our true vision, and betraying our highest ideals? This is what I shall attempt to answer and describe in the present work.

Practical Exercise

Preliminary: Find the right *place* (in your "home Temple" if you have one, on your favorite chair or on your bed) and the right *position* (sitting in the Egyptian position —spine erect with your hands on your knees—or in a comfortable position, or lying down) and take three deep, rhythmic breaths. Then, close your eyes.

Make an effort of *Introversion* (refocusing your attention and your psychic energies from the outer, physical, world to the inner, psychic world). Continue with an effort of *Supraversion* (focus your attention, thoughts, feelings and energies on a visualized sphere of white Light around your physical head and contact its Light, Power, and Vibrations). Conclude with an effort of *Infraversion* (visualize a ray of that Light and of those energies slowly descending into, and filling, your Heart Center, activating it). This is what is meant by centering yourself, entering the Temple of your Consciousness, and bringing the dynamic equilibrium of Peace and Life to your being. It is the basic preliminary work which has to be done *before* the actual work or exercises for this and all subsequent chapters.

Actual Work: Briefly, but vividly and concretely, review yourself and your life at present as a film unfolding on the screen of your imagination. Who are you and how do you function in today's world? What is your present self-image or conception of yourself, and *weltanschauung*,

9

or conception of the world? How do you perceive and define them? What are the basic tests, temptations, and experiences of your life at present and how do you cope with them. What do they mean to you?

What does the *law of polarization, intensification, acceleration, etherealization,* and of the *unfoldment of consciousness and energization,* as stated in this chapter, mean to you?

What are you doing, or are willling to do, *concretely* and *specifically,* to:

a. Explore your Inner Worlds
b. Harness your Inner Energies
c. Develop your Psychospiritual Faculties

Have you, or are you going through your personal Apocalypse (a major existential crisis) and Armageddon (major inner conflicts)? If so, how have you, or are you, coping with them? What are their basic features and significance for you? If you have not yet lived through them, how would you prepare yourself to do so?

Finally, how can you remain balanced, centered, and connected with the Light in today's world? What can you practically do to enhance this process and thus build character and become a more autonomous and responsible person with true integrity? Most important, what are you willing to do to change yourself and to transform your consciousness and your life?

When you have completed this meditation and self examination, make the appropriate entries in your workbook as to what you have discovered and how you are willing to act!

At this point, you might also want to review your library, your personal work tapes, your *inner* and *outer resources* (the "muscles of your consciousness" and the persons you work with), and the amount of time and energy you are willing to dedicate to the Great Work of personal Psychospiritual Transformation.

Note: At this time, please also refer to Appendix B, and make use of the Consciousness Checklist in connection with all the exercises and meditations suggested throughout this book.

Chapter Two

EMOTIONAL PURIFICATION

─────────

During the last Great Age which is now ending, the Piscean Age, the basic thrust of the evolutionary forces has focused squarely upon the building, coordination, and purification of the Astral body—of our emotional nature. It is this body and this aspect of our being that has been greatly sensitized, energized, and refined, much of the time through pain, suffering, and sacrifices of various sorts. During the previous Great Age, the Arian Age, it was the building, coordination, and perfection of the Physical and Etheric bodies that was the primary focus of the evolutionary forces. And during the coming, and now dawning, Great Age, the Aquarian Age, it will likewise be the mind and the mental body that will be the current focus of the evolutionary forces—its full development, activation, and coordination with the spiritual, the emotional, and the physical bodies.

It is within the general framework of this perspective that we can better locate and understand the great crisis of the 80's which has just begun and in which we shall all be both *spectators* and *actors*. Naturally, human beings have had a physical, an emotional, a mental, and a spiritual nature and vehicles for many hundreds of thousands of years, and the final purification, coordination, and perfection of these vehicles and their faculties will yet take a very long time. But, in each Great Age, the cosmic and telluric forces, the evolutionary *élan vital*, have a particular focus and direction, and human beings can respond to them and cooperate fully and consciously, and thus evolve faster and more effectively toward the full actualization of their being and the accomplishment of their destiny, or they can proceed in an impulsive and blind way and be caught by the inevitable swing of the emotional pendulum and by the inevitable consequences of what they have done and set in motion in themselves and others.

It is logical to assume that, if the major focus of the evolutionary forces in the last 2,000 years has been the development, purification, and coordination of the Astral body, or the emotional nature of man, the final crisis or "exam" of this period will involve this vehicle and dimension in a particular way. This means that the very crux of the crisis or exam will be psychological, psychic, and involving our emotions in a very intense and sharp way which, in turn, will have a deep impact upon our human relationships, our health and creativity, and generate a feedback loop with them. If we look at the various cultures that developed over the last 2,000 years we will find, amidst their infinite variations and nuances, that the emotional focus has dominated and left its imprint all over the world in Dionysian cultures that over-emphasized emotional expression as well as in Apollonian cultures that under-emphasized emotional expression and glorified reason and self-control with wild swings from one extreme to the other. Whether we look at religion, war, the economy, politics, the history of pathology, education, the family and, especially love and marriage, we find that it is the emotions that have been "hit," refined, activated, and intensified. One of the central symbols of early Christians, the Piscean fishes, or "ichtys," beautifully illustrate in a visual way the central dynamics of the swing of the pendulum, the principle of Enantiodromia, the going from one extreme to the other, polarization into opposites, and their underlying dualistic view and experience of reality. It is interesting to note how, in this historical period, charismatic persons and the religious, political, and military authorities have always used emotional appeal to motivate and direct the masses, whether for a religious cause, for a war, for political purposes, or for achieving any major collective endeavor.

What we are now called upon to do is to rise above the Astral world, the ocean of emotions that has ruled our lives up to now, to increase the vibrational rate of our consciousness and energies so that we may obtain a larger perspective of things and a deeper vision of the nature of our own being, of the world in which we live, and of our purpose in this world. In a nutshell, what we are now called upon to do is to *act rationally* rather than *recact emotionally*, to assume control over our own thoughts, feelings, words, and actions and, thereby, over *our lives* and its course. Now we are called to reconcile opposites, to manage and direct the many different faculties, energies, tendencies, impulses, aspirations, and energies that live in our being. We are called to achieve the "marriage of our personality," the proper coordination and functioning of our different vehicles and their faculties, energies, and tendencies—to synthesize our personality. We are also called to find the *right relationship* with all the persons who cross our path and to *live* right human relationships. And we are called to find at-one-ment, or union, with God, with the divine within and the divine without, which implies the right relationship and harmony with the physical and the spiritual part of our being (the body and the Divine Spark) and of the world (Nature and God). To achieve this, however, a profound purification and intensification, or awakening of our emotional nature is necessary as well as the development, activation of, and coordination with, other functions and energies of our psyche such as the mind, the intuition, the imagination, and especially, the *will* which should be the overall director and coordinator of our psyche and of our lives. But, this purification and intensification of our emotions and of our inner nature naturally involves pain and suffering, anxiety and anguish, yet also intense exhilarations and joys, agonies and ecstasies, trips through Hell and journeys through Heaven, and all this within the same personality and the same consciousness over a short period of time.

What we are now witnessing and living through is a great amplification and outpouring of the life forces which make our whole nature and being come alive and which greatly intensify the emotional swing of our ups and downs . . . until we either have a nervous breakdown and go to pieces, or finally assume control and direction over the energies and faculties of our personality. Our sensitivity is being greatly amplified and energized as Life pours through our Astral body and our consciousness, and this necessarily implies much greater and more conscious joys and sorrows, ups and downs, agonies and ecstasies; moreover, it also means that we are almost "forced" to direct our attention to controlling and directing these feelings, energies, and vibrations . . . or be rent asunder by them and experience the disintegration of our personality. As the famous Cure d'Ars (Jean Baptiste Vianney) put it succinctly:

> In this world, one must work and fight; for we will have plenty of time to rest and to enjoy ourselves in the next. And this spiritual fight can be explained by one key word: suffer-

ing or the cross.[1] In the invisible worlds, human beings can only ascend towards the Light by passing through various hells . . . Nothing is greater than man if we focus on his soul and nothing is smaller if we focus on his body alone; man is so great that only God can truly fulfill him, and he is so weak that without God he can do nothing. To really know ourselves, we must first explore and know Purgatory, Hell, and Heaven.[2]

Finally, he concluded beautifully, summarizing the essential position of the spiritual perspective concerning suffering:

There are basically two ways of suffering: to suffer loving (or with faith) and to suffer without loving (without faith). The Saints suffer (much more than ordinary people!) with patience, joy, and perseverence because they love. People in the world are very unhappy when they get crosses, trials, and sufferings; true Christians are unhappy when they don't have them! The Christian lives in the midst of crosses and sufferings like a fish in the water. For those who love God and whom he loves in particular, tests, trials, and sufferings are not punishmnets, they are graces and blessings . . . Crosses and sufferings transformed by the flames of love are like a bunch of small wood which one throws in the fire, the wood is hard but the ashes are soft.[3]

Practically and concretely, what does emotional purification entail; what is its nature, its psychodynamics, and its manifestations? Let us begin by looking at the nature of emotions, their place and function in the psyche. Emotions are the energies and materials that express through the function of *feeling*, one of the seven functions of the psyche. Emotions are powerful energies and impulses that can come from three areas of the psyche: the subconscious, the unconscious, and the superconscious as a result of stimuli or impressions coming from the conscious and unconscious part of our psyche and from the external universe. Emotions are really the great source of motivation, stimulation, and life in our daily existence. They are also the source of our greatest and highest joys and of our most intense and painful agonies. They are closely related, affecting and being affected by our thoughts, our imagination, our intuition, and our behavior. They can act as the wind behind the sail of a boat or as a millstone around our necks; and they can be the fountainhead of healing and rejuvenation as well as the root of disease and degradation according to whether they are positive or negative, with their positive or negative impact increasing in direct proportion to the period of time in which we experience them. For emotions are *life* flowing through and energizing our Astral body or emotional nature.

It is important that we learn how to recognize to what extent our emotional life and expression have been starved and poisoned in the past, then learn how to practice *emotional fasting* from both very strong negative and positive emotions for a while to put ourselves on a more functional "emotional diet." The essence of emotional purification and practical training could be summarized by the following central points:

1. One must learn to feel deeply and intensely—to refine one's sensitivity.

2. One must cultivate and express, more and more, positive emotions and higher feelings, and learn how to direct and control all emotions, and how to transmute negative emotions into positive emotions.

3. Then, one must learn emotional detachment and to be able to disidentify from persons, relationships and from one's desires and ideals.

4. One must learn how to use the will to direct and synthesize all the functions of the psyche and focus all the energies available, including feeling and the emotions, to achieve one's purpose and to do one's work.

5. It involves especially learning how to transform *destructive* into *constructive* suffering and how to take all the tests and trials of life as further opportunities for growth and self-actualization which will then enable one to become a better servant and vehicle for the divine Light and to accomplish God's will on earth.

6. It involves having the courage to open oneself up, to let oneself feel and love, and trust, and take the necessary risks that might cause suffering, pain, disappointment, and sacrifices to reach a higher goal and end.

7. In conclusion, it implies *feeling* more consciously and deeply, or becoming more *emotionally alive*, extending one's range of empathy and compassion from the self to others, from the part to the whole, and acquiring greater control and direction over one's emotional life; and, especially, to be able to cope with suffering, pain, anxiety, and frustration in a controlled and constructive fashion.

At the present moment, as we have entered the first phase of the *psychic dimension* of the Great Crisis (the economic and sociopolitical one following in its wake), it is imperative that we consciously strive to remain *balanced, centered,* and *connected* with the Light; that is, it is crucial that we observe ourselves and our relationships and activities so that we may have a healthy equilibrium of enough different kinds of relationships and activities and not too much of any one—be it one person, work, prayer, fun, food, or sleep. We must especially observe ourselves in terms of our emotional reactions and expressions so that we can learn to act rationally rather than react emotionally, impulsively, and irrationally to various external stimuli and situations and to our own inner needs and aspirations when it comes to making important decisions and taking vital actions. Finally, it is most important that we regularly draw in and suffuse ourselves and our consciousness with the spiritual Light of the divine Spark which, alone, can ultimately keep us balanced, emotionally centered, and connected with the source and essence of reality and life.

Moreover, today the "good fight" and the central arena where we are being tested and where we might be called, at times, to display nothing short of heroic behavior is the *emotional* one in the heart of our consciousness and being. Thus, it is in our Aura, not in the world, on the Astral rather than on the Physical plane that we must now face our "lions," our persecutions, our tests and trials, that we must face the emotional ordeal of "slow bleeding and dying" and make our heroic stand. What the early Christians and the true Initiates of old had to face in the world, or on the material plane, we must now face in the *depths of our own being*, in our emotional heart which has to be broken to be further opened to the Light and which has to "die" to be "resurrected." This time, the battle for self-conquest and self-mastery is now located squarely on the emotional plane and, therefore, it is with psychospiritual "swords," "weapons," and "tools" that we need to successfully face the ordeals which will culminate in our very own personal and emotional Armageddon. When this happens and it must, sooner or later, inevitably happen, our heightened sensitivity and our ever-increasing and rising life forces will be confronted with rejection, misunderstandings, injustices, abuses, hostility, and aggression, and that those who we love and trust the most will hurt us the most; for it is here that evil must be transformed into good, anger and rejection be answered with love and forgiveness, and that we must learn to truly love our enemies; and it is also here that the Holy Spirit will resurrect us when we have died to our old self. It is here that our Higher Self will confront our lower self and that we must choose between the most fundamental emotions of love and foregiveness or fear, guilt, and resentment which, ultimately, translate themselves as "life" or "death" for our very consciousness and being.

Our most vulnerable nature and aspect is, undoubtedly, the emotional one. Our emotional life has, most likely, been starved and poisoned in our childhood by inadequate and low quality relationships with our parents and with the larger sociocultural milieu which has been slowly degenerating and degrading for most of this century.

Thus, while most of us may have strong and healthy bodies and trained and effective minds, many of us are, unfortunately, emotional cripples. To compensate for this, the awakening of the intuition, the training of the will, and the control of the imagination are most important and all feed into the main "emotional stream" of our consciousness. Finally, the training of the mind and the ability to direct and control our thinking is also absolutely crucial for the way in which we perceive, define, and explain a given event or situation. This has a tremendous importance for the kinds of emotions and emotional responses that will be awakened and nurtured by this event or situation. This means that we have to be able to reframe or redefine, from the standpoint of a higher and vaster spiritual consciousness, the basic meaning and purpose of the many human events that happen to us and the various existential situations we find ourselves in, and which we would see as being negative, unjust, or painful from our normal state of consciousness. This implies mental clarification or purification which is the subject of our next chapter.

Practical Exercise

Preliminary: find the right place and the right position. Then make an effort of Introversion, Supraversion, and Infraversion.

Actual work: Meditation and exercises.

Focus your attention upon your Astral or Emotional body and Aura. If you know how and are so inclined, activate Netzach on your Tree of Life. Finally, review your emotional life and functioning at this point in time.

Have your emotional nature and needs been starved and poisoned in the past? What are you *now* doing to feed your emotional nature?

Do you feel overwhelmed by the Ocean of Emotions and driven by, or in prey of, *negative emotions?* What are you doing about this?

What are the basic tests, temptations, and experiences at the *emotional level* in your life now? How do you cope with negative emotions?

Are you able to transmute them into positive ones and to achieve emotional peace and life?

Can you effectively use your will, your mind, your imagination, Meditation and Theurgy, the Circle of Light Generator, Autogenic Training, or other appropriate techniques to achieve emotional balance, peace and life?

Read the remaining chapters of this work and

then go back to work upon your emotional nature and life.

1. Practice emotional fasting. That is, for 1-3 days make it a point to consciously abstain from all violent emotions.

2. Make a conscious effort to cultivate positive emotions by seeking beauty, good human relationships, Prayer, Meditation, and Theurgy.

3. Find a symbol, or an image, that represents your present emotional nature, your ideal emotional nature, and the obstacles that prevent you from being now what you would ideally like to be. Then, invoke the Light, Fire, and Life of your Divine Spark to energize the symbol, or image, that represents your ideal emotional nature.

   If you are Qabalistically knowledgeable and inclined, work on balancing Netzach and Hod drawing from Tiphareth and Yesod to complete this work.

4. Study yourself and your life to be able to identify the triggers that bring about negative emotions. What are your "sacred cows" that activate fear, anxiety, frustration, anger, depression, etc. How can you neutralize these by appropriate techniques and a transformation of your consciousness, perception and definition of these?

5. Practice conscious forgiveness and "letting go" of the past.

6. Select and then use symbols, images, and mantras that can function as "emotional energy and consciousness transformers" for you. For example: the presence of a beloved teacher, of a Circle of Light Generator, of a God Form, of a beloved person, of a

forest, a temple, a quiet lake in the mountains, of a time when you were in love and happy, or of techniques and formulae suggested in *The Invisible Temple.*

7. Reframe and redefine *mentally* and then *emotionally* the situations you are now living.

When you have completed this meditation, emotional self-examination, and psychospiritual transformation exercises, make the appropriate entries in your workbook, as to what you have discovered, what you have done, what has happened, and how you were able to cope.

Chapter Three

MENTAL CLARIFICATION

———————

Marcus Aurelius once stated that: "It is not what happens to us that is either 'good' or 'bad' but, rather, the way we think about what happens to us" and that: "Your mind will become like its habitual thoughts: for the soul becomes dyed with the color of its thoughts." This is perhaps the shortest and most succinct summary of the teachings of the Spiritual Tradition on this matter. It is also what I meant in the last article when I stated that "we have to be able to 're-frame' or 'redefine,' from the standpoint of a higher and vaster spiritual perspective the *basic meaning and purpose of the many events that happen to us* and the situations we cause ourselves to be in that would normally evoke anxiety, fear, pain, suffering, and which we would see as being 'negative' without this 'reframing'." Piero Ferrucci writes: "If our mind is only occupied with gossip, everyday worries, telephone bills, resentments, and the like, it will assume their hue. If we think about joy, infinity, or universality, its hue will again correspond ... Far from being ethereal and remote from life as we may sometimes believe, thoughts act on us in profound ways; indeed, we can literally say that thoughts are living beings."[1] The central principle here is simply that *our thoughts define our universe* and that each thought tends to actualize itself in the world. As Ferrucci concludes:

> Practice shows that we can create, vitalize, and strengthen an idea-force by thinking about it. As we observe its possibilities, dimensions, and applications it becomes more clearly defined. Feelings are attracted to it, and the new idea-force seeps into us, becoming part of our attitudes toward life and our habits of action. Thus by thinking about strength, love, or joy, we create strength, love or joy in ourselves.[2]

There are, perhaps, as many different ways of looking at the world, of defining events and occurrences, and of interpreting the significance of human experiences as there are different levels of consciousness and maturity which may, in fact, be different in every human being. The perspective we adopt in looking at human affairs, in judging good and evil, and in evaluating the meaning and purpose of a given situation is thus strictly dependent upon our *state of consciousness* which can vary greatly on the long continuum which stretches from the unconscious to the Superconscious, from Hell to Heaven, and from the myopic and immediate view to the much larger and higher, longer-range view. This is why when we reread a book several years after the first reading, or when we reflect upon a past love affair which seemed to us, at the moment, to be the "end of the world," or when we muse upon what we once considered a real tragedy, we can now see exactly the same events, the same basic materials, but in a very *different light* and with very *different meanings attached to them*. A good image here would be that of climbing a mountain and looking at the surrounding view and landscape. At each stage of the climb we see a certain portion of the view and landscape, which is absolutely correct from that point of reference, but which changes and transforms (itself) as we climb higher, for then we can see much farther and discover many things that were there all the time but which we could not see from a lower viewpoint. The same can be said to be true and to apply to *all human experiences and events*, regardless as to whether we judged them pleasant or unpleasant, and, especially, to our way of perceiving, defining, interpreting, and reacting to them.

What I called the "spiritual perspective or viewpoint" is simply the perspective, or outlook, which develops and unfolds when one reaches an altered and expanded state of consciousness which is called "spiritual consciousness." Actually, any perspective, viewpoint, or outlook toward oneself, toward the world, and toward human experiences and their meaning and purpose is always a direct function of our human consciousness with noticeable and qualitative differences unfolding as we descend from the field of consciousness into the subconscious and the unconscious, and as we ascend toward the superconscious, so that the very same event or situation can be perceived, defined and reacted to in very, very different forms as one moves up or down the scale of consciousness. Spiritual consciousness involves a much larger time framework, a much wider holistic connection of the various parts and pieces of our lives and beings to a greater whole, and very different standards for evaluating "good" and "evil," "desirable," and "undesirable," "real" and "unreal," "important" and "unimportant" which lead to a very different way of perceiving the true essence of the world, of human nature, and of the experiences one is living through. If we look at the human pilgrimage on earth and at the infinite variety of human experiences through the grid or glass of the "spiritual perspective," we find that its true nature and essence appears now to be a long series of very diversified *adventures, trials,* and *tests*. All of these now become "transparent" and reveal their nature and function as being that of self-actualization and self-realization—to enable a human being to fully develop his nature, consciousness, and their faculties so that he may be an effective vehicle and temple for the expression of spiritual energies, or God's will on earth in the physical dimension. Here, both the worst and the best have their meaning and purpose and fit beautifully in God's great plan for human evolution and thus reveal themselves to be essentially good even though they may be quite painful and unpleasant.

The very essence and central message of this perspective is that: *it is not what happens to us* that is crucial and where our area of freedom and choice lies, but, how we *perceive, define, and react* to the many experiences, lessons, and tests of life. An old theological maxim encapsulated the very heart of this approach when it stated: "the world can never hurt you, only your sins can." And this is because the world in all its richness and diversity is, ultimately, but a projection, creation, and externalization of our own thoughts, feelings, energies and vibratory rates. Thus, if we look at the world from the standpoint of the Superconscious, we will find ourselves in heaven, and if we look at it from the standpoint of the unconscious, we will find ourselves in hell. With the divine Light present in our field of consciousness, the whole world becomes God's gift and acquires meaning and purpose, whereas without this Light it becomes flat, dualistic, meaningless, and purposeless, and we are torn on the swing of the emotional pendulum with its dualistic expression of pain/pleasure, love/fear, attraction/repulsion.

As Antoine, the great French healer of the first half of this century, aptly put it:

> It is neither illness, poverty, injustice, nor even death (that are the great evils and enemies of mankind) but, rather, the false perception, the ignorance which makes the real

significance of these events, making them appear as catas-
trophies without remedy while they are but *natural steps* of
the human pilgrimage which no one can avoid at some point
in his evolution.[3]

From the standpoint of the spiritual tradition, human
beings are unhappy, miserable, and frustrated, thus dying
by inches and by minutes rather than moving toward fuller
consciousness and greater life, because they have lowered
their consciousness and closed themselves off from the
inflow of the divine Light which inevitably results in a
narrower, lower, and more materialistic and myopic perspective of human events and tests. If one accepts my fundamental thesis that there is a genuine spiritual perspective,
originating from higher states of consciousness, and showing the meaning and purpose of life and human experience
from a much higher and positive, *unitive* rather than *dualistic*, standpoint, then the importance of reminding human
beings of this perspective and of how life and human experience appear from its viewpoint become apparent. But
this must be done in such a way they can really understand
it and grasp it, each from his own level of consciousness and
unique personal experiences.

The psychospiritual foundation for a human being to
be open and receptive to the divine Light is *Worship* (the
love of God) and *Service* (the love of human beings and its
expression through action); it is through Faith, through
work, and especially, through suffering that one can purify
one's consciousness, raise one's vibrations, and slowly climb
unto the Sacred Mountain where God and the divine Light
dwell and from which top one can unfold the "spiritual
perspective" by which to look at oneself, at life, and at one's
experience in life in a transformed way.

Suffering, however, can be just as well *destructive* as it
can be *constructive* for a human being, breaking him physically
and psychologically, rendering him cynical, hardening his

heart, and making him bitter and resentful, thus cutting him off from the source of Light and Life, or purifying him, breaking his heart open, making him more sensitive and open to the source of Light and Life within him and in the universe. The razor-edge difference between the two is one's *state of consciousness and faith*, being open to the Light of the divine Spark or not, being able to forgive both those who have hurt and harmed us and ourselves for having been less than perfect and made mistakes, and being able to see that suffering does serve an important function and does fit in our pattern of growth, rather than perceiving it as useless and meaningless. Again, the central point here is not so much what happens to us or being able to change the external conditions or events as how we perceive those events and are able to change and expand our conscious-ness, our perspective, and our attitudes toward them. When-ever Antoine had to face something very painful or unpleasant, he would simply say to himself: "This is my test, which is a gift of God that I need for my progress on the Path."[4]

An interesting source of paradox, antinomy, and ten-sion, which can result in great inner stress for a human being, is the fact that the soul is calm and patient as it has eternity to accomplish its mission and find its way back home while the body and the personality have only this life, which makes time very precious, and they are very vulner-able to countless threats and sufferings. As Antoine again aptly puts it:

> Evil and suffering have countless faces, they constantly wait for us along our earthly pilgrimage, and they catch us and surprise us when we least expect. When one is young, one likes pleasure, health, and wealth, and, especially, love. But these come and go and do not last, and they deceive even our fondest and highest expectations. Pleasure leaves a strange "bite" and can eat one up both physically and psychologically.[5]

At the core of this spiritual perspective, we find a

paradoxical view concerning the nature and existence of evil. In the state of nature, in the world of duality perceived through a normal state of consciousness and at the existential level, both good and evil do exist and have powerful consequences upon our being and our lives, and one had better be able to discern which is which. But, in the state of grace, perceived through a heightened spiritual consciousness and at the ontological level, *evil does not exist*; that is, it exists only in our consciousness and thoughts which we can change as they are our creation. Therefore, from the standpoint of this higher and vaster perspective, all our enemies and all our tests, trials, and sufferings, *teach us valuable lessons* about ourselves and the world, and thus help us on our path of self-actualization and self-realization and are thus gifts of God or valuable opportunities. But, one may ask, if evil does not really exist, where do suffering, illness, and death come from? They come from our cognitive and affective perspective, from our present state of consciousness, which are rooted in the material, temporal world, and they truly constitute the great test and evolutionary trial which we must all face and overcome.

As Antoine concluded:

> Above all no violence. Violence is the sight of evil and the reaction to evil. To hate evil and to want to suppress it by force is to believe that it really exists. Yet, what to us appears as evil is but a *warning that we must work on some aspect of ourselves*, that we must perfect ourselves further. The true work to get close to God is to help and love one's fellowman, but to truly be able to do so, one must first *know oneself*. The essence here is to learn how to master the tree of the *sight of evil*. To heal is really to *show someone what meaning he can give and find in the test that he is now facing,* and to help him *change his state of consciousness and attitude* concerning what is happening to him.[6]

In the last years of his life, Antoine taught that evil, suffering, and illness are the result of a spiritual cause that originates in our minds and which depends upon our mind's particular focus and perception. For Antoine, ontological evil does not exist and there are always valid reasons and useful purposes for which a particular suffering or illness will manifest in a human being—even the most terrible and "unjust" one from a human standpoint. Thus, he says:

> Evil does not exist; it is our intelligence and mind which, focusing only upon the material temporal world, judges and defines a certain event or situation as "evil." The physical world, however, is but the projection and creation of the spiritual world, which is the real world and our true home. In this world, we are guided by our *intelligence* which classifies events into "good" and "evil." In the spiritual world, our guide is our *conscience* which does not see evil and which teaches us to love, to forgive, and to overcome the myopic physical side of things, and thus to get closer to God through the path of repeated tests and trials.[7]

For Antoine, the one and ultimate cause of illness and suffering is a consciousness focused on the material side of things—*the sight of evil*. Thus, while the natural tendency of human beings is to fear and flee from tests and sufferings, they should, instead, ask God to receive many of them for this is the royal way in which we can grow and become more than what we are. Padre Pio had exactly the same idea when he stated that: "If we truly understood the real nature and purpose of suffering and pain we would seek them as we now seek pleasures and joys." Matter, ultimately, is but an idea, a certain way of seeing things which corresponds to a certain level of consciousness and vibration which we can transform and raise.

The essence and final conclusion of Antoine is that the true nature of evil and of destructive suffering lies in the *sight of evil* which lasts so long as true love does not assume control of our heart and mind. And it is the very trials, tests, and sufferings which are the natural consequences of the sight of evil that will eventually lead to the triumph of love when divine Light and Faith will transform destructive suffering into constructive suffering. To turn unconscious living and emotional reacting into the art of living and act-ing, and destructive suffering into constructive suffering, one must know oneself at the right time and in the right fashion. That is the real key!

Practically and concretely, what is *mental clarification;* what is its nature, its psychodynamics, and its manifes-tations, and, most important, how does one achieve it? Before we turn our attention to these questions, let us bear in mind two important statements which encapsulate the very quintessence of the function and direction that the mind plays for a human being. The first comes from Albert Einstein who said: "The greatest discovery of any genera-tion is that human beings can alter their lives by altering their attitude of mind." The other comes from Jan Smuts, a South African Prime Minister, philosopher and mystic, who said: "To be whole and to live in the whole becomes the supreme principle, from which all the highest ethical and spiritual rules follow."

Mental clarification involves thinking in a clear, point-ed, and systematic fashion, and thinking involves develop-ing a cognitive grasp of the outer and inner reality of which we are aware and in which we live. The central psychologi-cal process through which we express and manifest think-ing is *meditation.* And meditation, according to psychosynthesis, involves four fundamental steps or phases: *reflective, recep-tive, contemplative,* and *creative* meditation.

The first two steps involve a psychological process only, operating on the level of the personality; reflective meditation implies gathering, bringing into the field of con-sciousness, and organizing all the knowledge one has—everything one has read, heard, seen, done or experienced —concerning the subject of meditation. Once this has been achieved and that one has before one's eyes and in full awareness all the knowledge and information concerning the selected topic, then one goes on to the next step, *receptive meditation*, by emptying one's mind of all ideas and data concerning the subject and by becoming as receptive and open to receive new ideas or insights about it that may then flow into the field of consciousness from the lower and higher subconscious and from the lower and higher unconscious. Once this is also accomplished to the best of one's ability, then we are ready to move on to the third and most important step, *contemplative meditation*, which leads one from the psychological into the spiritual level. This stage, however, cannot be reached by every person, as it does involve a spiritual gift: a genuine alteration and expansion of human consciousness to the point where "spiritual consciousness" begins to dawn and wherein the Light breaks through into one's awareness, and where one's center of consciousness has now ascended to the region of the Superconscious and has its materials and energies and inspiration available.

At this point, then, one will again contemplate the given subject letting the Light and the higher consciousness and vibrations now reveal and unveil its true essence with which we have become one. It is at this point that the real "reframing" and the new definition from a higher and vaster or spiritual perspective now occurs.

It is here that the sight of evil is finally overcome and that the true nature, meaning, and purpose of a given ordeal, test, trial, or suffering is revealed to one's consciousness, together with the energy and the strength to bear it and to cope adequately with whatever situation one finds himself in. It is also here that God's Will and God's Plan for human evolution and for a unique individual is ready to *receive it* and *live it*.

Finally, it is also at this level and point that knowledge is blended in and synthesized with *love* and *will*, which is a most important condition to truly make it serve God's purpose.

At the psychological level of *reflective* and *receptive* meditation, knowledge and the mind can be used or abused in the typical fashion of the existential world of the personality. As Ferrucci aptly puts it:

> We should stop to recall that if the mind can foster constructive personal attitudes and evoke superconscious energies, it can also be used for purposes far less commendable, even as an instrument of the worst irrational tendencies. Examples can be seen in those technological advances which are used without regard to some of the fundamental human issues, or even have a deliberately destructive aim to begin with, such as the sophisticated weapons in use today. In these cases, the mind—though functioning in a highly effective instrumental way—is divorced from human needs and ends, such as love, solidarity, aesthetic appreciation, intuitive understanding, and positive relating with the cosmos. When this occurs, the *mind becomes demonic*. In the individual, the hypertrophy of the mind presents dangers as disparate as they are deadly; you have aridity and abstraction from living experience, ruthlessness and contempt for the less brilliant. You have the eclipse of intuition and a reliance on empty logic alone. And then you have a cruelty unresponsive to anything that lives.[8]

The training of the mind and of thinking through meditation leads one to *clear, organized,* and *independent thinking*. In countless situations we can use our trained mind to clarify issues, to reflect on a given problem, and to disentangle the knots of a given situation, seeing the possible alternatives and their consequences. From this training and exercise then comes forth the ability to formulate an *ideal life model*; the kind of personality one would like to have and the lifestyle that is best suited to one's fullest development and ability to serve others in the most effective fashion.

Central to the training of clear and perceptive thinking at this stage is the development of concentration, visualization, and mental and emotional control; being able to remain calm, serene and disidentified, and thus objective in even the worst set of external conditions. These qualities are essential both for the inner cognitive work and for the last step in this process, *creative meditation*, whereby one will seek to objectify, incarnate, and live what one has seen and grasped mentally. The well-trained mind is characterized not so much by what we think about, but rather *how* we think—the style, penetration, level, and cogency of our mind—which has an enormous impact upon how we live and what we become. In a nutshell, the central features of the well-trained mind are:[9]

a. The ability to concentrate and visualize at will and to examine in depth any given topic, concrete or abstract, mundane or spiritual.

b. The capacity to organize ideas, memories, and images in inner files which can be brought out in the awareness at will.

c. Becoming aware of the grooves the mind functions in and be able to get out of them upon command.

d. Be able to see all sides of a question, not only those one is at ease with.

e. Be able to change mental universes easily and to be at home in all of them.

f. Be able to evaluate and modify the mind's own ways of functioning.

g. Be able to examine details without getting lost in them and to grasp principles without forgetting the details.

h. Be aware of its own limits and be able to transcend them or work to transcend them.

i. Be able to shift levels of consciousness, levels of vibrations, and perspective through which to become aware and look at anything one chooses to focus upon.

The very core and essence of *mental clarification* is to know what is happening to oneself and why it is happening in any and all situations, good and bad, pleasant and unpleasant; it is to be able to unveil and realize the deeper spiritual meaning and purpose of any situation, event, or trial, and to see how it fits into the patterns of one's life and one's self-actualization and self-realization, as well as into God's Plan and Will. It implies finding and creating the cognitive grasp of the situation one is in, of the event one is living, or the test one is undergoing, so that one's mental and emotional energies will not be dissipated in confusion or polarize on a negative frequency and expression. And, obviously, the more evolved, sensitive, bright, conscious, and alive one is, the greater are one's energies and sensitivity which require a greater emotional and mental control which makes this cognitive grasp evermore important, especially for mental types.

To take a very practical and concrete example, albeit a human difficult one: Suppose you go to work this morning and, two hours after you reached your office, you receive a pink slip saying that you have been "permanently laid off" in view of the financial difficulties of your company and its need to reduce costs and personnel. That piece of news really gives you a jolt and sends your heart up to your throat and butterflies to your stomach, and your mind begins to swim as you consider the practical implication of your "laid off" status. On your way home you drive nervously and a drunken driver hits your car, seriously damaging it but, fortunately, not hurting you. By the time you reach your home, you are emotionally and mentally in pieces and with your nerves raw. You are filled with confusion, fear, anxiety, frustration, hurt, and anger, and you are aware of the fact that this is what you are radiating and that you will probably communicate, by resonance, this confusion and fear to your spouse, thus generating a vicious and downward spiraling cycle. How would mental clarification be used here? First, you would have to make a great effort to pull yourself together by *being alone* and going for a walk or to visit a friend who has a sympathetic ear and who is a stable person. Then, you would pray and invoke the Light to bring some emotional centering and purification and, if necessary, you would let some time go by until you reach a minimum level of centeredness, concentration, and ability to use your key psychological tools: *willing, thinking, feeling, imagination,* and *intuition* and, at this point, you would begin the work of *mental clarification* in the following way:

First, begin with *reflective meditation* to get a clear idea and a comprehensive picture of where you stand in life, where you came from, and where you are going. Once this overall perspective is reached, then introduce the basic events of the day and consider their implications for yourself, those that depend on you, and your medium and long-range goals. Then, consider the various options that are open to you and the various ways in which you can respond to the new situation both psychologically and existentially, and try to weigh the consequences of these upon you and those that depend on you. Then, empty your mind and practice *receptive meditation* to see whether you can get new insights and inputs concerning both the implications of what happened to you in the world and the alternatives that are now open to you, and of your psychological reaction—i.e. your way of perceiving, defining, and responding to the new situation. If any insight or intuitions come, make sure to write them down or to record them on a tape. Finally, seek to alter your state of consciousness, to rise toward the worlds of Light and to get a breakthrough of the Superconscious into your field of consciousness. Then, from this new spiritual perspective now gain cognitive closure on what happened to you, its meaning, purpose, and consequences, and especially upon the best way in which you can respond psychologically to it—let go of certain goals, forgive others, become disidentified from the situation, accept the need to give up certain things or face sufferings, pain, and uncertainties. If necessary, give yourself time, make it a point to go and speak to trusted friends or a good counselor, and repeat the process later, one or more times if necessary. The central aim and ideal here is to get a clear and soul-satisfying picture of the situation and your ability to re-spond in a positive fashion to it, to remain balanced and not let yourself swing to a reactive extreme, to retain your inner peace and serenity and to remain emotionally centered, and to take positive action to integrate what has happened in your consciousness and in your life.

Practical Exercise

Preliminary: Find the right place and the right position. Then make an effort of Introversion, Supraversion, and Infraversion.

Actual work: Meditation and Exercises.

Focus your attention upon your Mental Body and Aura. If you know how and are so inclined, activate Hod on your Tree of Life. Finally, review your *mental life* and *functioning* at this point in time.

How is your mental nature, or mind, functioning at the present time? What are you doing to *feed* and *exercise* your mind? Are you able to think in a clear, organized, and effective fashion? Can you perceive the higher meaning and purpose of what is happening in your life and in that of others?

What are the basic tests, temptations, and experiences at the mental level in your life now?

Do you have negative thoughts and ideas? Can you recognize them? Can you transform them into positive ones?

If you are Qabalistically knowledgeable and inclined, work on balancing Hod with Netzach drawing from Tiphareth and Yesod to complete this work.

Do you practice meditation in a serious and regular fashion? Make it a habit to do so from now on.

1. Practice Meditation in the following way:

   a. Select a topic you would like to meditate about, or think upon in a systematic way, so as to gain a good, clear, and integrated cognitive grasp of it.

b. Practice reflective meditation by bringing into your field of consciousness and organizing all the information you have about that subject.

c. Practice receptive meditation by emptying your mind of all thoughts and ideas (mental fasting) to see if new insights concerning your subject will filter through.

d. Practice *contemplative meditation* by changing your state of consciousness, raising your field of consciousness toward the Superconscious and, in this expanded state of consciousness, look again at your subject and seek to become one with it, to "look at it from within" as it were.

e. Practice *creative meditation* by imagining and visualizing your self *being*, or *doing*, what your ideals tell you.

2. Make a conscious effort to train your mind by reading good books, having meaningful discussions with clear thinkers, and by energizing your mind through meditation, prayer, and theurgy.

3. Find a symbol, or an image, that represents your present mental nature, your ideal mental nature, and the obstacles that prevent you from being now what you ideally would like to be. Invoke the Light, Fire, and Life of your Divine Spark to energize the image, or symbol, that represents your ideal mental nature.

4. Study your mind and your present mental functioning to understand what are its strengths and its weaknesses, and how you can reframe or redefine the basic situations in your life.

5. Select symbols, images, and mantras that can function as mental energy and consciousness transformers. For example: a crystal, a laser beam, ideal models for thinking that you have personally known, or know, from history or myth, or use the Circle of Light Generator or an appropriate God form.

When you have completed this meditation, mental self-examination, and psychospiritual transformation exercises, make the appropriate entries in your workbook, as to what you have discovered, what you have done, what has happened, and how you were able to cope.

Chapter Four

PERSONAL CONSECRATION

————————

Important as *emotional purification* and *mental clarification* are, they are still but a means to an end, a preliminary foundation and a set of psychological tools, processes, or skills for the real work that is to follow and for which they are being prepared. This grand ultimate and final end is, of course, *self-realization*—the offering of the temple of the personality and the human self to the Divine Spark, the true Self, so that It can consciously, and in a clear and unobstructed fashion, express Its attributes in creation, in the body and in the world. These attributes are: Divine Wisdom, Divine Love, and Divine Creative Energies.

But, naturally, before one can reach this final and exalted end, there is much work that must be undertaken, many tests and trials that must be faced and passed successfully, and many accomplishments that must be realized, the aim of which is *self-actualization*—the full development, coordination, and completion of the personality. Personal consecration is the core element and the central process necessary to achieve both *self-actualization* and *self-realization*, as it involves the use and training of the will, both human and then divine, the giving of one's whole self with all of one's heart, mind, and soul to a given purpose or task. When one finally achieves personal consecration, then one can truly concentrate, meditate, express love and devotion, and visualize one's purpose and its progressive incarnation, and thus lose one's self in one's work and purpose; thereby transcending one's present personality and human self and all of one's human problems and concerns to obtain a genuine breakthrough of the Light and the activation of the intuition. Emotional purification and mental clarification thus provide the base from which true personal consecration can be achieved and manifested in one's being and life. They are the first two preliminary steps which lead to and culminate in the third: *being one's true Self and doing one's true work here*. Universal mysticism and the Spiritual Tradition have long recognized this and called it briefly: purification, consecration, and unification, seeing them as the necessary and unavoidable springboard to union with God, the end and the purpose of the Great Work. This is also precisely what transpersonal psychology now calls the "marriage of the personality with the soul" that then culminates in the "marriage of the soul and the spirit." Catholic religion has called this, in symbolic language, "the marriage of Christ with the Church," and the ancient Sages and Initiates called it the "building of the Temple of Solomon" and the "Quest for God." The symbols, images, and descriptions vary but the fundamentals, at the experiential level, ever remain the same.

Personal consecration involves, basically, two central elements: a strong, well-developed, and skillful will and a high and well-deliberated cause of purpose to which to dedicate one's self and one's time, energies and resources. The will is simply the expression of personal autonomy and integrity; it is the focused energies of the self which enable the personality to function freely according to its own intrinsic nature rather than under the compulsion of external forces. As such, it is one of the most vital and important functions of the psyche that must be consciously cultivated and progressively developed on the path of human and spiritual evolution. Many brilliant and inspired thinkers and authors have reflected and analyzed this central problem of human becoming, and realization from different angles and with different images and insights. Some of the most important I have encountered and which beautifully confirm and complement each other, providing a very rich soil and batch of seeds for meditation and contemplation, are the following:

Robert de Ropp puts it very succinctly when he writes of this:

> It is our privilege to live either as *Warriors* or as *Slaves*. A Warrior is the master of his fate. No matter what fate throws at him, fame or infamy, health or sickness, poverty or riches, he uses the situation for his inner development. He takes his motto from Nietzsche "That which does not destroy me strengthens me." The slave, on the other hand, is completely at the mercy of *external events*. If fortune smiles on him, he struts and boasts and attributes her favors to his own power and wisdom —which, as often as not, has nothing to do with it. If fortune frowns, he weeps and grovels, putting blame for his sufferings on everything and everybody except himself. I learned that *all life games* can be played either in the spirit of the warrior or in the spirit of the slave![1]

Castaneda has Don Juan state:

> The basic difference between an ordinary man and a warrior is that the warrior takes everything as a challenge while an ordinary man takes everything either as a blessing or a curse.[2]

And de Ropp concludes:

> It has been stated by Thomas Szasz that what people really need and demand from life is not wealth, comfort or esteem but *games worth playing* (ideals or basic objectives to

realize). He who cannot find a game worth playing is apt to fall prey to *accidie*, defined by the Fathers of the Church as one of the Deadly Sins, but now regarded as a symptom of sickness. Accidie is a paralysis of the will, a failure of the appetite, a condition of generalized boredom, a total disenchantment—"God, oh God, how weary, stale, flat and unprofitable seem to me all the uses of this world!" Such a state of mind, Szasz tells us, is a prelude to what is loosely called "mental illness," which, though Szasz defines this illness as a myth, nevertheless fills half the beds in hospitals and makes multitudes of people a burden to themselves and society . . . Seek, above all, *for a game worth playing* (look for a high ideal or purpose to which to consecrate your life and energies). Such is the advice of the oracle to modern man. Having found the game, *play it with intensity*—play it as if your life and sanity depended on it . . . Follow the example of the French Existentialists and flourish a banner bearing the word "engagement." Though nothing means anything and all the roads are marked "no exit," yet move as if your movements had some purpose. If life does not seem to offer a game worth playing, *then invent one.*[3]

For de Ropp, life games reflect life aims and purposes, and thus indicate the level of being and the level of consciousness of a human being, and what he will strive toward and thus become in this world—how he will grow and in which direction. Moreover, he distinguishes between three higher games, four lower ones, and a final Master Game. The three higher games one can play in this world he calls: the Religion Game or striving for salvation and peace of mind, the Science Game or striving for knowledge, and the Art Game or striving for beauty. The four lower games are: the Household Game or raising a family, Hog in Trough or the pursuit of wealth, Cock on the Dunghill or the pursuit of fame, Moloch Game or the pursuit of physical, military conquest, and No Game leading to insanity. Finally, the Master Game for him is the pursuit of wisdom, enlightenment, spiritual awakening, or Intuition.

At this point, it is also very important to bear in mind the connection that exists between thinking, visualization, awareness and will, which was analyzed previously in

"Mental Clarification," for indeed we become what we think, as ideas and images have a motor element which draws energies and materials from the unconscious and the superconscious to realize them in the physical world. Thus, William James once declared, paraphrasing Albert Einstein, that "the greatest discovery of my generation is that human beings can *alter their lives* by altering their *attitude of mind.*" Marcus Aurelius stated simply that "a man's life is what his thoughts make of it." And Albert Einstein, when asked what he considered to be the greatest problem of our age replied, "Men simply don't think."

It is interesting and sad to note that we live today in the richest land that has ever existed, in a golden land of opportunity where everyone dreams of and aspires to wealth and prosperity, but where out of 20 persons, only one will succeed financially! Out of a hundred persons, one will be rich; four will be financially independent; five will still be working at the age of 65; and 54 will be broke at the end of their productive lives! Why do so few succeed and so many fail? What has happened to all the sparkle and enthusiasm, to all the dreams, visions, and aspirations of their youth? They have been frittered away, says Earl Nightingale, the dean of human motivation and self-improvement theory, because people "don't know where they are going" and because they "cannot discipline themselves to achieve their fleeting and contradictory aims." They fail, in other words, because they are unable to set worthy goals and ideals for themselves and then to cultivate the discipline necessary to achieve these goals. In this life, one either becomes the *captain of his own ship* and the maker of his destiny, or he will become a *creature of circumstances,* fashioned and molded by the ideals and wills of others. As Rollo May perceptively pointed out: "The opposite of courage and integrity in our society is not *fear* and *dishonesty* but *conformity.*

In this life, there is, indeed, one truly fundamental

choice: to be free and in charge of one's being and destiny—
to have autonomy and integrity—or to be a slave—to remain
a creature of circumstances. To be free and successful means
to *do what one really wants to do* and what one has chosen consciously and deliberately. And here success breeds success
as failure engenders further failure. The central difference
is that between knowing where one is going (having developed one's will) or not. Take the analogy of a ship. Think of
a ship leaving a harbor with a crew, a captain, and a definite
destination or goal to reach. Sooner or later, even if the ship
encounters storms at sea or other obstacles, it will reach its
predetermined destination. Now take another ship just like
the first but with no captain at the helm and with no set destination or goal—with no aiming point. Then, get the crew to
start the engine and get the ship going. If it gets out of the
harbor at all, it will either sink, wander aimlessly about, or
wind up derelict on a deserted beach. The ship cannot possi-
bly go anywhere because it has no set course or destination—
and exactly the same is true for a human being who has no
basic set of objectives to pursue, or high ideals to realize!

A human being's character and life are what his thoughts
make them because we literally become and fashion our personality by what we think about, behold, and contemplate.
This is the central and most important, yet so simple, psychological and spiritual truth which literally holds the future,
integrity, and autonomy of our being and life in its power,
provided that we *act* as though what we think and behold
inwardly is *real* so as to make it real and incarnate it in this
world. Also we must be careful to really want what we focus
upon and not adulterate it with contradictory thoughts and
desires that would end up by cancelling each other out.

Why do we become what we think about? Because
thoughts and images have a "motor element" in them that
leads them to objectify and materialize themselves on the
emotional and physical planes. To use an inspiring image

and analogy: the mind can be compared to a good, fertile plot of land. On this plot, a farmer can plant what he chooses, the decision is up to him, the land does not care in the least! Thus, he can plant corn or wheat just as well as weeds or poisoned plants; the land will simply "grow" whatever is there and multiply many times whatever has been planted in it. The human psyche is exactly like this plot of land, and operates with precisely the same laws even though it is far more complex and fertile and functioning on different levels of being than the former: *it will grow and multiply whatever we plant in it.*

Another fertile image for the human mind is that of a huge tractor driven by a little man perched on its top. The psyche, as Norbert Wiener the father of modern cybernetics has shown, it is just such a machine, but a far more powerful and wondrous machine than any devised by the human mind which draws from within itself any model for an outer physical invention, and the human self, the conscious ego, is the man at the top. This machine and therefore the human psyche, can remain unused for centuries, or it can be driven into a ditch or a human settlement, thus creating untold ravages and catastrophes for its driver or other human beings, or it can be used and directed to specific and worthwhile human and spiritual goals. Hence we must learn to understand, emotionally as well as intellectually, that we literally become what we think and that we reap what we sow. We must learn to activate our will and intuition and refuse to accept that there are any circumstances that can prevent us from reaching our consciously chosen ideals and objectives that are part of God's Plan for us. This is why Earl Nightingale concludes that true human success is but "the progressive realization of a high and noble ideal."[4]

From the perspective of psychosynthesis, Piero Ferrucci offers the following insights:

> True, at any moment we may find ourselves going along with outer pressures: social constraint, propaganda, and so on. We may fall into the grooves of habit and act on automatic pilot. More rarely, we may even function purely according to instinctive mechanisms. But—and here lies the great novelty—we can also invent *new behavior* and become an intelligent cause. We can truly and freely choose, bearing the full responsibility and self-determination. It is to this evolutionary acquisition, still very much in development, that we give here the name of *will*. At times we are dramatically confronted with situations which invite us to make use of the will. If so, our psychic voltage rises and we can move on to greater freedom. But if we don't, we are crushed by the circumstances of life.[5]

And, he adds, pointing out a most important point concerning the psychological and physical well-being of a person, which all too often has been neglected or relegated to a secondary role by orthodox psychotherapy:

> Whenever the will of an individual is *ignored, suppressed,* or *violated* in a consistent and enduring way—or if it is stillborn or even nonexistent —*pain* and *illness* arise. And because the will is the faculty closest to our self, when it is infringed upon, the hurt goes all the way to the core.[6]

When working with the will, it is important to remember that *"any action* can be transformed into an exercise of will, provided it is not done from *habit* or experienced as *duty*.[7] By consistently using our will, an "avalanche process" is thereby set in motion, for once we have discovered our will it enables us to perform further acts of will. It is in this way that we can consciously increase our reservoir of "will energy" and, therefore, become able to develop it even further. Here, we create a virtuous circle: *will generates will*. Just because many people, especially in the mental health professions, have been calling "will" what, in fact, was merely stern self-restraint, should not lead us to throw out the baby of the true Will with the bathwater of Victorian self-denial.[8] for the real and synthetic function of the will is *to direct, not to impose*. An excellent allegory is given by

Ferrucci to illustrate the preceding principle. He suggests:

> Suppose you are in a rowboat in the middle of a lake, and that you want to return to the shore. To do so you will have to make use of two functions: first, you must decide in which direction to steer the boat and maintain that direction; second, you must use your own muscular energy to row the boat. Now suppose, again, that instead of handling a rowboat you are working a sailboat in a mild breeze. What you need this time is *skill* in handling rudder and sail so as to take advantage of the interplay of natural energies. No *muscular effort* on your part is required to move the boat. Your only function is to choose and maintain the *direction* in which you want to sail—a much easier and more relaxing task than that of supplying the propelling force, as before. In the sailboat you are not the agent: you are a *meta-agent*. This means that you let the wind, the sail, the waves, and the currents interact with one another. All you have to do is skillfully regulate this interaction without directly participating in it, as you would have done in a rowboat. True will is likewise a meta-agent . . . a "meta-force" which *can direct the play of the various elements of the personality* from an independent standpoint, without mingling or identifying with any of them.[9]

In his allegory of the rowboat and sailboat Ferrucci has really gone to the very core of the question of the will, its nature and functions. For the will is, indeed, or functionally should become, the *director* or *organizer* of the manyfold elements, dimensions, energies, and resources of the personality and, eventually, of the Soul. Thus, the will should integrate and direct the work and energies of the seven functions of the psyche—concentration, meditation, devotion, visualization, and intuition in particular. It should be able to draw upon the vastly greater resources of the subconscious, unconscious, and Superconscious, as well as working with and coordinating the energies and qualities of the various subpersonalities that are available or that can be created by the personality. Finally, it should also utilize, coordinate and work with the outer resources of the personality, the psychosocial network and resource persons in particular, and with the professional skills and the material and financial assets that are available to the personality as well. It is in this fashion, and in this fashion alone, that the will can become the "focused energies of the self," disidentifying from the various functions and materials of their personality, and express the full energy, vibration, and resources of the Self.

In psychosynthesis, the will is viewed clearly as the key function of the psyche, as diagrammatically shown in the star picture of the seven functions. And, as it is not of biopsychic or of psychosocial nature but ultimately of *spiritual nature*, it is no wonder that Assagioli considered it the "Cinderella of modern psychology"—being grossly misunderstood and sadly neglected, in its true nature and functions, since the birth of modern psychology and the discovery of the unconscious. Yet, there has always been a light of recognition of what it really is and of its central role. Thus, Otto Rank

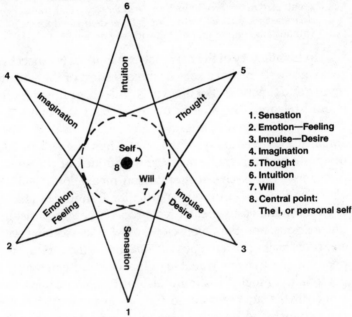

1. Sensation
2. Emotion—Feeling
3. Impulse—Desire
4. Imagination
5. Thought
6. Intuition
7. Will
8. Central point:
   The I, or personal self

From *The Act of Will*, Assagioli, Penguin Books.

explicitly stated: "The human being experiences his individuality in terms of his will, and this means that his *personal existence* is identical with his *capacity to express his will in the world*.[10] And Chaikowsky went even further when he declared, not as Descartes, "I think therefore I am" but "I will and, therefore, I think I am."

At the very heart and core of personal consecration we find two central elements: a high ideal or noble purpose to which to "consecrate oneself" and an activated and developed will. Let us now explore each in detail.

A. A high ideal or noble purpose to which to dedicate oneself:

Roberto Assagioli tells us that the simplest and the most usual unifying and integrating principle of the psyche, or ideal, is a *dominating passion* whether for a person, for a position, or for a given cause. He analyzes its nature and psychodynamic expression in the following terms:

> A strong passion tends to absorb all the internal energies and to direct all the external activities. It is like a jealous and exigent despot who does not tolerate oppositions or deviations and who aims at utilizing every faculty, resource, and energy of a person. In such a person, the physical energies, the will, thinking, feeling, the imagination, memory, and even biopsychic drives and sensations, and all other psychic energies are put to the service of the given passion. Everything is subordinated to and, if necessary, sacrificed for the end it seeks to achieve at all cost. A passion also awakens and mobilizes energies and resources that were hitherto latent or ignored, and enables a human being to do things which he would never have thought himself capable of doing. It can bind him to a very rigorous discipline and asceticism, to put away food and sleep, and to work 16 to 18 hours a day. One only has to think of what a love passion can do to a person; transform him from a quiet and shy person into an ardent and courageous person full of unsuspected resources, who cannot be stopped by any obstacle or danger.[11]

A strong passion represents all of the advantages and all of the disadvantages of powerful but rigid synthesis brought about from a lower state of consciousness and being. As such, it is at the same time clairvoyant and blind, compelling and egocentric. It perceives accurately all that which pertains to the achievement of its ends, but it is blind, deaf, and insensitive to all other concerns of life and to other people. It can be just as well constructive as destructive; it can create a new industry or party from nothing, or it can ruin a family, a community, or even an entire nation; it can bring a new masterpiece into the world, or it can sow ruin as a tornado; and it can intensify and exalt a person's energies and consciousness so that he can rise above himself and become more than what he presently is, or it can depress his consciousness and vampirize his life force, consume him and destroy his being and his life as a malignant cancer.

Passion, therefore, is a powerful but dangerous force which can be just as much a blessing as it can be a curse, depending on whether one can *direct it and control it or become controlled by it*. As Assagioli incisively and perceptively writes:

> For a passion to be benevolent and a blessing, two things are necessary: its end must be noble and elevated and it must be controlled by a higher principle and put into a proper perspective. For even an egoistical passion can bring about good and a noble passion can also be dangerous and highly detrimental if it is excessive. The *excesses of passion* often turn into their *opposites* with the swing of the pendulum; thus love turns into hatred, attraction into repulsion, and fascination into disgust. Noble passions have other insidious dangers as well: fanaticism, intolerance, pride, and hardness of heart. An ideal can so fascinate a person as to blind him to everything except its central goal, and it can lead him to believe that all is moral and good that leads to its realization; it can, in other words, lead one to *lose his sense of proportions*, of justice, and make one fanatical, intolerant, and cruel. This is the reason why one must be the master and not the slave of passions, *even the highest and best ones*. And this demands the presence and activity of a Higher Center, of a vaster vision, of an awakened and strong will which can keep the passion "in hand" or controlled, and subordinated to a vaster personal and transpersonal synthesis. But (and this is most important),

to *control* a passion does not mean to *destroy* it. For in a passion there is Life, Power, and Fire which are sacred in their
nature and origins and which are God's Gift to us.[12]

Another very basic integrating and unifying principle
of the psyche is the professional or personal role that a person occupies in a society, such as that of being a professor,
an artist, a scientist, a mother, or a husband. What is truly
important here is not *what* one does, but *how* one does it.
Thus it is crucial to have a clear vision and comprehension
of the ideal model of the special function one has chosen in
life so as to be able to actualize it and incarnate it in the best
possible fashion. Different cultures and ages have produced a diversified array of ideal types for people to choose
from and emulate. Thus we have: the *Saint*, who represents
a purification and exaltation of love, the *Sage*, who represents a development and exaltation of knowledge, and
the *Hero*, who represents the refinement and exaltation of
will and courage; then we have the Knight, the Nobleman,
the Gentleman, the Poet, the Artist, the Scientist, the Indus-
trialist, the Philanthropist, the Muse, the Sister, Helpmate,
and the "Energy and Consciousness Equilibrator," etc.

In the East, the Supreme Ideal has always been Illumination or Spiritual Awakening. And here, the concept of
Dharma plays a central role. Dharma is one's duty, the law of
life, and the particular ideal which one has to seek to realize
one's personal life. Thus, there is the Dharma of the Brah-
man, of the Kshatryia, of the Vasyia, of the Sudra, and even
of the Pariah. And there is the Dharma of the Father, the
Mother, the Son, and the Daughter. Moreover, in the East,
seven basic Yogas or Paths are recognized to lead one to
Illumination and union with God—which depend on one's
character, personality traits, and personal circumstances.
These are: Karma Yoga, Bakti Yoga, Jnani Yoga, Raja Yoga,
Mantra Yoga, Kriya Yoga, and Kundalini Yoga. Here, each
person must follow his own nature and develop to the

fullest extent possible every possible aspect of his natural faculties and tendencies. But, whatever a human being is or does, he must keep his mind focused on God, for here the battlefield is the soul and the enemies are the various parts and unbalanced energies and tendencies of the personality.

In the West, there are three Royal Paths to God, Reality and Self-Realization: *Mysticism*, the path of Love and Faith, which involves an amplification and intensification, as well as purification and consecration, of one's ability to *feel*; *Occultism*, the path of Wisdom and Knowledge, which involves a transformation and expansion of our cognitive universe, of our perception and definition of reality: ourselves, God, the world, good, and evil, and love; and finally, *Magic*, the path of Will and Power, which involves a magnification and consecration of our creative energies and of our abilities to create and to express our self in a conscious and productive way which is aligned with God's Will and Plan. Of these, it is the first, the Path of Love, that is for me, the royal path to union with God and the path that, in the end, fuses and synthesizes all three Paths at the Soul level.

There is also the full development and realization of one's *male* and *female* nature at the inner level, and the psychosynthesis of the couple at the lower level. Hence, one can strive to become a fully actualized Man and Woman, who are Hermaphroditic Beings, a Mother and a Wife or a Father and a Husband. As Assagioli comments further:

> The woman who has a husband but not children can give more of herself to practical and intellectual collaboration with her husband and to a deeper communion with him. She can also be a little maternal with him—protective, sweet, indulgent, generous, and can add new notes to and render richer and more harmonious the union of the two personalities and then of the two souls.[13]

A most important point and insight from the standpoint of psychosynthesis and one that is valid for all types of partial or human syntheses is that: one must never let oneself become absorbed or express oneself exclusively from any one of the functions of the psyche or any social role, whichever it might be and however noble and elevated it is. All functions must be used harmoniously and in mutual cooperation just as all the subpersonalities and all the social roles must be synchronized and integrated to enrich oneself and those we love. Balance, synthesis, and variety are absolutely crucial for the holistic and full functioning and expression of any human being.

The fully actualized woman has two very important gifts to bestow, those of *spiritual maternity* and of being a *muse*, a source of the highest inspiration and enthusiasm for a man and for the world. The first manifests as a high expression of love, understanding, healing, illuminating, and revitalizing energies, energies that can protect, heal, console, and elevate both one's personality and that of others. The second manifests in such a way as to fertilize and integrate the masculine and feminine polarities within the psyche and to bring through a stream of inspiration and intuition. Men and women in this world are incomplete beings, almost psychologically mutilated, and thus unable to truly express themselves. This is also what makes the proper integration and harmony of the couple so difficult. Many of the qualities and defects that we see in the opposite sex are really manifestations, external projections of latent, repressed, or undeveloped faculties, energies, and traits which we have in our unconscious. And this is why before we can have a successful interpersonal marriage, one must experience the marriage of his personality.

Finally, one of the most natural and effective ways of achieving a higher type of partial psychosynthesis is the use of ideal models. The essence of this approach consists in venerating and emulating a more evolved soul, a Great Person . . . One of the greatest deficiencies of our times is that our culture lacks truly valid cultural heroes for the youth and for the common person. As Assagioli explains:

> We must now mention another type of "ideal model" which is particularly important and efficacious: that of the great mythical or historical personalities, the cult of Heroes or Great Men. Such a cult of heroes, the admiration and veneration for great men is a natural and inextinguishable tendency of the human soul and one of the most powerful springs for its elevation.[14]

Here, it is interesting to note that the word "Duke" comes from *Dux* which means "Guide." Ultimately, we can say, as Max Weber pointed out, that all hierarchies and early and valid forms of social stratification are really "herohierarchies." And Assagioli writes further:

> Social stability, according to Carlyle, depends upon the fact that those who govern nations not be too unworthy of their function. These high dignitaries, he argues, are like bank bills which represent and should be convertible in gold. Unfortunately, many of them like bank bills, are false. Then come revolutions in which Democracy, Liberty, and Equality are proclaimed. Considering all bank bills (i.e. all leaders) to be false and being unable to have real gold, the people say that gold does not exist and has never existed! And yet, the cult of Heroes has always existed and will always exist (because there are, in fact, real Heroes and more evolved Souls) everywhere and cannot cease as long as men will live on earth.[15]

Ever since the Renaissance, and especially during the last three centuries, because of the materialistic, positivistic, and hedonistic intellectual climate, there has developed a tendency to negate or deny any manifestation of superiority, not only spiritual but moral and intellectual as well. As Assagioli puts it succinctly: "There has been a series of 'denigrators of men' who, with an incredible tenacity, have sought every possible way to demolish and cover with mud every higher human figure. They have insisted to see pathology in genius and sanctity and to reduce everything to its lowest common denominator."[16]

The positive and ennobling function and impact of Great Persons upon human beings is twofold: first, we have the direct action of a Superior Person and then we have its introjection in our personality which brings out the same in us. Assagioli beautifully describes this process in the following words:

> The Great Man vivifies us, enriches us, and radiates his Light and Warmth as the Sun does upon the seed, actualizing its true nature ... Looking where others look or talking about the same things, we can become drawn by the same fascination that drives them, i.e. we become like them ... The Great Man is like a focal point, an "image" that we project upon his personality, which in turn, impacts our own personality. This psychological projection becomes even more evident when its object is grossly inadequate as, for example, the person in love who sees in his beloved an *ideal, perfect being.* The classical example is Don Quixote who idealizes the woman he loves, but who is but an uncouth peasant! But even such a projection is useful in that it can evoke and activate our higher energies ... This psychological projection is very easily achieved when we do have truly Great Souls and Higher Types of human beings to look up to.[17]

Here it is important to note that the veneration of Great Souls and the *projection* we make should be followed by *introjection*, i.e. to internalize, reproduce, and thus actualize and bring forth this ideal in ourselves to become that which we behold and venerate. Finally, we should also note here that this projection and introjection of qualities that are yet unconscious and undeveloped in one self is one of the easiest ways to bring them forth and to actualize them in ourselves. Thus, a truly creative relationship between a man and a woman can act as the basic mechanism to bring forth the projection and internalization of the male and female polarities through which one can reach self-integration, as each one of us carries in himself the projection and the latent potential of the other polarity. But this emulation and imitation of Great Persons must be *conscious* and *willed;*

one must use all of one's consciousness, will, and energies to incorporate and develop the qualities and aspects which we admire in others to become, ourselves, what they are and to become even more . . . to actualize the unique qualities of our unique self.

There are some basic dangers involved with the use of "ideal models" and the veneration and emulation of more evolved and actualized human beings. The central ones are: becoming overwhelmed, blinded, and dominated by the powerful energies and thoughts of such persons leading one to lose himself and model himself on something or someone external and extrinsic to his own nature which, in turn, leads to fanaticism, dependency, and idolatry, or the projection of power to an immature and unworthy person, to a power seeker, who can then use it to harm others and himself. Particularly the unconscious projection of power from the part of a group to an individual can also go to the head of that individual, blow up his or her ego, and unbalance his or her emotional energies, mental perspective, and judgment.

The other danger is that of projection without introjection: admiring the qualities and attributes of another person without seeking to unfold them, incarnate them, and live them in our own being and lives. The final danger is that of mechanical, unconscious imitation which catches the letter but loses the spirit, the life-giving actualizing force of this process. In each one of these cases, the psychological center of gravity of our consciousness is taken outside of ourselves instead of truly awakening and bringing to light and full expressions our true Self and nature. The greatness, power, and energies of a hero should not overwhelm us and make us forget ourselves, but find and help us realize our true Self for, as Emerson states: "The true Genius does not impoverish others, he enriches and elevates them." And, we must remember that our image and conception of a Great Being is, inevitably, a mixture of reality and of our idealization and perceptions of that Being. Thus, it is vital that we learn to distinguish the *spiritual message* and Light, Love, and Life of that Being which come from God, from the Self that is in all of us, from the *personality* of that Being. For it is not the empirical personality of the Great Being, but the *Spirit* in Him and the expression of Its Attributes of wisdom, love, creative energies, and of beauty and goodness that we should venerate and behold to activate and bring to consciousness and expression our very own and unique ones. As Assagioli succinctly concludes: "The Spirit is always limited in His personal manifestations; one must, therefore, not imitate these but move up to and reach its Source . . . *Love the Flame and not the Lamp.*"[18] The central point here is that by seeing embodied in this world what we strive and hope to become, and that by interacting with energies and presence of a person who functions on the higher octaves of consciousness, being, and energy, we can *activate* the same in ourselves and we can contact our true Self and thus bring out our own unique traits and contributions to humanity. Moreover, the Hindus have a beautiful saying which claims that: "The Ganges River purifies one when it is seen and touched, but Great Beings purify even when they are merely remembered." This raises the important but thorny question of "where to find the real Hero today"? Obviously, the coming Aquarian Hero, in contradistinction with the passing Piscean Hero, must be found *within oneself* rather than in the world. When Man's consciousness was more focused on the outer physical dimension, he needed and sought external, embodied heroes of various types, both authentic and false, according to his own level of spiritual discernment and inner drive. Higher Beings and genuine Heroes were provided by the Hierarchies who watched over and guided the evolution of humankind. Thus, spiritual, religious, political, intellectual, economic, artistic, and social "Ideal Models" were given to a race and to a nation as parents are given to a child. Many of these were, unfortunately, worshipped with a personality cult being built around them. Others, as various historical aristocracies clearly show, were corrupted by power, personal interests, egoism and hedonism, and served themselves and their own interests rather than the common good. Thus many revolutions and rebellions occurred turning yesterday's "gods" into today's "devils."

In the coming Age, the authentic Hero must be found and activated within. This is why, in my own experience, the most humanly developed and spiritually awakened human beings I have ever had the pleasure of meeting and knowing have, one and all, kept a very *low profile*. They have sought to hide and veil their true Powers and Light rather than to assert them and to have them become publicly recognized.

The question, therefore, is "how to find or awaken the real Hero Within"? Available to us, we have a whole panoply of approaches and techniques such as the "Ideal Model" exercise, activating the Hero within by a legendary or historical study of great Persons of the past, by a psychological study of basic Archetypes, and by the evocation of the symbolic Hero of one's choice, by the Qabalistic construction of a God form, and by Occult Meditation and the Magical formulation of selected Telesmatic Images.

B. An activated and developed will:

The will is the focused energies of the Self which can activate, coordinate, and direct all the other functions of the psyche, and which controls the behavior of the organism. As such, the will is neither a great deal of raw energy nor a blind determination to do what one wants to do at any cost but, like the director of a play, the will focuses, directs, and utilizes all the energies and resources of the psyche and of a person's subpersonalities in a harmonious way to achieve the goals and objectives that are focused upon and desired. More than a physical or biopsychic energy, the will is a *psychospiritual energy*, the energy and life of the self, working through the mind and the biological organism to realize and accomplish a person's objectives and desires. As such, there is hardly anything that an individual can do—physically, emotionally, imaginatively, mentally, or spiritually—which does not require the proper focusing and use of the will. A strong, healthy, properly developed and skillful will is, therefore, absolutely indispensable to achieve anything worthwhile in the three most important areas of human activity:

    a. The worldly, professional, economic, and social area;

    b. The psychological, emotional, and mental area which defines one's "state of consciousness" and "being in control of one's personality and destiny" or not;

    c. The spiritual area or the area of human growth, self-actualization and self-realization.

It is the function of willing which determines whether one can say "yes" or "no" to oneself and to others in everyday life. And it is "willing" which enables a person to resist his own biopsychic drives, passions, and irrational impulses and desires, as well as the wishes and aims of other persons who are seeking their own self-interest. It is also "willing" which enables a person to persevere and to be successful in the pursuit of his goals and objectives in spite of all the obstacles and difficulties which may arise and bar the way. Finally, it is the will that energizes and directs the psychic energies of a person toward behavior, feelings, thinking, imagining, and intuition, as well as toward observation and the regulation of the biopsychic drives; it is the will that coordinates the various resources, functions, and subpersonalities of a person to help that person live according to his ideals and to implement his life objectives. As such, it is the will and the ability to *concentrate*—which best describes the action of the will on the energies and resources of the psyche—that are the first and most important of the psychological faculties and "tools" to be developed by the pioneer and explorer of the inner worlds and to be cultivated by the aspirant of the Mysteries.

The will can best be compared to an electrical battery: it can be charged or discharged by our various attitudes and activities. Whenever we truly know what we want and then go ahead and achieve it in spite of all the obstacles that may bar the way, we charge and strengthen our will; or, when we know clearly what we do not want and we avoid it and do not give in to it, in spite of all the temptations and inducements to do so, we strengthen and charge our will. On the other hand, if we do not truly know what we want and let ourselves be swayed by external agents or circumstances, other people, or even by the cravings and desires of our own being, we weaken and discharge our will.

The will can be seen as the fundamental expression of personal *autonomy* and *integrity*—the capacity of a person to function freely according to his own intrinsic nature rather than under the compulsion of external forces or of inner unconscious forces. It is to the voluntary development of being truly and freely able to choose, being the full responsibility of self-determination, that we give the name of *will*. At times, we are all dramatically confronted with situations that invite us to use our will. If we do so, then our psychic voltage rises and we can move on to greater freedom. If we don't, then more and more we lose our will and autonomy and are crushed by the circumstances of life. Any action or activity whatever can be transformed into an *exercise of will*, provided it is not done by habit or experienced as duty. Then, a chain reaction is set in motion: once we have discovered our will, it enables us to perform further acts of will. Like a bank account that grows with accrued interest, the reservoir of our will energies can grow, establishing a positive circle: will generates and increases the ability to will. It is by *using* it, that we discover and intensify our will.

The real function of the will is to *direct*, not to *impose*; hence, the central aspect of working with the will consists in being fully conscious of what we want and of how we are going to get it. In this process, there are four key stages in the exercise and expression of the will, which are:

Deliberation:	Setting goals and objectives that provide adequate motivation;
Decision:	Making a choice and a commitment to one goal and objective to be realized;
Planning:	Organizing the best means and the ways to achieve this goal;
Execution:	The actual implementation and realization of these goals and objectives.

To conclude, the will is a capacity which is eminently human: *the power to choose.* By selecting the right goals and objectives and then realizing them progressively, we can simplify, beautify, and turn our life into a real work of art!

The systematic training of the will and development of the ability to concentrate are a complex science and art, but there are certain central insights and exercises that can be most useful to begin and get to the core of this process. These are:

First, undertake a serious and accurate study of yourself, of your present strengths and weaknesses, as a minimum amount of self-knowledge is indispensable for the proper training of the will.

Second, study the nature, function, and purpose of the will so as to have a minimum understanding of what it is that you want to develop (e.g. *The Act of Will* by Roberto Assagioli).

Third, do something you have never done before; perform an act of courage; make a plan and follow it; do something very slowly; act contrary to the expectations that significant others have of you; behave independently of what people say or do; postpone an action you would like to begin right now or begin at once something you want to postpone; finally, undertake something that makes you feel insecure; face squarely some of your worst fears and anxieties, first in the *inner theater of the imagination* (through a guided daydream), and then in the *outer theater of real life*.

Fourth, work with the following practices or exercises that greatly help and intensify the growth and expression of the will:

   a. Never abandon a plan, project, or undertaking that you have carefully selected and in which you believe because of the difficulties that may arise. Meditate on the saying: "If something is worth starting it is worth completing."

   b. Learn how to say "no" to people, to desires and longings in yourself and to various inducements by life or circumstances, no matter what is the attraction of the temptations. For whenever we resist ourselves orothers, or deny ourselves something we really crave, we charge our will and, conversely, whenever we give in to temptations and desires, and seek instant gratification, we discharge and weaken our will.

c. Purposely cultivate activities that you dislike or find hard to do (e.g. physical exercises, unpleasant chores and tasks, etc.) or that have no other purpose than to enable you to do what you want.

d. When confused, in doubt, or torn between two or more contradictory tendencies, goals, or desires, take the time to meditate, to clarify your motivations and objections until clarity and focus are found once again, and then act, but not before. To act when confused, unsure, or torn between contradictory tendencies is another major way of discharging the will.

e. Meditate on all the disadvantages and problems that have resulted during the last year because you did not have a developed, strong, and skillful will. Then, meditate on all the advantages of having a strong, effective, and skillful will, and *visualize* both situations very clearly, ending by seeing yourself as already having and using a strong and skillfull will.

f. Meditate upon, integrate, and use the following insights and principles: Images and ideas have a motor element in them that will bring about their realization in your consciousness and then in your life and being. Ideas and images tend to awaken and intensify the emotions and feelings that are connected to them. Attention, interest, affirmation, and repetition reinforce the ideas, images, and psychological states that correspond to them.

g. Learn to concentrate your *full attention* upon a physical object (e.g. the hands of a watch that are slowly turning), then upon a mental image, an emotion, a thought, an inspiration, and finally a plan of action to achieve a given objective, at the exclusion of everything else, so that your mind can turn into a magnifying glass focusing all your attention and consciousness upon the chosen subject.

h. Study the laws and practices that will enable you to raise your physical, emotional, mental, and spiritual energies—so that you can deliberately raise your vitality and energies through proper nutrition, sleep, physical, psychological, and spiritual exercises.

i. Learn how to focus upon and use all the functions of the psyche to energize the will—thought, emotion, imagination, intuition, and biopsychic drives.

j. Finally, bear in mind that the training of the will begins with the *will to train the will.* Here are four traditional steps presented by the Spiritual Tradition that cna be used very profitably, namely:

Preparation: Alignment with the Higher Self through physical relaxation, emotional centering, and mental focusing.

Purification and Elevation: Direct the aspirations and feelings of the heart and the attention of the mind toward the Higher Self.

Identification: Imagine, affirm, and experience identifcation with the Self.

Meditation: On the nature, characteristics, and significance of the will in your life.

Conclusion:

Personal consecration involves two fundamental steps; developing a strong and skilled will and finding or choosing a well-deliberated and noble purpose to which to consecrate one's time, energies, resources, self and life. This, in turn, requires a minimum of *self-knowledge*, obtained through self-observation and consciously living through many experiences in life. It also requires an attunement with our Higher Self, obtained through a breakthrough of the Super-conscious into the conscious, and the activation of our intuition, which can be achieved through living Prayer, so as to make us aware of God's Will and Plan for us in this life, and which our Higher Self knows. As such, it is the logical step after emotional purification and mental clarification.

At the level of the *personality*, personal consecration will train and activate our will and personality so as to make us "Warriors," the captain of our personality, and in control of our behavior, life, and destiny, and thus to achieve true autonomy, integrity, and the power of conscious choice. It will enable us to do and get what we want in this world. At the level of the *Soul*, personal consecration will enable us to align our vehicles and consciousness to those of our Higher Self so as to make us aware of what is God's Will and Purpose for us in this life, to attune our personality and lives to them; and to have the guidance, inspiration, courage, and strength to fully accomplish them . . . and thus to fulfill our highest purpose and reason for being on Earth. It will enable us to know and to do what God wants from us and for us in this world.

Here, the choice of goals and objectives, of the life path one wants to follow, and of what one wants to do to serve God and Man, and thus to become, is truly crucial. It will necessarily involve many hours of reflection and meditation, and much observation and testing of one's self in the real life experience, and a genuine breakthrough of the intuition with ensuing readjustments as one grows and matures. For this is the quintessence of personal consecration: to find a noble and worthy ideal to which to dedicate one's self and one's life, and then to follow and *live the discipline* that is necessary to achieve and realize this noble ideal!

Practical Exercise

Preliminary: Find the right place and the right position. Then make an effort of Introversion, Supraversion, and Infraversion.

Actual work: Meditation (to be inserted before actual exercises suggested in text)

Focus your attention upon your Will and your Creative Energies. If you are Qabalistically knowledgeable and inclined, work on activating Geburah and Chesed on your Tree of Life and review the functioning of your Will at this point in time. How is your Will functioning at the present time? Are you able to do what you want to do and not to do what you really don't want to do?

Have you been able to identify and crystallize worthy goals and ideals to which to dedicate your time, energies, and resources—to consecrate your life?

Write them down! Meditate upon what you are really living for at this point in time.

Have you been able to develop and practice a *discipline* to enable you to realize and enflesh what you really want?

Are you able to organize and direct the many elements, dimensions, energies, and faculties—the resources of your personality, of your sociocultural environment, and of your Soul to achieve the ideals and objectives you are living for? Make a list of them and identify the strengths and weaknesses you perceive in yourself, and discuss these with others who might help you by sharing with you how they perceive you.

Find a symbol or an image that represents your Will as it now is, as you would *ideally like it to be*, and of the *obstacles* that prevent you from being what you would ideally like to be. Invoke the Light, Fire, and Life of your Divine Spark to energize the symbol or image that represents your ideal Will.

When you have completed this meditation, will self-examination, and psychospiritual exercises, make the appropriate entries in your workbook as to what you have discovered, what you have done, what has happened, and how you were able to cope.

Chapter Five

VISIONARY UNFOLDMENT:
The Opening, Training, and Utilization of
Imagination through Visualization

There is a proverb that is as old as humankind which claims that "when individuals or groups lose their visionary powers, they lose themselves and the power to consciously grow, unfold their unique being, and express themselves creatively." Moreover, a little thought will soon reveal that anything, and I mean *anything*, that a human being has ever created was first an image or a thought in his mind—which shows the tremendous power and importance of the imagination. In most civilizations, the imagination was revered and highly prized as the creative power par excellence, as the very link and life line between the inner and the outer worlds. After the Renaissance, however, and especially after the Enlightenment with their emphasis upon the conquest of the outer, physical world and the development of positive, rational knowledge, the imagination was relegated to children, women, lovers, poets and mystics. Now, however, with the rediscovery of the feminine principle in human nature, the higher reaches of human nature, and the unfoldment of human consciousness with breakthroughs of the Superconscious into the conscious, the power and importance of the imagination with its process of visualization are finally coming into their own.

Consider the following basic points, drawn from different traditions, which beautifully illustrate the true nature and power of the imagination:

1. The Western Spiritual tradition clearly tells its students and devotees that: "By Names and Images are all Powers (of the Psyche) awakened and re-awakened."

2. One of the most important psychological principles of Psychosynthesis is that: "Every image has in itself a motor drive" and that "images and mental pictures tend to produce the physical conditions and the external acts corresponding to them."

3. Carl Jung, in one of his most perceptive statements about the nature and use of the imagination, declared succinctly: "The psychological machinery which transmutes energy and consciousness is the symbol."

4. Erich Fromm has rightly called the "language of the imagination"—images, symbols, myths and rituals —the "Forgotten Language," the lost language of the Deep Mind, of the unconscious and the Superconscious, which "speaks" and manifests in dreams, guided daydreams and in visions.

5. In the light of the foregoing, it is easy to understand why the imagination and its accompanying process of visualization is one of the essential components of Theurgy or Ritual which is designed to activate the intuitive flow: inspiration and creative energy.

Thus, in conclusion, we may say that while in the outer world we have an emphasis upon *observation* to gather scientific data and many languages with their related alphabets, sounds, and concepts to communicate, in the inner worlds of the psyche we have *visualization,* or inner observation, and the universal language of the depths and heights which is the language of the imagination—images, symbols, myths, and rituals with their vibratory, energy, and consciousness frequencies that release a tremendous power of evocation and creative expression.

The central thesis of this writer is that we are now on the very threshold of a new culture that will put a great deal of value on introversion and supraversion—on the exploration of the inner worlds of the human psyche and on the harnessing of its latent higher energies and faculties. As man has learned in the last 500 years to observe, study and control the forces of the outer, physical universe, so he must now learn to observe, study and master the potentialities of the inner worlds of his own being. One of the most important keys to accomplish this task is to understand and be able to use the imagination and the power of visualization which can be studied and trained as we did with the power of observation.

Just as the power of outer observation is crucial to gather knowledge about the physical world and to orient oneself in that world, so the power of inner observation, or visualization, is essential to gather knowledge of the inner world and to orient oneself in them. Both faculties can be compared to our physical "muscles" and their training and coordination. Unfortunately, so far our civilization has emphasized and privileged only outer observation which is necessary to make our way in the physical world. But when it comes to the functioning and education of inner visualization, most people are like little children who must begin at the very beginning.

It is interesting to note, however, that children generally have a very vivid imagination which has become atrophied because of lack of use and training, and that so-called primitive people were also believed to have a very vivid imagination, or eidetic faculty, which slowly faded away with the oncoming of modern industrial societies. Among adults, only artists, poets, lovers, and mystics are generally endowed with a well-functioning and creative imagination. And women, too, who are believed to be more emotional and intuitive than men, are seen to have a well-functioning imagination—a belief which seems to link the power of imagination and the faculty of visualization with the female side of human nature.

In the last three decades more and more psychologists and psychotherapists have become interested in the image-making function which was too long considered to be an interior faculty representing a lower level of mental development of their disciplines. Freud, Jung, Desoille, Singer, Pope, and Assagioli have now paved the way for a more mature and serious scientific study of such activities as dreaming, daydreaming, fantasy, suggestion, and guided imagery—all of which are, ultimately largely based upon the nature and proper working of the imagination and of visualization. Religion, on the other hand, with its intimate relationship with symbols, archetypal images, myth, and ritual that grew out of an earlier phase of story-telling and drama with their great evocative power has always been deeply interested and practically involved with the imagination and the power of visualization—sometimes praising it as divine inspiration coming from the Higher Worlds and, at other times, condemning it as a satanic influence leading to idolatry. But it is the Sacred Traditions of the past—in their occult, mystical, and magical teachings—which are now converging into an *emerging and unfolding spiritual science*, incorporating the best and the latest developments of humanistic psychology, that we can find the fullest comprehension and application of the nature and workings of the imagination and visualization to draw upon their latent potentialities. In sum: one cannot be a true "spiritual scientist" without having mastered them and neither can one become a full human being without knowing what they are and how to use them. But to be able to use the imagination and to visualize anything effectively, one must have developed and coordinated, to a certain extent, the will and concentration, thinking and meditation, and feeling and devotion—which is why these faculties and processes are all interrelated and interacting.

What then is the imagination and the power of visualization? The very etymological meaning of the word "imagination" reveals its true mature: it is the *image-making function*. It is the psychological function which evokes, reproduces, and creates images of all kinds. It is also the synthetic function par excellence as it can evoke and reproduce the functions and materials of the other functions (such as sensations, feelings, desires, thinking) and it includes various types of imaginings such as the evocation of visual images, mental crystallizations, auditory, tactile, and artistic imagination. Visualization is simply: the power to see things with the "eyes of the mind." Roberto Assagioli puts it succinctly in the following words:

> The imagination in the precise sense of the function of evoking and creating images is one of the most important and spontaneously active functions of the hyman psyche, both in its con-scious and in its unconscious aspects or levels. Therefore, it is one of the functions which has to be utilized owing to its great potency. This explains why in psychosynthetic therapy we are particularly interested in the regulation, development, and utilization of imagination, since the practice of the technique of imagination is one of the best ways toward a synthesis of the different functions.[1]

And he concludes:

> The imagination has a close relationship with intuition as intuitions often present themselves to our consciousness

not in an abstract and simple way but in the form of complex images. This entails a primary task of learning how to distinguish the contents, the essence, the idea inherent in an intuition from the form, the vestments which it assumes. The character of the form being symbolic, the complex and important question of symbolism arises. Essentially, the symbol can both *veil* and *unveil*. When mistaken for the reality that it expresses, it veils it and is thus a source of illusion. When recognized for what it is—a means of expression—it constitutes a useful and, at times, indispensable aid to "catching" and then illuminating a transcendental reality.[2]

In the Mystery Tradition, the imagination is often referred to as the "Ass which carries Jesus into the city of Jerusalem," that is, it is the vehicle and the channel through which the energies and the materials of the Superconscious and of the Spiritual Self are conveyed to the field of consciousness and to the human self.

The imagination contains, within itself, various important subfunctions or ways of manifesting itself. The most important of these are *receptive* or *reproductive* imagination and *creative* imagination (its "female" and "male" polarities) as well as *subjective* and *objective* imagination. The imagination, moreover functions at all levels of the psyche: in the field of consciousness as well as in the subconscious, unconscious, and Superconscious, embodying and giving shape to the most ephemeral and trivial ideas, emotions, and sensations all the way to the most exalted and universal archetypes and intuitions of true Vision.

Reproductive imagination is the ability to invoke, remember, or recreate on the "screen of the mind" anything, or event, one has ever seen or experienced. Whereas *creative imagination* is the ability to generate new ideas, combinations, associations, events and stories.

Subjective imagination can be conceived as the purely *personal* imagination of one person focusing his attention and consciousness within his own being.

Objective imagination, on the other hand, is the direct

and transpersonal perception and vision of the Inner Worlds which can be entered into by the proper use of a focused and energized imagination—in particular those of the Etheric, Astral, and Mental worlds.

Finally, the imagination and the power of visualization have an immense evocative and awakening power for our other functions (emotions, thoughts, and intuitions) by resonating with an "opening up" of the various regions of the psyche—the subconscious, the unconscious, and the Superconscious mind, with their related energies, vibrations, and state of consciousness. *Visualization*, the power to see things with the "eyes of the mind" also entails two basic processes: one that is purely mental and nonvisual in the sensory way (talking to oneself, conceptualizing ideas, the daydreaming) and the other that is fully visual and eidetic in the sensory way (dreaming, hallucinating, or seeing things through astral or etheric clairvoyance). Here, the most important point is not to seek to "see things" in the same way as one sees them with the physical eye but, rather, to become so absorbed and immersed in what is happening in the inner dimension that one forgets and withdraws completely from the external environment, physical stimuli and events, and loses all sense of time. The key factor, in other words, is *full concentration and absorption in the fantasy one is living*. For it is this way only that the imagination will unlock the doors of the unconscious and of the Superconscious and that we will be able to enter consciously in the inner worlds.

The cardinal axiom for the development of the imagination and the power of visualization is the same as that which applies to the training of all the other functions of the psyche: it is practice, practice and, again, PRACTICE: And, as we mentioned before, certain prerequisites are very important. Namely, the will must be trained together with a good capacity for concentration, and so must thinking with a capacity for meditation and feeling with a good capacity for devotion be trained and coordinated. For it is only at this point that visualization and the proper use of the imagination can truly be realized as they involve and depend upon the proper and synthetic functioning of thinking, feeling, and willing. Without the coordinated development of these, the imagination will remain "flat," ever-shifting, and lifeless with the subject being unable to fully immerse himself into and live the scenarios and events that are being imagined.

The training and proper functioning of the imagination is vital for both the actualization of the personality, the psychological part of the Work, and for the realization of the Self, the spiritual part of the Work. And it can be utilized both for psychotherapeutic work (the exploration, purification, and integration of the personality) and for spiritual work proper (the training for the Mysteries and the realization of the spiritual Light). The most important and integrated exercise to train the imagination and develop the power of visualization is known today as "mental imagery," the guided daydream or what I would call the inward journey. For, just as we can take journeys in the outer, physical world, so we can also take journeys in the psychological, psychic, and spiritual worlds of the psyche—provided we have a vivid imagination, a trained power of visualization, and the ability to get completely absorbed by unfoldment of inner events. Young children, people from primitive societies, artists and poets, inventors and creative persons of all types, some psychotherapists and, of course, those who are interested or trained in the occult, mystical, or magical traditions have, consciously or unconsciously, taken all kinds of inner journeys. Most forms of effective prayer and worship, magical and occult exercises, and all basic spiritual exercises, including work on the Tree of Life, Path Work, Inner Plane or Out-of-the-Body work involves some variant of the Inward Journey using either the subjective or the objective, or both aspects of the imagination.

A human being can live in essentially two worlds: the outer, physical world of nature and the inner, psychic and spiritual worlds of the soul. Ever since the Renaissance, modern man in the West has made a tremendous effort of *extroversion*, the projection of his consciousness and psychic energies toward the outer, physical world of nature. This he did to an unprecedented extent in the history of humankind by developing modern science and its offspring, technology, which has enabled him to bring about industrialization, urbanization, and bureaucratization—in short, modern industrial society. But he had a price to pay for this, and a price which is now just about to really make itself felt: alienation from his own self and from the inner worlds of his psyche. To gain knowledge and mastery of nature, it is now imperative, for the very survival of Life and of this planet that man again get in touch with his very own inner worlds, energies, and faculties which he sacrificed to achieve the former. Thus *extroversion* must now be balanced by *introversion* and *infraversion* (directing one's attention toward the physical dimension) must be balanced by *supraversion* (directing one's attention toward the spiritual dimension). It is interesting to note that the English word *eccentric* means "away from the center" and that the French word *désaxé* means "to have lost one's axis or center," both of which beautifully describe the condition of the average person in our society! And here, it is the *imagination* and its major process, *visualization* that hold the key, or passport, for the systematic exploration and integration of the inner, psychic, and spiritual worlds of the human soul—of the subconscious, unconscious, and Superconscious.

The proper use of guided imagery can also provide an excellent diagnostic tool to externalize and project a microcosmic picture of a person's personality and life. In a similar fashion, guided imagery and the guided daydream

can also be utilized as a cathartic, expressive, and therapeutic tool to bring into consciousness and to work with
repressed emotions and traumas—to bring light to the dark
caves and labyrinths of the unconscious. Finally, the structured use of the imagination through visualization can be
used as a powerful tool for *personal growth*—for self-actualization and self-realization—to complete the development
and integration of the personality and of its functions, and
to bring through into expression, in the field of consciousness, the higher energies and the latent potentialities of the
Superconscious and of the Spiritual Self. Thus it is equally
and perhaps even more so a powerful and indispensable
instrument for true spiritual work. In fact, the "male aspect"
of Prayer, Theurgy or Ritual works essentially through the
process of visualization—which must become as real and
as compelling a reality for the student as the outer, physical
world is for the ordinary person! Here, the imagination is
used first in its *subjective aspect*, then in its *objective aspect*,
when the student is fully immersed in this inner world, to
finally culminate in true spiritual visions which are endowed
with a reality and transforming power of their own.

To better understand and appreciate the impact or psychodynamics of the imagination and of the process of visualization upon the psyche, it is important to keep in mind the
following psychological laws:

1. That every idea or image tends to produce the state
   of mind, the physical state, and the acts that correspond to it.
2. That proper attention and repetition greatly reinforce the effectiveness of the idea or image that is
   being used and rendered "alive" in the psyche.
3. That, most of the time for most people, the effects of
   the idea or image, that is the activation of that to
   which it is related, are produced without one being

aware of them as they take place in the unconscious, both lower and higher.

4. That, whatever we think about, direct our attention to, or visualize, we will actually nourish, energize and activate by sending our psychic energies toward, and awakening in our nature, the layers of consciousness and the energies to which it corresponds.

As Carl Jung aptly summarized it, in describing the role and properties of the imagination:

> . . . . *Looking*, psychologically, brings about the activation of the object: it is as if something were emanating from one's spiritual eye that evokes or activates the object of one's vision. The English verb "to look at" does not convey this meaning but the German "betrachten," which is an equivalent, means also to *make pregnant* . . . So to look or concentrate upon a thing, "betrachten," gives the quality of being pregnant to the object. And if it is pregnant, then something is due to come out of it; it is alive, it produces, it multiplies. That is the case with any fantasy image; one concentrates upon it, and then one finds that one has great difficulty in keeping the thing quiet, it gets restless, it shifts, something is added, or it multiplies itself; one fills it with living power and it becomes pregnant.[3]

One of the major tools for training the imagination and the power of visualization is guided imagery or the guided daydream. This method can be used with a trained guide or alone or even in a group situation. The basic rules are very simple, but they can only be understood and mastered with plenty of *actual practice*. They are:

1. Select a comfortable place that is quiet, with little noise and not too much light, and where one is not likely to be disturbed for one or two hours. Then, make yourself as comfortable as possible by taking off your shoes, unbuckling your belt, and finding a truly relaxed position for your body. Finally, close your eyes, bring the focus of your attention upon

yourself, take three deep breaths to signal the beginning of the inward journey, shift the gears of your consciousness, and enter into the inner worlds.

2. As the actual starting point, you can choose an image, a symbol, or even a given situation and begin the inner voyage by making a thorough study of your consciousness (use the checklist developed for that purpose). I generally have the student visualize and describe what he is wearing, the place in which he finds himself, and his present sensations, desires, emotions, thoughts, and general state of mind.

3. The inner voyage then begins with a definite *intention* and purpose in mind (e.g. looking for an object or a symbol—a cup, a sword, a house, a place, or a person).

4. During the actual inner voyage, the student who is now functioning in the world of his imagination and who has completely withdrawn his senses and attention from the outer world to focus upon the inner worlds where *anything is possible*, can move in his imaginary space in three basic ways:

   a. He can remain on the same "ground level" by walking into a meadow, a forest, or a field. In psychodynamic terms this would bring him in touch with his preconscious and subconscious mind.

   b. He can begin a descent into a cave, under water, or in the basement of a house. In psychodynamic terms, this would bring him in touch with his lower unconscious and repressed, negative and threatening events of the past, arousing anxiety, depression, or a state of heaviness and being ill at ease.

   c. He can begin an ascent toward the top of a mountain, toward the clouds or the sun, or toward the higher floors of a house. And this would bring him in touch with his higher consciousness or Superconscious and awaken a sensation of lightness and warmth, of well-being, joy, and, perhaps, even *illumination*.

5. It is very important to keep in mind here that, in the world of the imagination, *all is possible* and the normal restrictions of the physical world do not apply. Thus, here a person can fly, pass through walls, transform himself into another being, and acquire "magical" powers.

6. The events and the sequence of the inner journey can be either well structured by the guide or left unstructured for the voyager to determine for himself as he moves along and faces various situations in his imaginary world. Some basic guidelines, however, do exist with standard situations, encounters, and events to be faced. Briefly, these are:

   a. Take a trip to the sea and explore its depths. Take a trip to a mountain to find the Temple of the Sun, the Temple of Silence, or a Guardian of the Mysteries. Take a trip under the earth to explore its caverns and depths. Go somewhere to meet a Wise Man, a Wise Woman, or an Angel, or other characters in their mythical or realistic expressions.

   b. Encounters with other beings—human, animal, or mythical—are very important and generally involve meeting with persons of the same or the opposite sex, dialoguing with them, giving them something or receiving something from them; asking questions and answering questions; exposing one's dilemmas or discussing existential, philosophical, or religious matters.

c. While doing all of this, it is important to study oneself and to observe and note any changes that might occur in one's state of consciousness (using the appropriate checklist), particularly one's emotional, mental, and intuitive states, and to be able to describe them. It is also important to bear in mind that every being and event encountered in the inner voyage actually represents, symbolically and analogically, a part of one's being and life.

d. One can also take these beings with oneself in moving through the psychological space, going up or down, and watching for transformations that are likely to occur in them and/or in oneself. For example, one can meet an octopus in the sea and see this creature transform itself into a human form, the face of one's mother, a friend, or an enemy, as one moves back to the surface of the sea, and then become an angel as one further moves towards the sky or the sun.

7. Finally, one returns to one's present place and state of consciousness by using the same means one used to begin the trip. At this point, one would take three deep breaths and reopen one's eyes after having "shifted the gears" of one's consciousness from the inner to the outer world. One might also want to take notes of what happened, describing the events that took place and one's reactions to them, or transcribe the session that has been recorded for a later analysis of it with the guide.

Taking his clue from Carlyle who stated that "in a symbol lies *concealment* or revelation," Assagioli contends that: "symbols properly recognized and understood possess great value: they are 'evocative' and induce direct under-standing."[4] Indeed, for him the fact that words indicating higher realities have their roots in sensuous experience serves to emphasize the essential analogical correspondence bet-ween the external and the inner worlds (remember the Hermetic Axiom: "As above so below, as below so above"). In fact, the person who takes them literally and does not pass beyond the symbol to its underlying reality will never know the "truth." For Assagioli, there are 14 basic types of symbols leading the student of guided imagery to contact the transpersonal energies and the high potentials of his psyche. These are:

1. *Symbols of introversion, of inner orientation:* Introver-sion is an urgent necessity for modern man and for our present civilization which is far too extrovert-ed, man being caught in a vortex of activities that become ends in themselves. Thus, the external life must be counterbalanced by an adequate inner life. Recognition must be given to the existence not only of the external world, but of different inner worlds, and that it is possible, indeed, man's duty, to know them, explore them, and conquer them.

2. *Symbols of deepening, of descending to the "ground" of our being:* The exploration of the unconscious is symbolically regarded as the descent into the abyss of human nature, as the investigation of the "under-world" of the psyche. The person who is willing and courageous enough to recognize the lower sides of his personality, without allowing this knowl-edge to overwhelm him, achieves a true spiritual victory.

3. *Symbols of elevation and ascent:* The conquest of the "inner space" in an upward direction. There is a series of inner worlds, each of which has its specific

characteristics and levels; the world of inner sensations, of passions and drives, of the imagination, of the intuition, of the will, and of the Light. Here the symbol of the sky and of the Holy Mountain as a superior realm, the habitation of the gods and the goal of human aspiration, is universal.

As is well-known, the Hindus believed the peaks of the Himalayas to be the home of the gods, while the Greeks regarded Mount Olympus as the habitation of their divine beings. The Japanese have Mount Fujiyama, Moses received his revelation on Mount Sinai, the transfiguration of Jesus took place on Mount Tabor, and he gave his Sermon on the Mount.

4. *Symbols of expansion, of broadening of consciousness:* The spectrum of consciousness, like the spectrum of light, contains only a fraction of the total spectrum which is conscious or visible. Thus our consciousness can be enlarged on three basic directions: laterally, up, and down, to include increasingly larger zones of impression and contents. Time also provides another direction in which expansion can take place, from the present to the past and the future.

5. *Symbols of awakening:* The state of consciousness of the average man can be termed a "dream state in a world of illusions:" the illusions of the "reality" of the external world as our senses perceive it, and of the many illusions created by the imagination, the emotions, and mental concepts. Thus, "awakening" demands first of all *an act of courage* and confrontation with reality.

6. *The symbols of light and illumination:* Just as ordinary waking marks the passage from darkness of the

night to the light of the sun, so awakening spiritual awareness marks the transition called "illumination" and the activation of true inspiration and intuition.

7. *The symbols of fire:* The worship and veneration of fire are found in all religions. Everywhere, on altars, in torches (e.g. the Olympic Torch), and in lamps, the sacred fire burns and the flames glitter. The inner experience of fire has been experienced by many mystics.

8. *The symbols of growth and development:* The seed and the flower—the seed which enfolds within itself the potentiality of the tree and the flower which opens from the closed bud and which contains the fruit. Development signifies release from encumbrances and denotes the passage from the potential to the actual.

9. *Symbols of strengthening or intensification:* Spiritual experiences can be regarded as intensifying the life, consciousness, and love capacity of a person —as amplifying the "psychic voltage' with which the average man lives. This can also involve the passage from the potential to the actual, from latency into manifestation, and the passage from the personal to the transpersonal.

10. *The symbols of love:* Human love is, in one respect, a desire and an attempt to "come out" of oneself, to transcend the limits of separate existence and enter into communion with, to fuse oneself, with another being, with a greater reality.

11. *The symbols of the way, the path, and of pilgrimage:* These have been universally used to denote human evolution toward the completion and perfection

of one's being and destiny.

12. *The symbols of transmutation:* Both the body and the psyche can be transmuted, or refined and perfected, by means of a regenerative transformation which is psycho-spiritual alchemy. Transmutation can be achieved in two complementary ways: by an elevation of one's field of consciousness, or by a descent of the spiritual energies and inspirations into one's field of consciousness.

13. *The symbols of regeneration, of the "new birth":* These are related to the former since a complete transmutation opens the way to regeneration and a new birth, the birth of the spiritual Self in the personality.

14. *The symbols of liberation which are related to those of development:* These imply the elimination of distortions and resistances, a process of liberation from our complexes, our illusions, from identification with the variouis parts we play in life, the masks we assume. It is a release, a freeing and activation of latent potentialities.

Roberto Assagioli offers many basic spiritual exercises to be carried through by guided imagery (e.g. the Blossoming of the Rose, the Legend of the Grail, and Dante's *Divine Comedy*.

The *Divine Comedy* is a perfect syumbol of a complete psychosynthesis. The first part—the Pilgrimage through Hell—indicates the exploration of the unconscious. The second part—the Ascent to the Mountain of Purgatory—indicates the exploration of the subconscious and the process of moral purification and the gradual raising of the level of consciousness. The third part—the visit to Paradise or Heaven—depicts the various stages of Superconscious realization, up to the final vision of God in which Love and Will are fused. Here, we find a specific symbolism and process of visualization. At the beginning, Dante (the student) finds himself in a dark forest and is in despair. Then, he sees a hill illuminated by the sun and meets Virgil, who symbolizes human reason. Dante sets out to climb the hill, but three wild beasts, representing different aspects of the unredeemed unconscious, bar the way. Virgil then explains to him that he cannot climb the hill directly, but has to first make the Pilgrimage through Hell; that is, explore his unconscious and release the energies that are bound there. Virgil then leads Dante on this journey through Hell, helping him, encouraging him, and explaining to him the various phases of the process. Virgil accompanies Dante through his Journey in Hell and his ascent of the Mount of Purgatory, but once Dante has reached that summit, he disappears and is replaced by Beatrice who represents Intuition, Divine Wisdom, which alone is competent to lead him into the various regions of the Superconscious.

To this exercise, I would add another one: the visualization of the exercise representing the complete process of psychosynthesis: self-actualization and self-realization. Here, one begins with Introversion and refocusing one's attention upon the inner worlds. Then, Ascent and elevation of the center of one's consciousness to contact and be infused by the Light and Fire of the Self. Leading to Descent, bringing that Light and Fire into the center of consciousness and then into the unconscious to cleanse it and reintegrate it. Finally, radiation of the Light and Fire into the world and dynamized and inspired action therein.

When it comes to spiritual training proper, we find that all the key exercises of the Occult, Mystical, and Magical paths rely heavily upon the utilization of the imagination, of the power of visualization, and of the method of guided imagery. Visualization, together with concentration, meditation, and devotion form the base of the Pyramid which will eventually set the intuition in motion through the process of Invocation-Evocation. Moreover, by visualizing a given image of symbol, we are creating a thought form and a pathway by means of which higher, Superconscious energies and materials can be concretized and directed. Without a form, they would dissipate and never manifest in a specific fashion, and without a proper pathway, they could not have a direction or channel of expression. Thus, as we take the basic spiritual exercises and the more advanced and specialized ones based upon the Qabalah and the Tree of Life, in each we find a major role that is played by the use of the imagination, the power of visualization, and the method of guided imagery. Some specific examples are:

1. *Divine Names:* When vibrating Divine Names or Words of Power, we must use visualization in its pictorial, auditory, and sensory aspects; that is, we vibrate the chosen Name in a given location and Center, wherein we perceive Light (colors), Form (a given shape), Fire (sensations of heat and warmth), we might hear sounds and rumblings (the shifting of the vibratory rates), and we may sense energy and life being activated and circulated through our being that comes "alive."

2. *The Sign of the Cross:* When using the Ritual of the Cross, we have to use the imagination to visualize a sphere of dazzling white Light overshadowing our Head Center, sending a ray of its Light, Fire, and Life in a pillar of Light descending first into our Heart Center and then to the Feet Center. Then, from the Heart Center we visualize another ray of that Light, whose colors now change, radiating and spreading to the Shoulder Centers which must also be visualized. And, as in the former exercise, we

may also have auditory and sensory phenomena related to the visual part—as well as mental crystallizations and new insights. This Cross of Light may then be traced and projected upon our own Aura, that of others, in the Temple and in the city wherein this ritual is being carried out.

3. *The Lord's Prayer, the Creed, the Beatitudes, the Ten Commandments, the Hail Mary,* and *the Invocation to the Holy Spirit:* All of these exercises, in their component parts and as a whole, involve an active part being played by the imagination, visualization, and guided imagery. For each key symbol that is being used (e.g. Father, Heaven, Kingdom), one or more images and symbols should appear on the screen of the imagination to focus and manifest the energies and inspirations that are related to the image or symbol. Finally, connections between various symbols and the centers on the Tree of Life are also established through the proper use of visualization in its pictorial, auditory, sensory, and mental forms. Thus, crosses, lines, circles, spirals, etc. are formed in our imagination through which the energies of the Superconscious can flow to the various parts and levels of our being and of the world.

4. *The Qabalah:* All the main exercises and training programs of the Qabalah are based upon the active use of the imagination, visualization and guided imagery; first at the subjective level, then at the objective level, and finally, for some at least, at the level of true Vision.

Thus the formulation of the Tree of Life in our own Aura with each of its Centers and Paths, their colors, images, and connections are, basically, a form of guided imagery. Each Center has its own Divine Name, Archangelic Name,

Angelic Name, and correspondence in the physical world, its own symbols, images, colors, and specific inner experiences. Likewise, traveling on the 22 Paths connecting these Centers, with the experiences and ordeals that are related to each Center involves, basically, a guided imagery to be performed on three basic levels: the subjective, the objective, and the level of true Vision or Contemplation wherein one becomes, momentarily, *that which one beholds*, or its vehicle of expression, and where one is transformed by the experience.

For example, take the Heart Center, Tiphareth: this Center has a specific location—overshadowing the heart region in the middle of the Pillar of Equilibrium. It has various images linked with it: a King, a Child, and a sacrificed God. It has a God Name: Jehovah Aloah ve Daath; an Archangelic Name: Raphael; an Angelic Name: Malachim; and a Mundane Name: the Sun. Its title means beauty and equilibrium; its spiritual experience is the Vision of the Harmony of things and the Mysteries of Crucifixion; its virtue is Devotion to the Great Work and its vice, Pride. Its symbols are the Calvary Cross, the Rosy Cross, the truncated Pyramid, and the Cube. Its colors are clear, rose-pink (Atziluth), yellow (Briah), salmon pink (Yetzirah), and golden amber (Assiah).

Finally, Pathwork on the Tree of Life is actually a structured guided daydream which should lead one from the level of subjective imagination, or of one's own fantasy, to objective imagination, the Astral World, and perhaps for some, beyond to the Mental and the Spiritual Worlds.

A very well informed and perceptive American writer, Theodore Roszack, writes:

> With the eclipse of God in the 19th and 20th Centuries, we have no other place to begin but with ourselves—*within ourselves*. All we have lost in the course of becoming this torn and tormented creature called modern man—the visionary energies, the discipline of the sacred—we discover again in the depths of our psyche. It is there or not at all! The Aquarian Age is characterized by high moral idealism and an open-

ness to visionary experience. Its main sign: bringing spiritual waters to a parched and dying culture. We have the guilt of *having lived and living below the level of our potentialities*, thus purgation and renewal are the themes of the day . . . What is at stake today, for our very survival on this planet, is the *survival of the visionary energies*, the survival of our ability to perceive, if only dimly, the life-enhancing truths to which myth, ritual, sacramental symbol, contemplative object, magical rites, the natural wonders, and ecstatic communion bear witness—the *Deus Absconditus*. At the climatic summit of industrialized civilization, as everything is beginning to crumble around us, we discover that there is also an ecology of the psychic environment which must be trusted to find its way to balance and compensation. Either that or the human personality, the richest of all the world's gardens, becomes waste and toxic. To create an ecology of the Spirit, that is the task we confront on the Aquarian frontier![6]

The central thesis of Roszack is that: We are the unfinished animal charged with the task of self-perfection—the very "discovery" that has ever been reborn and reawakened in the direct experience of every Saint, Sage, and Hero. If the fulfillment of one's highest nature and destiny is the true meaning of Salvation then, indeed, it is the task that must marshall and consecrate *every function of the human psyche:* willing, thinking, feeling, imagination, and intuition in particular. For, as he so well states: "Behind every drive for more and better, stands the *transcendent quest*, the pursuit of the highest of all goals: To be Godlike among Gods."[7]

His secondary thesis is that: it is possible that the entire inventory of human culture radiates out of the white-hot *visionary experiences* of the few (the Saints, the Sages, and the Heroes) as creators of the original human culture. "Imagine," he says, "that culture as wholly nonmaterial, a subtle landscape of myths and rituals, of cosmic wanderings and spectral explorations, of dance, chant, and rapture."[8] And he concludes: "The anthropology of Eliade, Campbell, and Castaneda recognize the visionary genius as the first world citizen, the prophet of a planetary culture we have yet to see born!"[9]

For him, the great battle is always within the arena of our own soul. Unfinished animals that we are, we engage in a life-long exorcism of demons that are, in reality, so many fragments of our own forbidden experience. Dichotomy is the heart of the problem and the purpose of the Aquarian frontier is to close the dichotomies that have for so long tyrannized Western society, to reunite flesh and spirit, intellect and instinct; and, above all, to bridge the rift that parts sacred from profane. Its search is for the Earth's epiphanies, for *experienced divinity*, in the world, in the here and now, it is synthesis. Its thrust is to find the sacred within the profane and the profane within the sacred. Thus, culture is what the few create in order to confer their vision upon the many!

How do we come to the visionary fire? Through Myth, Magic, and Mystery: these are the primary cultural channels the fire runs along on its way from the few to the many. Taken together, they form the sacred triangle which has always been at the core of Religion and Mystery Traditions. But, today, the sacred triangle has become the profane triangle:

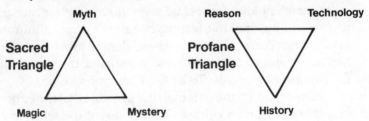

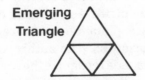

In the profane triangle of today, myth is synonymous for falsehood, magic is hocus-pocus and show business, and mystery has come down to the level of a thriller! Nothing of the original dignity of these three concepts penetrates the dense veil of trivialization that now screens them from a decent appreciation in the popular mind! But, within a few generations, a new sweeping revolution may occur, shooting through society like pent-up energies that have reached their critical point—toward resacralization. *Myths* govern the encounter of the person with time, hence with mortality. It uses the action of time to speak of eternal things. The purpose of myths is to imbue the randomness of events with instructive order, so that the intellect is not abandoned to the chaos of time. Myths have been given to us so that we may understand our personal and collective experiences. They educate us to the dramatic and dialectic structure of history: they offer the paradigms we need in order to read meaning into human conduct.

Magic governs the encounter of the person with nature and with human consciousness. At the root of the magical consciousness is the conviction that mind permeates the universe, filling every natural object with life, consciousness, and purpose. In the Western world, Hermetism, Alchemy, and the Qabalah made up the last widely recognized school of natural mysticism before the study of nature was monopolized by modern science. What authentic magic seeks is not power but security (connectedness), the security of being at one with nature. It seeks *being* power rather than *doing* power.

The *Mysteries* govern the second birth of the person, the encounter with spiritual crisis. Their purpose is to teach the Self within the self, whose discovery may be the end of one life and the beginning of another. They come down to us as the highest and riskiest of all *rites de passage*. One approached the Mysteries by way of Initiation, the original pattern of Initiation was invented by the Few out of their spiritual experiences—perhaps they were a reenactment of their life crises which might not be endured and resolved by others? It is a Gnosis we are still pursuing, a knowledge acquired on the threshold of ecstasy.

All psychiatry and psychotherapy is really a search for the hidden self, which is the traditional concern of religion! Freud's conviction was that the quest for the self must take us back and down—into juice and tissue of our physical nature, into its infantile fantasies and passions. The way to sanity lay through the history of the body and its many thwarted gratifications. For him, sanity meant the surrender of all illusions and the final acceptance of our total isolation in an alien universe. Actually, the very opposite is true: it is only by going within and up, toward the Light and the Self that the self can be discovered and integrated and that meaning, purpose, and beauty can be found in this life!

The higher sanity will take as its model of health the example of saints, shamans, prophets and seers—of those who must faithfully follow the path of the few. It will borrow heavily on the teachings and symbols of the *visionary quest*. The great lesson of the modern experience is that every tradition is only one tradition among many, none can claim exclusive validity. What the Higher Sanity demands of the philosophies and therapies that serve it is open, planetary dialogue between modern experience and sacred tradition, whatever its source.

The culture of the Few was one of material simplicity and visionary abundance. A sacred culture in which Myth, Magic, and Mystery were the prime preoccupations and qualities of experience the principal wealth. The psychotherapy of the future will not find the secret of the soul's distress in the futile and tormenting clash of instinctual drives, but in the *tension between potentiality and actuality*. It will see that, as evolution's unfinished animal, our task is to become what we are; but our neurotic burden is that we do not, except for the few amongst us, *know what we are*. What is most significantly and pathologically unconscious in us is the knowledge of our potential godlikeness.

Thus, now the goal is again to expand the limits of the personality, to unfold the higher reaches of consciousness, and to harness the latent energies of the psyche, with God-likeness as its distant goal. It is *spiritual* intelligence that the moment demands of us: the power to tell the greater from the lesser, the spiritual from the psychic, the sacred from its copies and secular counterfeits, for nothing in human experience is now left out. The spiritual intelligence can only be found in the Sacred Traditions. The beginnings of the Path of the Inward Quest lies in psychotherapy, but its end must be in the Sacred Traditions of the past and in the synthesis of the two.

The Inner Voyage is the emergent sign of our times. Here sexual emancipation is paralleled to the awakening of the spiritual quest and energies. The visionary energies can be compared to the white light which has been broken by the prism of history into separate colors: religion, art, science, law, and culture. Culture originated in high visionary experience of the few!

Practical Exercise

Preliminary: Find the right place and the right position. Then make an effort of Introversion, Supraversion, and Infraversion.

Actual work: Meditation.

Focus your attention upon your imagination and your power of Visualization. If you are Qabalistically knowledgeable and inclined, work on activating Yesod in your Tree of Life and review the functioning of your Imagination and power of Visualization at this point in time.

How well is your imagination functioning at the present time? Are you able to visualize symbols, images, events, and happenings you have already experienced and to create new ones?

How well can you work with the guided daydream approach? Meditate upon your present ability to visualize inwardly what you wish to and how you could *train* and *develop* this important function ("muscle of consciousness").

Are you able to live things in your imagination and then to translate them and manifest them objectively in your being and in your life? Make a list of what you presently consider to be the strengths and weaknesses of your power of Visualization.

Find a symbol, or an image, that represents your Imagination as it *now is*, as you would *ideally like it to be*, and of the *obstacles* that prevent you from using your imagination as you would ideally like to. Invoke the

Light, Fire, and Life of your Divine Spark to energize the symbol, or image, that represents the ideal functioning of your imagination.

When you have completed this meditation, imagination self-examination, and Psychospiritual exercises, make the appropriate entries in your workbook, as to what you have discovered, what you have done, what has happened, and how you were able to cope.

Chapter Six

THE OPENING OF THE INTUITION

━━━━━━━━━

It is at this point, after having resolved the basic questions, training, and challenges of emotional purification, mental clarification, personal consecration, and visionary unfoldment—which constitute the preliminary and foundational work at the level of the personality—that the truly *spiritual* aspect and phase of the Great Work of self-actualization and self-realization can begin in earnest. Up to this point, the personality remains in the world of nature and thus in darkness as to consciousness, perspective, will, and plans of the Higher Self—of God. Up to this stage, one remains caught up in the mesh of the elements, highly vulnerable to and controlled by external events and stimuli, and dependent upon external guides, authorities, and the letter of the Holy Scriptures. Now, a major "abyss" or qualitative threshold (in terms of consciousness and vibrations) must be crossed so as to be "born" to the world of Grace, to the Inner Kingdom of God, which is Spiritual

Consciousness. However, even to complete the work of emotional purification, mental clarification, personal consecration, and visionary unfoldment, it is necessary to have the Light and the Higher Perspective that only Spiritual Consciousness can bestow—for only a Higher Center and Energies, embedded in a spiritual perspective can, ultimately, truly center and purify the emotions, reveal the truth about one's self and one's nature and destiny, unfold the visionary energies and experiences, and can provide, as we have pointed out, the high and noble ideals and goals to pursue and to dedicate one's self to, and the Will to achieve the full coordination and integration of the functions of the psyche and of the various subpersonalities. Once, but only once, this abyss, or *qualitative threshold*, has been successfully crossed can one be truly inner directed, find the source of inspiration and guidance, love, and life within one's self rather than outside in other people, teachings, or traditions. Thus, the opening of the intuition is a truly crucial step in one's human and spiritual growth and the effective Initiation which can lead one to the rule of the Divine Spark and to the establishment of the Kingdom of God within—the dawning of genuine Spiritual Consciousness.

Intuition with its male-female processes of Invocation-Evocation, or aspiration-inspiration, is the only one of the seven functions of the psyche to be half psychological and half spiritual in nature, as it is the pathway, the bridge, or connection between the field of consciousness and the superconscious, and between the human and Spiritual Self. In order to consciously and systematically awaken it and cultivate it, rather than having it express spontaneously from time to time on rare occasion, a minimum amount of knowledge, experience with, and mastery of the other four basic functions (willing, thinking, feeling, and imagination), and of the other two secondary functions (biopsychic drives and sensations) is necessary and must be attended to first. Then, and only then, are we ready to begin the ascent to the Spiritual Mountain within our own being, the Superconscious, by activating the intuition. Before the higher Superconscious energies and vibrations of the Light, Fire, and Life of the spirit can descend and manifest themselves in the human temple of the personality and ensoul it, the temple must be developed, cleaned, and organized at least to a minimum extent. From time immemorial, ever since the human spirit and soul descended and incarnated on earth, the deepest and most important questions for human-kind—What am I? Where do I come from? Where am I going? What have I come here to accomplish?—could only be answered by the *awakened intuition* and by no other faculty or investigation process. For it is only the activated intuition that can truly penetrate into the spiritual realms and to the core of reality and of our being, establishing an open and conscious connection and communication be-tween them.

What then is intuition? Briefly put, intuition means "seeing from within," or the "teachings from within," as it is the channel that links up the conscious with the Supercon-scious and the human self with the Spiritual Self. It is the true and living Ladder of Jacob that exists in the microcosm, within each human being, waiting to be awakened and activated at its appropriate time. Genuine spiritual illum-ination, true spiritual intuition, or divine Revelation must all necessarily come through the channel of the intuition which must be "opened" and "activated" for such a pur-pose. And, once this channel or link is open and the higher spiritual energies (the Light, Fire, and Life of the Spiritual Self) flowing through it, they will energize, expand, and bring to life all the other functions of the psyche literally transforming man's consciousness, translating him from the realm of nature to the Kingdom of God, raise his center of consciousness and bring him a new Heaven and a new

Earth—to a major cognitive and existential transformation.

When the intuition is seen through the image of a channel, or ladder, it is easy to distinguish its two basic levels or poles: the one that begins at the personality level, extending through the various layers of consciousness to the Superconscious, and the other that ends (or vice versa) in the soul and that connects the Superconscious with the conscious. The first is the psychological end of the intuition and the other the spiritual end. Piero Ferrucci has interesting and illuminating insights to offer concerning these two levels of the intuition which he calls "ordinary" and "superconscious" intuition. Thus he writes:

> We should distinguish two levels of intuition, the ordinary and the superconscious. At the ordinary level, we can have, for example, an intuition about a person. More than just a feeling of empathy or a sudden intellectual understanding, such an intuition may reveal the present life situation of a person, with its many ramifications and implications. We can also have problem solving intuitions, as when a student sees a solution of a mathematical problem, or in general when one jumps directly to understanding rather than slowly walking to it with the aid of reasoning.
>
> At the superconscious level, the intuition gives access to vistas usually unimaginable by our ordinary personality. Thus we can have a direct intuitive realizaton of a psychological quality, a universal law, of the interconnectedness of everything with everything else, of the oneness of all reality, of eternity, and so on. The content of an intuition at this level is normally impersonal. There is often a sense of wonder; talking about the intuitive vision of the scientist, Einstein said: "His religious feeling takes the form of a rapturous amazement at the harmony of natural laws which reveal an intelligence of such superiority that compared with it, all the systematic thinking and acting of human beings is an utterly insignificant reflection."
>
> We may, also, however, have superconscious intuition concerning a person. But in this case, it does not relate to the specific mood or the present situation of that person: it reveals, instead, that person's life purpose, or his other higher possibilities or destiny—something to which the individual's ordinary appearance and lifestyle do not give

any clue. Intuition perceives in *wholes*, while our everyday analytical mind is used to dealing with *parts* and therefore finds the synthesizing grasp of the intuition unfamiliar.[1]

Finally, Ferrucci concludes:

Intuitions are often registered at the level of feelings, without any involvement on the part of the mind. In this case, they can trigger a sense of exhilaration, expansion, and peace. Frequently, however, when the feeling dies away the intuition often vanishes, leaving no permanent trace or significant contribution to growth.

In my work with people I have found time and again that only when intuitions are registered also at the mental level can they be fully assimilated. The right coordination of intuition and mind seems to be the best way in which the riches offered can be correctly interpreted, connected with everyday reality, and clearly communicated. In this way, intuitions of a superconscious sort can become permanent landmarks of our growth, sources of continuing inspiration, luminous points in a living, growing web of insights.

A peculiar effect of intuition, which accounts for its synthetic character, is that it has spontaneous ramifications in several dimensions of an individual's life. A single intuition may often throw light on previously unrelated issues, showing the existence of the same pattern in all of them.[2]

Carl Jung, affirming the existence, validity, and importance of the intuition as a psychic function writes:

I regard intuition as a basic psychological function. It is the function that mediates perception in an unconscious way. Everything, whether outer or inner objects or their relationships, can be the focus of this perception. The peculiarity of intuition is that it is neither sense perception, nor feeling, nor intellectual inference, although it may also appear in these forms. In intuition a content presents itself *whole* and *complete*, without our being able to explain or discover how this content came into existence. Intuition is a kind of instinctive apprehension, no matter of what contents. Like sensation, it is an irrational function of perception. As with sensation, its contents have the character of being "given," in contrast to the "derived" or "produced" character of thinking and feeling contents. Intuitive knowledge possesses an intrinsic certainty and conviction, which enabled Spinoza (and Bergson) to uphold the *scienza intuitiva* as the highest form of knowledge. Intuition shares this quality with sensation, whose certainty rests on its physical foundation. The certainty of intuition rests equally on a definite state of psychic "alertness" of whose origin the subject is unconscious.[3]

Roberto Assagioli writes as follows concerning the nature and expression of intuition:

The types of intuition are three in number. There are first of all the sensory intuitions associated with the conscious perception of visual, auditory, tactile, etc., impressions produced by stimuli originating in the environment. This class need not detain us, as it is limited to personal psychic levels and does not concern the superconscious.

Then we have intuitions of ideas, in the Platonic sense, and since these come from a higher region than that in which the ordinary mind functions, they may be considered to be transpersonal. The same can be said of the third kind of higher intuition, that is to say the aesthetic, the religious, the mystical and even the scientific. This denotes the difference between the personal psychological and the transpersonal life.

Intuitions present themselves to the consciousness, or are perceived by it, in two ways. The first, which adheres more closely to the etymological meaning, can be described as the opening of an "inner eye," thus permitting the "sight" or perception of some reality inaccessible to normal mental vision. The other way is characterized by a brilliant, lightning-like flash of light, which, "descending" into the field of consciousness, is perceived by the "I," the center of consciousness at its normal level or "seat." The common and specific characteristic of intuitions is their "authenticity." They convey the perception of their object in its totality, like an organic whole, and thereby differ from the mental consciousness, which is analytical.

This points to the intuition's capacity to pass beyond the acquisition of knowledge about an object's every quality to capture its *very essence*, i.e., what it IS. Thus the intuition qualifies as one of the fields of investigation of the new psychology of Being, in which Maslow was the pioneer.[4]

Keyserling tells us:

Man, like all animals, is intimately linked to the total mass of beings and things, and if instinct is lacking in him or is so atrophied that he cannot depend upon his elementary

impulses, then the human equivalent of instinct must inter-
vene in order that man may freely orient himself in the cosmos.
In this sense only the intuitives are free: and that is why they
alone provide all the great revealers, the leaders and the
innovators . . .

The intuition penetrates the veils of the future and,
therefore, of the possible. But reality is in perpetual transformation, and therefore only he is able to see it who grasps
directly what from time to time is possible, and this in a dou-
ble sense. Firstly, because above all the facts some "possibilities" exist; and in the second place, because he perceives
directly, among these possibilities, those which at times and
in determined conditions, can be realized. Both can be
derived from a primordial interior experience of the all.[5]

After the activation and flowering of the intuition,
there follows an even higher stage and development which
has generally been called "spiritual Illumination" and which I
would call the "birth of Christ within" and the "dawning of
true spiritual consciousness." As Ferrucci has aptly put it:
"While intuition can be thought of as giving us a glimpse of
the world in which the Self lives, illumination is the act of
reaching the Self and contacting It fully."[6] Assagioli, after
having experienced his own personal degree of illumination and studied a number of cases involving illumination
in others, has described its essence in the following words:

(Illumination involves) an inner perception of light
which in certain cases is so intense as to be described as a
dazzling glory and an impression of *fire*. It is from these
characteristics that the term "illumination" has arisen, the
term by which the superconscious states are often designated.
In many cases this illumination extends to the external
world, which is perceived as transfigured and bathed in an
effable light. A sense of release from ordinary self-conscious-
ness and self-centeredness and an enormous expansion and
elevation of conscious awareness. A sense of oneness with
the whole. This inner realization has the paradoxical character that, while it is associated with the previously mentioned
sense of loss or of oblivion of one's personality, there is at
the same time a sense of fuller, wider, and more real life.

An impression of beauty, both of the inner formless
beauty and a revelation of a hitherto unperceived beauty of

the external world, even in its most common and ordinary aspects. Feelings of joy, of peace, of love, mingled in various proportions. A loss of the sense of time; a rising above the "flux of becoming," above past, present, and future. The realization of the External Now and of the essential permanence, indestructibility, and immortality of one's own spiritual Self, of the Center of one's being. An unshakable certainty and inner assurance of the reality of this inner experience. An urge to express—to communicate to others —the illumination, to share this precious treasure, and a sense of compassionate love for those still wandering and suffering in darkness and illusion.[7]

At the practical level, the central question is ever the same: how can we awaken and activate our own intuition so that it can guide us through the jungles of human experience and human decision, illumine our minds and hearts, and reveal to us what is God's Will for us, God's Plan, for humanity and our own specific and unique role and contribution therein? To develop the intuition in a conscious and systematic way there are two basic approaches: the *female* and the *male*, and two major Paths, the *Mystical* and the *Occult Path*. And there are certain universal and central guidelines or rules.

The first basic rule is simply to recognize that we have, potentially, an intuitive faculty that can be awakened and trained and to give it *attention*: time, energy, and thought. And this, naturally, applies to the development and cultivation of all our faculties and potentialities, for the law of growth and consciousness development is ever the same on all planes and for all aspects of our being. As Ferrucci puts it succinctly: "We can increase our intuitive capacity if we will acknowledge the possiblity of our receiving intuitions, recognize their value, cherish them when they come, and finally, learn to *trust* them—when carefully interpreted— rather than relying exclusively on logical reasoning and material evidence."[8] Then, we should learn how to use and interpret the symbols, the images, and the rituals and arche-

types that are linked with the intuition and its manifestation—
we should learn, in other words, *the language and the alphabet
of the intuition* and of the Deep Mind, the subconscious,
unconscious, and Superconscious. For this is the language
of the sages and the script of wisdom. Finally, we should
practice over and over again those exercises and muscles
(energies and vibrations and states of consciousness)
which give one access to the intuition. And then carefully
record their manifestations and breakthroughs in our consciousness—make a written or verbal diary of all insights,
hunches, brilliant ideas, and inspirations that come to us in
dreams, guided daydreams, or in daily life, both in meditation and in reflection, and in activities and action. Again, as
Ferrucci puts it:

> Intuitions often tend to come in clusters, rather than
> separately, and the act of writing (or recording) down the
> first one facilitates the arrival of others connected with it.
> Moreover, the most original ideas do not appear fully blown,
> but, on the contrary, make themselves known little by little,
> first as vague perceptions, then in clearer outline. Later they
> form themselves into patterns and finally stand revealed in
> their full meaning. So by recording intuitions at their outset
> we firmly anchor the beginning of this process of gradual
> revelation and give it a firm basis for unfolding.[9]

The female approach to intuition simply consists in
learning the technique of practicing *silence* on the four
planes: the physical, emotional, mental, and spiritual, and
to *listen* and observe *inwardly* what happens to our stream of
consciousness as we do so. The male approach to intuition,
on the other hand, consists in mastering and practicing the
technique of Ritual or Theurgy—to use images, symbols,
and archetypes, individually and in groups, to deliberately
bring down their Light and Fire, the spiritual Energies from
the Superconscious and from the Self, to raise our center of
consciousness. And this is what constitutes the true essence
of prayer or worship which are designed to prepare and

open a channel going from the field of consciousness to the Superconscious and from the human to the Spiritual Self.

The Mystical Path to intuition simply involves loving God with all our souls, all our hearts, and all our minds, and our fellow human beings as ourselves. It involves the purification, sanctification, and expansion of our ability to *feel* and to *love* God and His Creation and thus ourselves and others. The Occult Path, on the other hand, involves a deliberate and sequential process which is called invocation, the "male" polarity, and evocation, the "female" polarity.

As Assagioli describes it:

> The etymological meaning of Invocation is "calling down," "calling into." It is essentially *a demand*, an appeal to something higher, asking for help or intervention . . . Invocation is an inner action which includes and combines the use of *all our inner functions*. It is a simultaneous activity of the mind (meditation), of feeling (devotion), and of the imagination (visualization), and of the will (concentration and affirmation). It is obvious that this comprehensive and synthesized action of our whole being (consciousness), when rightly carried out, gives invocation a potency incomparably greater and richer than the separate use of any single inner activity.
>
> Such combined action is certainly not easy; in fact it is very difficult, and requires much training and the definite use of appropriate techniques. But the time and energy spent in achieving proficiency in invocation are well repaid by its powerful beneficent effects, and, as in the case of other skills, once developed it remains a permanent acquisition.
>
> As invocation is a synthesis of various other activities, it is necessary to learn first the technique of each one separately, as we have been doing. The four inner activities, though different and distinct, are interrelated, and each of them stimulates and facilitates the use of the others.[10]

Evocation, Assagioli describes as:

> Evocation—etymologically "to carry out" or "call forth" —is the response from "above," the "answer" to the invocative demand. Such a response is sure and we can rely upon it with an assured conviction because it is brought about by the universal and unfailing Law of Cause and Effect.

But the *recognition* of the response may be difficult: it comes in ways that are often unexpected and not apparent, and also may not be immediate. While the evocation at its start can be considered essentially instantaneous, an immediate "reflex action" by the Power invoked and its manifestation in our consciousness and in the outer world may often be delayed or indirect; its causal relationship with the previous invocation may therefore escape us ...

Sometimes, while the appeal, the invocation of our personality, may have been sincere and rightly motivated, the response may reveal truths about ourselves which we dislike, or may require commitments which we, in our personalities, are afraid or unwilling to undertake ... Such reactions are normal to human nature, but they should be recognized as mistaken, and consequently eliminated in order to give free scope to the inflow and manifestation of the evoked energies. We can be sure that the higher energies produce beneficent effects in ourselves and in the world that are out of all proportion to any temporary discomfort they may cause. These reactions, however, do not always occur; often the inpouring of Light, Love, and Power is immediate and easily sweeps away all obstructions. When this happens, our task is to absorb and make the best use of the evoked energies, radiating them, and expressing them in outer action.[11]

Finally, Assagioli concludes:

(There is another form of invocation) It is the *call* or *pull* which reaches us from the Self, or from some other higher Source—"within," "without," and "above" our conscious personality. Its first and simplest manifestation is the "voice of the conscience" which calls us to follow some higher standard of conduct, to recognize ethical values and to adhere to them. It is present in every human being, even in most of those who have been criminals or are mentally disturbed; the difference between such people and those of higher integrity lies in the degree of obedience and disobedience to this "voice of conscience." In this lies the privilege and the burden of our inner freedom.

Accounts of religious experiences often speak of a "call" from God, or a "pull" from some higher Power. This sometimes starts a "dialogue" between the man and this "higher Source" in which each alternately invokes and evokes the other.[12]

To recapitulate: in *invocation*, the first four basic functions of the psyche—willing, thinking, feeling, and imagination—are used in a synchronous fashion so as to concentrate, focus, and direct all our attention and awareness upon the Spiritual Self residing in our "Head Center" in the Superconscious, direct all our thoughts and meditations to Him, send Him all our love and feelings, and visualize Him in our favorite image or symbol. This generates an upward-thrusting triangle of subtle and etheric energies with concentration and meditation at the two outer angles, devotion in the center, and visualization at the base. When this is done to the utmost of our present abilities and in a growing fashion as we use it, invocation will then be answered by evocation, which is the downpouring of spiritual energies into our field of consciousness wherein spiritual Life energizes our human will and concentration; spiritual Light illuminates our meditation and thinking; spiritual Fire warms and expands our feelings and devotion; and spiritual Vision opens and crowns our visualization. Thus it is that to an aspiration of the human heart utilizing the four key psychological functions to their utmost corresponds an inspiration of spiritual energies transforming these very functions and their processes, and bringing in additional, *sui generis*, factors that are truly spiritual in nature. Ultimately, however, the intuition with its accompanying inspiration and revelation are spiritual gifts and mysteries and not human or psychological achievements. As such, a life of devoted prayer, selfless service to others, and proper perspective and balance in the way one lives and all the things one does, is, perhaps, the best way to obtain the gift of true intuition which only the Spiritual Self can bestow.

Key exercises and practices to develop and train the intuition:

Since the very essence of intuition is to set up a channel between the field of consciousness and the Superconscious, between the human and the Spiritual Self, it is obvious that, in order for higher energies and materials to flow into our field of consciousness through this channel, we must be relaxed on all levels. Thus, the first and most important step is to learn how to systematically relax on the physical, then the emotional, and finally on the mental level, for any tension, stress, or "storm" on these levels would immediately either block or distort the downpouring stream of intuition or higher energies. And it would lead one to the major problem or pitfall of training the intuition: confusing emotion and imagination with true intuition which is always "right" or linked with reality.

Basic ways to open the intuition are:

1. First and foremost, we have Prayer in the full meaning of this word: the systematic and regular practice of Silence, on the four Planes, and of Ritual or Theurgy to maximize sensitivity and receptivity, on the one hand, and the downpouring of Light and spiritual Energies on the other. This is truly the royal road to intuition as we develop our Faith which is a psychospiritual faculty.

2. Then we have the many spontaneous breakthroughs of intuition and inspiration which occur when we truly forget ourselves or lose ourselves, when we truly give ourselves fully to some task, to contemplating beauty, to listening to beautiful music, to reading a truly inspired book, and, especially, when we love someone or something and open our love channels letting its Fire and Life flow unimpeded through our being. Then, intuition is activated almost by itself and without our doing anything about it; or, what we had previously set in motion at some levels, but blocked at others, can then be released and flow freely.

3. The inner dialogue with a symbol or image of the Spiritual Self or of the Superconscious.

4. The Letter to the Higher Self expressing our needs, fears, hopes, and aspirations, and our demand for help and inspiration.

5. The Guided Daydream ascending to meet (or have a diaglogue) with the Sage, the Angel, or any other spiritual Archetype as well as with the Sun, the Light, or Fire.

The Temple of Silence:[13]

This is a very old and effective exercise, the essence of which is the following: Imagine a hill covered with greenery. A path leads to the top where you can see the Temple of Silence. Give that temple the shape of your highest aspiration—noble, harmonious, and radiant (as people of old would embody in their churches or cathedrals).

It is a spring morning, sunny and pleasantly warm. Notice how you are dressed. Become conscious of your body ascending the path, and feel the contact of your feet with the ground. Feel the breeze on your cheeks. Look about you at the trees and the bushes, the grass, and the wildflowers as you go up.

Now you are approaching the top of the hill. Ageless stillness pervades the atmosphere of the temple of silence. No word has ever been uttered here. You are close to its big wooden portals: see your hands on them and feel the wood. Before opening the doors, know that when you do so, you will be surrounded by silence. You enter the Temple now. You feel and experience the atmosphere of stillness and peace all around you. Then, you walk forward into the silence, looking all about you as you go. You see a big, luminous dome. Its luminosity not only comes from the rays of the sun, but also seems to spring from within and to be concentrated in an area of radiance just in front of you.

You enter this luminous silence and feel absorbed by it. You become one with it and feel this luminous silence permeate your whole being; physical, emotional, mental, and spiritual. Feel it and experience it enveloping your whole being, flowing through your veins, and suffusing every cell in your being.

Remain in this luminous and living silence for two to three minutes, recollected and alert. During this time, *listen* to the silence and receive its blessing and its message, for silence is a living, pulsating, vibrating quality, not merely the absence of sounds or noise!

Finally, slowly leave the area of radiance; walk back through the temple and out the portals. Outside, open yourself to the impact of the spring, feel its gentle breeze once more and listen to the singing of the birds, and notice, by self-observation and introspection, the changes that have taken place in your consciousness and what your consciousness and being now reveal to you. Then, come back down the path and return to your normal, waking state of consciousness and open your eyes.

Practical Exercise

Preliminary: Find the right place and the right position. Then make an effort of Introversion, Supraversion, and Infraversion.

Actual work: Meditation and Psychospiritual Exercises

Focus your attention upon your Intuition and your ability to contact your Superconscious and your spiritual Self, through Invocation-Evocation, to bring through (in your field of consciousness) their energies and materials: the Light, Fire, and Life that will feed and make your Head, Heart, and Shoulder Centers "come alive." Activate Tiphareth in your Tree of Life and review the functioning of your intuition and your ability to contact the spiritual part of your being at this point in time.

How well is your intuition functioning at this point in time? Are you able to invoke, effectively and experientially, the Light, Fire, and Life of your spiritual Self and to bring through the energies and materials of your Superconscious? Which method, or technique works best for you? Prayer, Silence and Theurgy, the Inner Dialogue, the Letter to the Higher Self, the Guided Daydream, or other? Meditate upon your present ability to activate your intuition and to get the "inspirational glow" going and reflect upon how you could further expand this important function.

When confronted with crucial existential situations which could greatly benefit from an intuitive response from your part (such as making basic decisions, evaluating potential relationships, or setting upon a new course of action) are you able to get your Intuition going—effectively and experientially? And, if so, how do you test your intuitions to distinguish them from possible emotions, impulses, fantasies, or wish-fulfillment?

Find an image, or a symbol, that represents your Intuition as it now is, as you would ideally like it to be, and representing the obstacles that prevent you from utilizing your Intuition as you would like to. Invoke the Light, Fire, and Life of your Divine Spark to energize the image, or symbol, that represents the ideal functioning of your Intuition . . . and SEE WHAT HAPPENS!

If you are Qabalistically knowledgeable and inclined, work on activating Tiphareth with Chesed and Geburah, Netzach and Hod, to complete this work.

When you have completed this meditation, intuition self-examination, and psychospiritual exercises, make the appropriate entries in your workbook, as to what you have discovered, what you have done, what has happened, and how you were able to cope.

Chapter Seven

THE DESCENT OF THE LIGHT:
Personal Christmas

━━━━━━━━━━

Thus far in our previous chapters, we have focused upon the development of the personality, the slow and gradual "building of the temple made without hands." This is the process which psychosynthesis calls *personal psychosynthesis* leading to *self-actualization*. It is also what the Spiritual Tradition calls the Lesser Mysteries, or the Elemental Initiations, and the foundation of which lies in what I have called emotional purification, mental clarification, personal consecration, visionary unfoldment and the opening of the intuition. Naturally, some elements of self-realization and of establishing a link and a contact with the Self and the Superconscious were also involved as even that part of the Great Work cannot be accomplished without some guidance from on high, without some directing breakthroughs of our Higher Self, especially in the last aspect of the work on the quadrant of our personality involving the opening of the intuition. Now, we shall put the finishing touch to this work and then proceed with the true and experiential quest for God, for the Self, for self-realization and what the Spiritual Tradition calls the Greater Mysteries which lead one from the domain of the personality to that of the Soul. We have dealt at length and examined in detail the training and purification of the emotions, the development and use of the mind, the unfoldment of the visionary energy, the development and use of the will and the opening of the intuition through the use and training of the imagination and of visualization. Now we shall turn our attention to the remaining core aspects of the personality which are the health and care of the physical body, the knowledge and control of the biopsychic drives and energy transformations, and the training of the senses with the use of outer and inner observation. Then, we shall leave the realm of the personality and take a leap into that of the Soul, and the blending or marriage of the Soul with the personality.

A vital, healthy, and properly functioning physical body is very important, even though not absolutely indispensable for the descent of the Light and the dawning of true spiritual consciousness which is depicted in the West under the symbols and festival of Christmas. Thus, it is most important that students and candidates for spiritual initiation take proper care of their physical organism through the proper application and living of seven interrelated areas that culminate in true vital, and holistic physical health, balance, and functioning of the biological organism. These are *nutrition, sleep, exercise, sex,* and *positive emotions* and *thoughts, social life,* and *spiritual life* all of which play an interrelated and mutually supporting role and creating and maintaining proper physical health by awakening the "wisdom of the body" and the intuition to guide us in our daily life.

The vital role of nutrition for physical health hardly

needs to be elaborated here as it has become common knowledge in the last two decades. Reading good nutrition books and, especially, applying the basic rules of nutrition in one's daily diet, are very important and must be adhered to as violating any basic law on any level always brings about negative consequences for one's consciousness and overall functioning. In a nutshell, one must eat good food, in the right mixture, and neither too much or too little of it, preferably at regular intervals.

Getting the right amount and quality of sleep is equally important as getting right nutrition as sleep is as important as food if not *more* so, as evidenced by what happens to us when we get too little or too much, or poor quality sleep even over a very short period of time. One point that is generally overlooked, however, is that in order to get good quality sleep and to fall asleep naturally and easily one must be tired, i.e. one must have used up in constructive activities the multi-layered energies that flow through our being. Thus, working too little or not giving freely and fully of ourselves—physically, emotionally, and mentally, and later, even spiritually—can be as harmful to a good quality sleep as can working too much and being under too much stress, tension, or anxiety of one kind or another.

Recent physiological and psychological research is also demonstrating a very ancient truth that was always taught by the spiritual traditions, namely that our sex and lovelife play a vital role for our physical as well as psychological health. This means that too much sexual activity as well as too little or, especially, poor sexual exchanges can have a deleterious effect on our energies, balance, and creative self-expression. Here, each individual has to get "in tune" with his own nature and needs, at a given point in one's life cycle, to avoid the twin traps of repression and license as well as routine and low quality sexual sharing. Even more important, each individual has to work consciously and deliberately to raise and refine, purify and consecrate his love energies, and exchange them with a suitable partner where there are natural affinities and genuine esteem, trust, and love. The deepest and ultimate problem of human life is, indeed, the problem of learning how to love more freely, deeply, intensely, and purely. It is most interesting to note that even exoteric religion has characterized the same act as being both a *sin* and a *sacrament*, i.e. acting as a degrading and degenerating force or as an elevating and sanctifying force. The crucial difference coming not from what one does but from one's *attitude* and *consciousness* in doing it! When sex involves the emotional, mental, and spiritual dimensions, and when one is a channel for God's Light and Fire then, indeed, it is one of the greatest sacraments. But when only the physical and the emotional dimensions are involved and when a person is not really concerned with the well-being of the other but rather seeks personal gratification and pleasure, then it becomes a sin that lowers rather than expands consciousness.

Finally, when it comes to cultivating, expressing, and living positive emotions and thoughts rather than negative ones, psychosomatic medicine has established once and for all that there is a very close connection between the body and the mind, via the endocrine and the nervous systems, and that negative thoughts and emotions are the ultimate cause of many forms of disease. I personally believe that once human beings will have learned and be able to express the higher levels and qualities of love with all those with whom they interact, sickness and disease will vanish and become a nightmare of the past except for occasional cuts and fractures caused by purely physical agents which will also heal much more rapidly and efficiently. The point here is not to render oneself completely immune to negative thoughts and feelings for, as long as one is a human being living on Earth this is not possible, but, rather, to be able to transform and transmute, in a short period of time, the negative thoughts and feelings that occasionally attack us so that they will not dwell in us and obsess us for a long period of time.

Recent studies in medical sociology, social psychology and network therapy have shown conclusively that the *quantity* and *quality* of our human relationships have powerful consequences for our physical, emotional, and mental well-being, that human interaction is to our human consciousness what food is to our bodies, and that negative human relationships or the lack of certain "love vitamins" can have a devastating effect upon our psychosomatic well-being.

As for having a spiritual life, after the works and conclusions of Carl Jung and Roberto Assagioli, it has become increasingly clear that it is an indispensable component of our lives. If food is the nourishment of the body and human interaction that of our consciousness, then our spiritual life, and prayer in particular, is the nourishment of our Soul. Without some form and expression of a spiritual life, it is not possible for a human being to be balanced, fulfilled, and, at the same time, growing and becoming more than what he is.

Biopsychic drives, which used to be called instincts, are energies welling up from the unconscious and providing the basic drives and urges that we call hunger, thirst, fatigue, and sexual desire. They also include anger or aggressive energies and repressed emotionally charged energies that, unless otherwise discharged, will flow back into the field of consciousness and are experienced as compulsive and obsessive behavior as well as affect the biological organism with stress that eventually results in various illnesses. The major function of these drives, the giants and dragons that live in the labyrinths of the unconscious, is to keep the biological organism healthy and functioning properly, as a vehicle for the Soul and the Self, and to continue the race so that physical vehicles will be provided for incoming Souls which incarnate on earth to continue their journey in this "school of experience." These drives, therefore, are neither "good" nor "evil." They simply fulfill a natural purpose which is vital for mankind. Being very powerful and unconsciously propelled, these drives—sex and agression in particular—must be understood and controlled by the self which must learn to consciously direct their expression and manifestations rather than being controlled by them, which is *true slavery*. A great deal of raw energy and life force can be found at the root of these drives and can be harnessed and expressed in many constructive ways. For millenia, mankind has been battling with the outer elements of fire, water, earth, and air and has gradually learned about their nature, dynamics, and laws so as to harness them to provide a higher standard of living and greater personal security. It is now time for all of us to get acquainted with and to control the *inner elements* of the psyche: drives, passions, emotions, imagination, intuition and will to harness them for our spiritual growth and development —to "redeem" them and consecrate them for the Great Work— for becoming conscious Sons and Daughters of God. The process of tapping and consciously directing and utilizing these powerful "subterranean energies," on various levels and in different ways, is called *sublimination, energy transformation, and transmutation*. This process and capacity must be mastered and possessed by anyone who wishes to make serious human and spiritual progress, and by the "Knight of the Spirit," the "Initiate," in particular, for he must learn to become conscious of and utilize all the energies and resources of his own being and of the universe for the Great Work—for becoming at one with God. And the central key is to link them with the Higher Energies, with the Light that comes down from on high.

Some of the basic techniques and procedures to accomplish the foregoing are:

a. To be transmuted and controlled, sexual and aggressive energies must be firmly and consciously grasped and brought into consciousness, not feared or repressed. Physical exercises and breathing techniques, artistic, intellectual, and spiritual endeavors and projects, the pursuit of high and noble ideals, and giving oneself fully to a given task can be of great help. And so can the realization and affirmation that every human being is *sacred* and should not be used and harmed as an object to exploit or to satisfy one's uncontrolled needs.

b. The conscious evocation, unfoldment, and expression of all the aspects and qualities of human and spiritual love—friendship, brotherhood, compassion, altruistic and spiritual love.

c. A firm concentration upon and involvement with a given project or interest to which one can project all his attention and energies, and love.

d. The proper use of symbols and archetypes in the imagination which are *energy* and *consciousness transformers*; the evocation of a Hero, a Sage, or a Saint, an ideal model and the patterning of one's life, attitude, and being around this model can also be of great help.

e. Seeking and cultivating the company of like-minded people, or groups, who are also interested and working toward transforming and controlling these energies. For these can act as genuine "catalysts" through the atmosphere they create around themselves, the example they provide, and the energies they radiate for anyone attempting psychological transformations of this type.

Assagioli looked at the essence of aggression as "*a blind impulse to self-affirmation*, the expression of all the elements of one's being, without any discrimination or choice, without any concern for the consequences, without any consideration for others."[1] We can and should look at aggressive energies as a *natural process*—a wave of aggressive energy wells up in an individual, becomes more and more powerful, and pushes forward to express itself. At this point, the individual is faced with three basic choices: two natural, unconscious, and destructive ones, and one conscious and constructive one. First, the individual may be frightened, shy, or unwilling to break his or her own standards of courtesy, so the aggressive wave is repressed causing all kinds of psychological harm, from psychosomatic to purely psychological ills. Second, in extroverted, action oriented people, the wave may express itself in destructive words or deeds. Third, the individual may consciously work toward transforming his aggressive energies that can then be expressed in many positive and constructive tasks. An excellent and very practical way to achieve the foregoing is to:[2]

a. Pick a project or an activity that you want to give more "steam" to.
b. Then, lay that project aside for a moment and get in touch with your aggressive energies and feelings. Feel their vigor, their vibrancy, the effect they have on your body and the hurt that they cause you. Give them "space," i.e. observe them without judging them or immediately categorizing them.
c. Realize that these feelings are *energy* at your disposal, energy that is precious and that can *do* things. It can hurt or destroy, but it can also become the propelling power for the project or activity you

have chosen.

d. Now vividly imagine yourself in the midst of your project or activity. Call to mind as many details as you can with your imagination. Imagine the moves involved, but now see them vivified and intensified by the vitality you have chosen to invest in them.

We are all endowed by nature with five basic physical senses: seeing, hearing, touching, tasting, and smelling, and the ability to observe physical things in the world and the flow of consciousness in ourselves. While sensory awareness training is not crucial for most types of psychological and spiritual development, the proper use of *observation*, both at the outer and at the inner levels, definitely is. Unless one can properly train oneself to observe what exists and happens in the outer world and what one does therein, from the standpoint of the "fair witness," one would find it difficult to observe oneself in the inner worlds with their far more complex and subtle events and differences. Hence, analogically, *inner training* can greatly benefit by *outer training*. This means that if one can learn to observe precisely and systematically in the outer world, one will then find it much easier to do the same in the inner worlds. Two basic practical exercises here are:

a. Learn to observe in a systematic, objective, and comprehensive fashion the interaction of two human beings who stand in front of you for 10-15 minutes.

b. Learn how to observe, from the standpoint of the fair witness, in an objective and detached fashion, how your emotions and thoughts operate for a period of 10-15 minutes.

The inner work of man, the first major portion of the Great Work is based essentially on the systematic study and training of the seven functions and processes of the psyche on three major levels:

a. The *psychological*, involving the development of the personality.
b. The *psychic*, the exploration and use of the latent energies of the mind, ESP and PSI phenomena, but not *for their own sake*, only as a byproduct of genuine spiritual work.
c. The *spiritual*, the exploration of the Superconscious and the discovery of the Spiritual Self to achieve a proper harmony and alignment with its life, will, and consciousness.

These functions and processes are the basic tools that are used, consciously and unconsciously, by the practical man, the scientists, and the artist, as well as by the mystic, the occultist, and the magician, though on different levels and to varying degrees. The three highest types of human beings known and venerated by mankind, the Saint, the Sage, and the Hero are, actually, personality types in which *feeling, thinking,* and *willing* have been purified, sanctified, and amplified so that they can be properly aligned with the higher energies, vibrations, and will of the Spiritual Self. Just as the Seer is the person in whom the imagination has been purified, activated, and exalted, the Prophet is the person in whom the intuition has been activated to link the Spiritual with the human self. To begin a serious and sequential work on one's personality and on one's self for psychological and/or spiritual reasons, it is of paramount importance to understand, train, and work with these functions and processes. There is simply and absolutely no substitute for this kind of knowledge and training, as these form the very foundation and core instruments for acquiring self-knowledge, self-mastery, and self-integration—for achieving self-actualization and self-realization.

Once this work has been accomplished, to a certain

extent, the next major phase of one's growth and spiritual development can begin in earnest and is characterized by the *Descent of the Light in the Personality*, the dawning of true Spiritual Consciousness, which has been beautifully and simply described by the Christmas story and celebration in the Western Tradition. When we apply the Christmas Glyph to the microcosm and when we interpret it in terms of the Lesser Mysteries, there are certain points that stand out. These are:

1. That this event and glyph does not apply to "Christians" only, but to all human beings who have achieved a certain level of consciousness and being, regardless of their race and religion.

2. That it celebrates and applies not so much to something that happened in human history some 2,000 years ago as to something that must happen to each of us individually, in the future or as soon as we are truly ready for it to happen, and that it takes place in our Soul or consciousness.

3. Finally, that far from being a *fait accompli* or something that we can passively observe happening to us, it is something which we can and must actively bring about, as well as receive as a free gift from our Higher Self, by involving and utilizing all of our human and spiritual faculties and resources. Unless we fully and consciously participate and cooperate in bringing it about, it will never take place. As the great poet Silesius put it: "Though Christ a thousand times in Bethlehem be born, and not within thyself, thy soul will be forlorn and lost."

The central and spiritual meaning of Christmas is, actually, plainly described by the etymology of the word Christmas or *Christ making*. Christmas thus means "making

Christ" or "becoming a Christ" which is what happens to us when the Light of the divine Spark really descends and lives in our personality. The birth of Jesus, who became the Christ at age 30 some 2,000 years ago in Bethlehem is the universal and timeless glyph, image, archetype or blueprint of the *birth of spiritual consciousness within our own soul or human consciousness*. It represents in images which are the "language of the Sages" the conscious linkage and alignment of our human self with the Spiritual Self, of our human consciousness and will with the divine Consciousness and Will, so that we may be reborn anew as *spiritual beings*, as Children of God in whom it is the Lord that rules and lives. As such, this event is one of the most important landmarks not only of this lifetime but of our entire evolution: it is the crossroads and the culminating point for a very long unconscious and conscious preparation for entering another qualitatively different level of consciousness and being. It is an evolutionary leap or mutational jump which is as great, if not greater than our crossing into the human realm from the animal one and moving from nature to society. And, like the former, it takes place over a long incubationary period and not instantaneously—at least in its preparation. The story of the birth of Jesus, with its many events, symbols, and images is thus the universal glyph and prototype of what is to occur to each of us, in our own soul or consciousness, at its appointed time, and which we have to collaborate fully and consciously in bringing about. This myth with its central symbols is thus like a map and the guilding light leading us by degrees to this long-coveted, deeply yearned for, but dimly imagined goal: *the descent of the Light in our personality.*

Focusing our attention upon the Christmas story, the symbol of our spiritual Initiation, we find the following *dramatis personae*, basic events, and core images: the Christ child enveloped in golden-white Light, Mary and Joseph clothed in blue and red garments, the Three Magi or Kings of the East, and Shepherds. The core images here are: the Star of the Savior, the Manger where the Birth occurs, the Animals watching the Christ child while a choir of Angels sing "Glory to God in the Highest and on earth peace to men of good will. The Three Gifts brought by the Magi to the Christ child are Gold, Myrrh, and Frankincense, and finally the Christmas Tree. Most of these persons and images can be found in the composite glyph of the Christmas manger or *crèche*. Interestingly enough there are seven basic *dramatis personae* and seven basic images which are not a coincidence.

All of these, seen through the perspective of the Lesser Mysteries of the Western Spiritual Tradition, apply to the microcosm, and the soul and consciousness of a human being and must be decoded and translated with that basic key in mind. This work, moreover, is quite complex and gradual, involving several of the key functions of the psyche and their basic processes. Thus, one can use the composite glyph of the Christmas story and Manger to practice and develop the power of *concentration, meditation, devotion, visualization, invocation-evocation,* and *energy and consciousness transformation.* Finally, it can and should be used for the purpose of meditation, contemplation and theurgic work for it both describes and brings about the Descent of the Light in our personality, our spiritual Initiation. In meditation, we discover the deeper meanings and applications of these symbols as applied to the microcosm—to our own soul and consciousness; while in contemplation we behold and realize their truly esoteric and spiritual Mysteries, their essence for us at this point in our evolution; and in theurgic work we realize and incarnate this process in our consciousness now—we enable the image and the work to "become flesh" in us now.

Focusing on the meditation and contemplation aspects

of this master glyph of spiritual Initiation, here are some of the central meanings and correspondences we find: the Christ-child enveloped in golden-white Light represents the personification and manifestation of the divine Spark incarnating progressively in our field of consciousness bringing the Descent of the Light in our personality. Mary and Joseph represent and personify, respectively, the essence and expression of the feminine and of the masculine principles in their manyfold manifestations. To give birth to anything in creation, be it a child, an idea, an emotion, a work of art, an artifact, or spiritual consciousness the interplay of a male and female principle, Ying and Yang, Ida and Pingala, positive and negative, and Anima and Animus, is indispensable. Human nature and thus all human beings have a divine, human, physical and demonic aspect which is also brought into manifestation and expression by a male and female principle. Therefore, to give birth to the Divine in Man and to awaken spiritual Consciousness, the same interplay between the masculine and feminine principle is vital. For this law is the same on all planes of being and for all levels of expression. Here Mary represents *Divine Grace*, Light, or Spiritual Energies, coming down from Above while Joseph represents *human effort* striving from Below and thrusting Above for the Star of higher consciousness and spiritual realization. Joseph symbolizes the *psychological and human work* that must be accomplished as the necessary foundation while Mary symbolizes the *spiritual response* which always follows and crowns authentic aspirations and efforts of the human mind, heart, and will. Joseph is thus the symbol of the *Promethean thrust* toward the Superconscious and the Spiritual Self while Mary is the symbol of the *Epimethean response* and manifestation of the Light in the field of consciousness.

In psychological terms Joseph is lined with *Invocation*, the synthesis of concentration (will), meditation (thinking), devotion (feeling), and visualization (imagination) upon the Divine Spark while Mary is linked with *Evocation*, the downpouring and outpouring of the spiritual Energies, Inspiration and Intuition which revitalize, transform, and amplify willing, thinking, feeling, and imagination. In the Grail symbolism, Joseph represents the Spear and Mary the Cup. Mary here is the earthly and psychic womb or matrix, while Joseph is the earthly stimulus necessary to activate and extend the divine Light and the spiritual Energies to manifest consciously in the field of consciousness.

The Virgin Birth of Jesus, or the Immaculate Conception, has many meanings and implications on different levels of consciousness and being. Its basic spiritual meaning, however, is twofold: First, it indicates that the Soul of Jesus is an "immaculate Conception," i.e. that it freely incarnates for the sake of the world and not because it has to for its own growth and evolution—that it is free from sin, karma, or imperfections that must be worked out on earth in the physical world. While normal human beings are born to sin, that is, they have to incarnate by necessity to continue their evolution, to become more than they are, to polish out their imperfections, and to actualize their human faculties and realize their Self. Jesus was born without sin, that is, did not have to incarnate by necessity but freely chose to do so in order to provide a pure and trained vehicle to the Christ Spirit coming to the world. Second, it indicates that the Birth of the Divine Spark in the soul, or the dawning of true spiritual Consciousness, involves psychological and spiritual forces and processes and not physical ones, i.e. that both conception and birth occur within *one's consciousness* by the use of one's psychospiritual tools and resources to which God adds the free gift of Grace.

The Three Magi or Kings of the East symbolize, in the microcosm, the royal faculties of the human psyche: *will, thought, feeling* that have to work in unison to realize spiritual

Initiation by bringing their archetypal presents to the divine Spark: Gold which represents human knowledge and consciousness, Myrrh being the human creative energies and will, and Frankincense being human love and feeling. For it is only when a human being will give and open all his mind, heart, and Soul, all his human knowledge, love, and energies, that these can be purified, vivified, and transmuted by the spiritual Light into spiritual Wisdom, spiritual Love, and spiritual Energies or Will. Hence each one of us must bring his gifts, the best and highest of himself, to the Divine within, to the Inner Christ and His ever-shining Light, for these are the human energies, vibrations, and substance upon which the Divine can work and through which he can express and reveal Himself. For, without this offering and sacrifice on our part to act as channels and vehicles for the spiritual Light, neither can our human knowledge, love, and creative energies be transformed and amplified, nor can the Divine manifest consciously within our psyche and lives.

The fact that Mary could not find a place to deliver in the local inns and that she had to give birth to Jesus in a manger symbolically tells us that the Astral body and consciousness of human beings are generally so filled with worldly desires and preoccupations that there is no "place" or "room" for the spiritual Energies and the divine Light to come in, and these never force their way in but patiently wait and knock to be wanted and bid to "come in." The Manger represents the psychospiritual Heart Center of a human being which is located in the very center of his being and which is the core Center where the spiritual energies and the divine Light have to flow in and activate so that the Spiritual Self can be connected with and, eventually, direct the human self and the personality. The presence of various animals there shows two basic things: that the human heart still has animal passions operating in it when spiritual consciousness is born and that the energy of these animal passions and biopsychic drives should not be killed or repressed but rather harnessed and put to work by the Divine within so as to accomplish their appointed work in the biopsychic economy of human nature. While there are many animals that are symbolically present at the birth of the Christ child, two stand out more prominently than others and represent important universal archetypes. These are the Bull and the Ass. The first symbolizes the sexual drive and power, while the second the imagination and the stubbornness of the human ego or lower self. As these are present and breathing upon the Christ child, they tell us, in the symbolic language of the Sages, that the sexual energy, the imagination, and the determination of the lower self can and should be harnessed by the divine Light, transmuted, and put to work in their rightful place when a human being finally becomes a child of God and a citizen of the Kingdom of Heaven.

The Three Magi, who come inside and worship the Christ child, are also contrasted with the Shepherds who stand outside recognizing the tremendous event that is taking place but without understanding it. These two archetypes represent the polar opposite types of human beings: the *Magi* symbolizing the Faustian types who have to go through the entire range of human experiences and investigation to finally come to the supreme Truth and Reality—if they do not stop and get lost on the way! The Shepherds on the other hand, represent the Intuitive or Mystical types who are drawn to the ultimate Truth and Reality spontaneously and inwardly without needing all the experiences and studies of the former. Gold, Myrrh, and Frankincense also show, in the macrocosm, that Jesus was being recognized as a King: a being who is the master of himself and a channel for the divine Will, a Priest: a being who acts as a link and an energy and consciousness transformer for the spiritual Energies in this world, and a Prophet: an Initiate and a revealer of the Mysteries.

The Star of the Savior, the five-pointed Pentagram that guided the Magi to Bethlehem and to the Manger and that stood over Jesus, is the symbol and emblem of the *perfected Soul* who is coming down the planes to incarnate on earth and clearly shows that a great Soul is coming to earth for a special mission. Any highly spiritually developed person and clairvoyant can attest to this fact which is visible to him on the inner planes. For, in the inner planes, every human being is a glowing *star* and appears as such to clairvoyant sight which reveals his evolutionary and spiritual status. This star that we shall find again, this time at the top of the Christmas tree, is also the symbol and expression of a *perfected human being*, what all of us will eventually become.

The choir of Angels singing "glory to God in the highest and on earth peace to men of good will" represent the spiritual Energies flowing from the Spiritual Self to the human self, from the Superconscious to the conscious, affecting our intuitions, thoughts, feelings, and decisions which are now linked to God's Will and Consciousness and are instruments for their conscious manifestation. These psychospiritual energies "light up" and activate the core Centers on the Tree of Life and bring a sense of peace or harmony and integration at the core of the personality which are consciously experienced and realized. "Glory" is the spiritual Light and Splendor which always shine "on high" and which are now recognized and consciously experienced by the candidate. "Peace to men of good will" establishes and represents true harmony within the psyche and its many levels, components, and faculties which now form a "living psychosynthesis." This, in fact, is one of the major goals for any living human being, representing the marriage of the personality and the marriage of the personality and the Soul, but it can only be fully realized and experienced when the Divine Spark has indrawn in its vehicles and is ensouling them and when spiritual Consciousness is activated and consciously experienced.

The Christmas tree, another central symbol of the Christmas glyph, represents the Tree of Life, the psycho-spiritual Centers and their connections within our being, which we have to activate and "light up," and which can become fully lit up only when the Divine has descended into it and its abode in it. Thus, when we make a Christmas tree, decorate it, and light up its candles, and put a five-pointed star at the top of it, we are, in fact, creating an *external projected symbol* of what we have to do and become inwardly: purify and sanctify our souls (decorate the tree), progressively light up and activate each of the psycho-spiritual Centers, and finally become the fully lit tree and are recognized as such by the spiritual Beings who have the Inner Vision.

Finally, human beings also get together and exchange cards and presents to celebrate this event and rejoice in it. This is a manifestation on the physical and human planes of a process that takes place on *all* planes of being at that time. A tremendous infusion of Light and spiritual energy is released in the atmosphere of the earth and in the Aura of the person who undergoes his "personal Christmas" or the descent of the Light. While the Spirit gives spiritual things: His Light, Life, and Being, human beings respond by wanting to give and share human things which are meaningful to them on their respective levels. Moreover, when the Divine is slowly born and awakes in every human soul, it always brings many gifts and the spirit of giving in its wake, a process which is reenacted by human beings on their own levels.

In conclusion, Christmas is both the blueprint and the prototype of our *own individual Spiritual Initiation*, the conscious birth of the Divine Spark in our Souls. It is the Great

Event toward which we are all, consciously or unconsciously, striving and which was prefigured and historically enacted for us by the Glyph of the birth of Jesus the Christ told in the Christmas story, thus becoming the great symbolic archetype for all humanity. It is also the central objective of the great work of human growth and spiritual regeneration toward which all psychological and spiritual systems that are authentic are aiming; and it is the culmination of the psychospiritual work which is being outlined and described in the present work. Each of the symbols, images and events connected with this Event, great or small, single or composite, can be used for a great deal of personal, psychological, and spiritual work. Each, therefore, can be and should be used as a theme and object for *concentration, meditation, contemplation,* and for *theurgic work,* which combines and integrates experientially the functions of thinking, feeling, willing, imagination, and intuition, to become more than one is and to consciously collaborate in one's true BECOMING. Each symbol, image, and event must in particular, be used as a subject for meditation—for reflective, receptive, contemplative, and creative meditation—to decode its deeper meanings and correspondences. For this is the process whereby we can make them come alive in one's consciousness and being, incarnate them and incorporate them in one's life so that, in the end, each one of us may go through and experience one's own personal Christmas or spiritual Initiation—for that is, after all, the central reason for our being here on earth, on the physical plane of being.

As the central concept of the present chapter is Light and its Descent into the Personality, it behooves us, at the end, to focus in depth on the various meetings and the essence of "Light." To begin with, we can, analytically, focus on five basic dimensions of the Light even though, in reality, the Light is one with many different expressions and manifestations on different planes of being. While the Light is one but with different vibrations and forms of expression at the conscious level, it still remains, essentially, as GOD-IN-EXPRESSION OR MANIFESTATION, and this we should ever bear in mind. Thus, Light exists and manifests itself on the divine level, the Plane of God, and in the four basic planes of manifestation, the spiritual, mental, emotional, and physical planes.

On the divine level, Light is simply the "Garment of the Eternal," the Energy and Manifestation of God in the triune expression of Light, Fire, and Life which are three in expression but one in essence. All that ever was, is, and ever will be is thus an expression and manifestation, an emanation and creation, of the Light which constitutes its essence.

On the spiritual level, Light is the very source and essence of consciousness and wisdom, of love and feeling, and of energy and will. Here Light is also one in essence but threefold in its manifestations and is the underlying Life essence behind all forms of consciousness and awareness. It is also the great unifying and integrating force that links up, relates, and synthesizes everything it comes in contact with. At the spiritual level, the manifestation of Light reveals the Self and enables the Self to express itself in consciousness, love, and power. Its conscious realization brings faith in its true and deepest sense.

On the mental level, Light manifests itself as consciousness, knowledge, awareness, and clarity. It is the "fuel of the mind" and that energy which enables the mind to function properly and to bring into awareness and, later, to comprehend all that which it focuses upon. Here the manifestations of the Light translates itself as a clear, penetrating mind that can comprehend that which it focuses upon both in the outer and in the inner world.

On the emotional level, Light manifests itself as love and feeling. It is the "emotional fuel" that makes us feel

toward whatever we focus upon. Here, it is the great ener-
gizer and motivator to the personality and it translates itself
as deep, intense, and clear feeling, and as Courage, in the
old French meaning of the word, which means "a new
heart" or a "change of heart."

On the physical level, Light manifests itself as life,
vitality, and energy—the ability to use the physical vehicle
as a responsive and well-trained instrument to achieve
whatever purpose we have in mind in the physical world. If
the body is sick or in a state of disease or lack of proper
integration, the Light can heal it and help the various organs
and systems of the body to carry out their natural functions.

In conclusion, on all levels of being, the Light is the
ultimate Life force and sustaining element which, when
properly circulating, brings about true health and well-
being and without which no plane of being or function can
be activated and function. The Light is thus not only the
manifestation of God in the world and in our own being but
also the necessary energy fuel which keeps us going on all
planes of being and which, ultimately, enables us to become
and express our true Self. The Descent of the Light into the
personality creates a link and a harmony between the personality, the Soul, and the Self, and enables us to raise our
"center of gravity" and our basic level of consciousness
from the personality level to the Soul level where, for the
first time, we really discover and become our "Self" and
become children of God.

Practical Exercise

Preliminary: Find the right place and the right position. Then make an effort of Introversion, Supraversion, and Infraversion.

Actual work: Review and Meditation

At this point, you should have completed your study and training leading to self-actualization and to the mastery of your basic "muscles of consciousness." Thus you should reflect and test yourself out on how well you understand and can utilize, either singly or together, what I call the "muscles of consciousness": Feeling, Thinking, Willing, Imagination, and Intuition together with their related psychological processes of Devotion, Meditation, Concentration, Visualization, and Invocation-Evocation. Use the Consciousness Checklist (see Appendix B) and carefully go through its basic categories. Which are more or less developed at this point in time? What are you practically doing now to develop and coordinate them?

Then, focus your attention upon your Biopsychic Drives; sexuality and aggression in particular, to see how well you can handle them at this point in your life: face them transmute them, and then in a conscious and constructive fashion, harness their energies and power. How do you handle your sexuality and aggressive energies? Have you achieved conscious control over them or do they still "drive" and control you to some extent?

Now turn your attention upon your *sensations*. Can you easily get in touch with them? Which is more or less developed? Do you have a program of "sensory awareness" development? Can you work with outer and inner Observation in a satisfactory way? How adept are you at this point in working with inner Observation? Are you doing anything to develop it further?

Finally, turn your attention to your daily life and the way you handle your personal hygiene and energy. How well acquainted are you with the seven basic laws of preventive and holistic medicine? To what extent do you abide by them in your personal life? At present, which is your strong and your weak point (nutrition, sleep, physical exercise, sexual life, emotional and mental life, social life, or spiritual life)? Are you presently doing something about it? And, if not, what could you do to improve the quality of your health and of your bio-psycho-social functioning? Remember that YOU are building the "Temple made without human hands" which is your personality, your human consciousness!

Having dealt, as best as you can, with the process of self-actualization, you are now ready to pass on to the next phase, that of self-realization: becoming aware of, nurturing, and aligning your personality with your Soul and with the Divine Spark. To do this: Meditate upon the Christmas story as a symbolic representation of your own Spiritual Initiation to come. Read the Christmas story in the four Gospels and meditate upon the meanings and correspondences of each one of its major symbols in the *microcosm*, in your own being and consciousness.

Find an artistic representation of the manger scene or draw it up. Then recreate it in your imagination and use its symbols and images, both individually and collectively, for concentration, meditation, contemplation, and theurgic purposes . . . . and see what happens. What is it that you have to change in your life, to eliminate or to add, so as to create the sacred space, the sacred time, and the sacred efforts to facilitate the descent of the Light into your heart Center and Consciousness? When you have completed this review, meditation, and psychospiritual exercises, make the appropriate entries in your workbook, as to what you have discovered, what you have done, what has happened, and how you were able to cope.

Chapter Eight

ARMAGEDDON:
The Last Great Inner War

No matter what spiritual tradition we look at, we always find a dualistic conception of human nature as being torn between a "lower self" and a "higher self," between the personality and the individuality, or the personality and the Soul. The higher part of our being is generally linked with the spiritual aspects and the spiritual worlds, whereas the lower part of our being is connected with the material world and mundane perceptions and activities. Actually, the entire structure of human nature from the Divine Spark and the Soul all the way down to the physical body and the physical world are *divine* and thus just as sacred or important. But the central distinction we just saw, which is as old and universal as the distinction between the sacred and the profane, refers to the connection between our various vehicles and the Self as well as to the focus of our consciousness as being partial and limited and thus *egoistical* and *separative*, or holistic and unlimited and thus *altruistic* and

151

inclusive. These are truly fundamental concepts and insights that we must understand and experience in our quest for true and integral self-knowledge, self-mastery and self-integration.

The Higher Self has, sometimes, been symbolized by the Sun, and the lower self by the Earth. The Higher Self includes the Divine Spark and the three higher vehicles of consciousness, the higher and lower spiritual, and the higher mental. The lower self, on the other hand, includes the lower mental, the emotional and passional, and the etheric and physical vehicles. In terms of the chakras, the Higher Self includes the three higher ones while the lower self manifests itself through the three lower ones. The fourth, or Heart Center, stands astride the two basic natures, defining the upper limits of the lower self and the lower limits of the Higher Self, and the point where the crucial "shift of consciousness and center of gravity" between the two takes place. Just as the Earth rotates on an orbit around the Sun, so the lower self also rotates on an "orbit" around the Higher Self. The *right distance* is crucial in both cases for, should the Earth get too close to the Sun, it would burn, while if it gets too far from the Sun it would freeze. Should the lower self get too close to the Divine Spark, it would also burn, i.e. the tremendous energies and vibrations emanating from it could not be assimilated and integrated, and the personality would then become overwhelmed by them and dissociate. But, should the lower self get too far from the divine Spark, it would also freeze, i.e. lose its sense of identity, meaning, purpose and joy in life, and, being in "darkness," fall prey to external and internal stimuli, to hedonism, materialism, and self-will. Finally, it is only when the four lower vehicles of consciousness are dissociated from the Divine Spark and the three high ones that it is known as the *lower self.*

A well-known spiritual writer, Omraam M. Aivanhov,

declares: "The essential key to understand and resolve all the central problems of human existence is the proper understanding of the two basic and opposed natures of Man: the lower self, or personality; and the Higher Self, or Individuality."[1] For him, the lower self represents all that which is unstable, changing in human nature, thus it assumes different masks and plays different roles in the greater theater of life and its central goal is always the same: *to profit personally*, to take, to increase its possessions, its power, and its control so as to satisfy its interests and desires. Hence, it is basically *egoistical* and *egocentric*. The Higher Self, on the other hand, represents that which is most stable and lasting, that which is impersonal and disinterested, and its central goal is also always the same: *to give*, to share, to radiate, to enhance life and consciousness. The individuality, which includes the Divine Spark, also lives in perfect harmony with other human beings and with the whole of creation. Thus it is basically altruistic and selfless, or "heliocentric." This first strives for its self-interests and pleasures and is thus driven by self-will—which will, logically, clash with the self-interests and will of others. The second, on the other hand, ever strives for the good of the whole, being aligned with God's Will.

The central task of self-actualization and self-realization consists in creating roads, bridges, and valid connections between the personality and the individuality. But here, only those who are strong, audacious, and courageous, and who are willing and able to work and to sacrifice themselves to grow and become more than what they are, will succeed, for the weak and the lazy accept themselves and life as they are and will never take the risks and make the efforts to *become more than what they are and know*. Aivanhov represents both natures and describes their operations basically through the use of symbols and images which have multiple meanings and applications on different levels of consciousness and being. In his works, the personality is represented by the Earth and the Moon (which *take* rather than *give*) and as a multitude of animals with their teeth, claws, horns, and tough skins. It is an octopus which projects its tentacles, a tiger, a crocodile, a bat; it is the dragon of St. George, the horse Bucephalus that Alexander learned to master, and the bird of the Thousand and One Nights which covers the Sun and darkens the sky when it spreads its wings. The individuality is represented by the Sun which radiates Light, Warmth, and Life, by the princess who is captive and asleep, and by the pearl of great value that lies at the bottom of the ocean.

The basic teachings of Aivanhov on this matter is that we must not fight against one's personality but harness it and master it to put it to work to accomplish its God-given tasks. Those who fight against it and its weaknesses fight against themselves and exhaust themselves to end up in hospitals. Repression is not better than licence (of which it is the other face!). Moreover, it is precisely the drive that leads a human being to fight against his lower nature and his basic weaknesses, or which let them predominate, that, by projection and externalization, produces all the basic conflicts and wars that tear apart both human nature and societies.

From the standpoint of the personality there is only division, separation, and thus conflicts without end. By learning to raise one's level of consciousness to the level of the individuality, however, one can then find lasting peace, harmony, and the right relationship with all the parts of one's being and with all the persons that make up one's psychosocial network. The individuality can use all the elements, faculties, and energies of one's being because it understands and respects the role, the place, and the tasks of every aspect of our being. Thus it is from its viewpoint alone that one can discover and establish the right relationship and well-being of all living beings and thus avoid the conflicts of the various facets and tendencies of our own nature, for interpsychic and intrapsychic conflicts are the two faces of the same reality.

The essential characteristics of the individuality is the perception and understanding of the fundamental unity and right function of all creation and of the incredibly rich harmony and diversity of all the parts, each of which has its proper note, song, and function in the universe. When our center of consciousness and being has finally reached and been properly rooted in the individuality, then we shall learn to operate and fight in the outer theater of life with the weapons of *love* and *light*. As Aivanhov puts it succinctly:

> Man only has the right to oppose a *wrong* to transform it into a *right*; he has the right to destroy something only when he can immediately transform that which he has torn down into something better. True struggling and "fighting" are thus *self-overcoming*, going beyond what we are at present in love and in offering that which is best in us, sacrificing something to improve it, beautify it, and benefit all concerned.[2]

One cannot fight against one's weakness alone. The central key here is to know how to find and redirect one's energies to transform them and project them toward what is on high, toward superior manifestations and expressions. If one has a real enemy, one does not fight against him but merely provoke him into a series of unending and escalating conflicts which take their toll on both parties. With true love, personal sacrifices, patience and justice, one can get the enemy to turn into a friend or, at least, to cease being an enemy. This is why, in a nutshell, a human being, by the proper knowledge and understanding of his two opposed natures, has the *essential secret* through which he can work for his happiness and his spiritual enrichment as well as those of the whole world.

Aivanhov's core assumptions and basic philosophy on

this subject, which are most inspiring and enlightening, are:

> The origin of the personality lies in the Spirit, for if the Spirit had not manifested it and emananted it, projected it from Itself, it would not exist. At the beginning we find the Spirit, and when the Spirit wanted to manifest Itself in the lower and more dense regions made with a denser and more opaque matter, It fashioned three bodies: first, the mental body, then the astral body, and finally the physical body with its etheric double. These are the basic "bodies," or vehicles of consciousness which form our personality. As for the Individuality, it is an integral part of God Himself, a Spark, a Flame, and Intelligent and Loving Energy. The Individuality has great possibilities: it wants to know, to feel, to see, to experience everything and to create in the worlds of manifestation. But, It can only manifest Itself in the lower regions through the Personality which is Its instrument, its *temple*. This is what can explain the paradox of why a human being is, here on earth, weak, ignorant, and sick while, at the same time, in the spiritual worlds, an entity endowed with Light, Knowledge, Power, and Immortality. This is what explains our limitations and imperfections in the lower worlds and our perfection and power in the higher worlds . . . When these vehicles will be fully developed and coordinated, the mental body will be so clear and sharp that it will be able to receive and comprehend the wisdom of the Individuality. The astral body will then be able to express the noblest and most disinterested feelings, and the physical body will be strong and healthy, and finally able to carry out in the physical world the will and commands of the Individuality. At present, however, while the Personality is fashioned by the Individuality, it often acts in ways contrary to the true motives of the Individuality: the Personality wants to be free and independent, and to carry out its own will, thus it opposes and does not obey the impulsions that come from the higher spheres. But one day, when we will be more conscious and evolved the Individuality will succeed in vivifying and controlling the Personality which will then be obedient and truly aligned with the Individuality so that the two will form one properly aligned and functioning whole. This is the true marriage, the true love, when the Bride and Groom will finally be mated and which the Spiritual Tradition calls "making the ends meet." One end is the Individuality and the other the Personality, both of which are triple like Cereberus, the dog with three heads

who guards the entrance to Hell. This, then is the true work
of the disciple: in the midst of all vicissitudes, variations, and
tribulations of life, he must succeed in aligning, harmoniz-
ing, and integrating the consciousness and will of the Personality with that of the Individuality so as to become a
living temple and instrument of the God within. This is the
quintessence of the true work of spiritual regeneration, of
the Great Work taught by all the genuine spiritual schools
and traditions.[3]

Later, he continues:

The Personality is opaque, heavy, and rigid like an
armor while the Individuality is transparent, light, and alive.
We all wear our physical body as the snail wears a shell
... The Personality leads us to the gates of Hell while the
Individuality to the gates of Paradise. The Personality is
egotistical in its decisions, hard in its judgments, and without
love or wisdom. It wants, demands, protests, and wants to
possess and to dominate; it is nervous, vulnerable, and anx-
ious; in short, it possesses all the human defects. But it is also
like a rich grandmother who owns treasures which are very
important for our well-being and self-realization. The problem is that we give in to it and that it acquires rulership over
our being and life. The Personality owns subterranean riches,
raw materials: the instincts, appetites, passions, and desires
which make her powerful and overwhelming. Its major
defect is to be bound to the lower self and to work for it
rather than for the Higher Self. In its egocentrism, the personality keeps, preserves, and increases the possessions of
its owner but what it lacks is a moral conscience, generosity,
impartiality, and self-sacrifice, for it is very close to the
animal level.

All of the inferior tendencies of the Personality can be
summarized by one word: the Devil. The old myth that we
have a demon on our left shoulder and an angel on the right
is true, but what they really symbolize is the Personality and
the Individuality. The first always to take while the second
to give. The predominance of the Personality is the true
cause of all the anomalies, contradictions, wars, revolutions,
and miseries of humanity. The divine nature whispers, speaks
softly and never uses violence, coercion, or a lot of noise: it
does not insist or compel anyone, it merely suggests and
waits. But most human beings who lack spiritual discernment are not even aware that their higher nature has spoken
to them and inspired them. Scientists, philosophers, writers,
and very cultivated persons identify themselves with the

Personality when they say: "*I want* (money, a car, a mate), *I am* (well, sick, inspired), *I have* (this desire, opinion, taste)." They think that it is they who act, but they are wrong, it is the Personality in them which desires, thinks, feels and suffers . . . and makes them work.[4]

Finally, Aivanhov concludes:

The Personality is an illusion, a partial and ephemeral reflection and not an eternal and lasting reality. It is not our true Self, it is a mirage which the Hindus have called "Maya." Thus, it is not the world which is "Maya" but our lower self because it always leads us to perceive ourselves as separate beings. The world is not maya, it is a reality just as lies and hell are also realities. The fundamental illusion is to perceive ourselves and to think that we are separated from the universal and eternal Life, from this unique Being Who is everywhere but Whom we can neither feel nor understand because our lower self makes this impossible . . . The Personality, like the masks and the roles that a person takes and plays in life, changes with every incarnation whereas all the qualities and wisdom that a person has acquired in any incarnation remain as his true heritage of inestimable wealth in the Individuality. The Individuality can be compared to the sun while the Personality to the moon. The moon goes through different phases and is always varying; it does not radiate its own light and is not the center of a solar system as is the sun. The Personality is just as unstable as the moon while the Individuality, like the sun, remains always luminous, radiating, and powerful.

The distinguishing feature of the Personality is that it always wants to take, to possess, and to hold on. It is an inverse trinity corresponding to the intellect, the heart and the will in their inferior manifestations. And when the personality enters into conflict with other forces and persons who prevent her from realizing its egotistical tendencies, it becomes irritated, violent, evil, vindictive, and cruel and does violence to others to release its own pain and frustrations. The Individuality, on the other hand, only wants to give, to radiate, to enlighten, and help others. It projects something of itself and emanates a light and an energy. It wants to make efforts, to sacrifice itself for the common good, to be generous, and self-effacing. This is why it does not keep that which it possesses and why it is not irritated if someone comes to take its riches. It is happy to see that others can be enlightened, fed, and helped by her presence and actions. It is also a trinity which manifests mind, heart, and will. The focus of its intelligence is to enlighten, of its heart to warm up, and of its will to animate and liberate all beings. And, as these two natures, so completely different, cohabit in the same organism and being, every person is ceaselessly torn and drawn by these two forces, the first egocentric and centripetal, the other heliocentric, altruistic, and centrifugal . . . The core virtue of the Individuality is to give and to radiate. All virtues are, in fact, but a radiation, a projection of one's Self, to give or "sacrifice" something . . . for something higher and better. When a person reaches this point and truly falls under the dominion of the Individuality, he is forced to master all the tendencies of the Personality in himself, and all of its fears and anxieties: the fear of dying, of not being loved and understood, of being poor and hungry. All fears and anxieties of the Personality, however, can be overcome by the desire of the Higher Self to give, to radiate, to extend Itself and uplift others.

Thus, anyone who is egotistical and self-centered cannot project and radiate Light for Light is something that a human being must draw and project for himself. Its essence is a manifestation of love, of life, of goodness, and of generosity. And when this occurs there is no more fear or anxiety for fear and anxiety cannot coexist with Light and Love. While the Personality is an abyss which engulfs everything, the Individuality can be compared to a river, a high peak, or the sun.[5]

For Aivanhov, the true essence of morality, responsibility, and maturity lies in knowing that we are all ONE and that that which one does unto others he does unto himself. This fundamental principle is clearly and directly realized by the individuality but it is foreign to and rejected by the personality which cannot experience and comprehend this oneness and interrelation of all forms of life. Thus, he states incisively: "When you harm someone else, you will then reflect: Oh, but I am harming myself because I live in that being and he also lives in me. This is how true morality can be realized and how evil is forced to flee."[6]

Lastly, Aivanhov also gives us very important insights on the subject of meditation, contemplation, and identification as related to the core functions of the psyche: thinking, feeling, and willing. Thus, he writes:

Meditation is an intellectual process the essence of which is to reflect and to seek light, wisdom, and knowledge. *Con templation* is linked with feeling. Here it is a question of consciously amplifying and awakening all the faculties of the heart and soul by developing and expressing love, admiration, and wonder. Then, contemplation can raise our con sciousness to the angelic realms. *Identification* is an act of the will through which one can bind and link oneself with God (or any other object). To conquer and overcome the Personality one must use and refine these three basic faculties. The Personality is very powerful and one is obliged to live with it and to feed it a little bit for, otherwise, it would perish. And it is the Personality which holds the keys of our worldly food and experience and of material wealth. Thus, it is useful and necessary for the Great Work but one must master it and put it to work and not become its slave. One must never kill it but, rather, control and direct it, and use all of its energies, treasures, and functions. If one falls too low and becomes ensnared by the Personality, identifying the self with the body, then one is in great danger for, in the lower regions, one is very, very vulnerable. Here, everyone can reach you and destroy you because you are heavy, blocked, and at the mercy of your enemies. But, if you know how to move, to change places and states of consciousness, or to fly like birds, then you are no longer at the mercy of circumstances. When one descends too low into matter, one becomes enslaved and it is others that rule our lives and being. In order to be able to glide above all human vicissitudes and not let oneself become prey of anxiety or despair, to rise above human tragedies and sufferings, one must climb and climb, and expand one's state of consciousness.[7]

The true key to life and happiness can be found, for Aivanhov, in the way in which one looks at the world and in proper understanding, which depends on one's level of being and consciousness. The personality is always vulnerable to fear because it feels itself *separated* and *isolated* and thus poor and very insecure. This is the real reason why the personality always seeks to take in order to insure its "security." But when one fears, one cannot love for love is incompatible with fear.

Internally, in the Microcosm, Light and Spiritual Energies of the Individuality transform themselves into gold, in human gold. And it is this gold which gives the initiate his unique conviction, certitude, and lucidity. As Aivanhov sums it up:

> The initiate only desires what his Individuality desires and this is his liberation, for the only true liberation is that from the dominion of the Personality or of the Lower Self. Then, he is the master and his Personality is the servant. One must feed, wash, and take care of the Personality, but not become ensnared in its caprices and yearnings. Do you ever leave a servant without food and lodging? One never becomes a divinity by following only the laws of the earth, one becomes a divinity by subjecting oneself to the laws of the sun . . . The Personality is a link, an open door between our field of consciousness and Hell, thus it is through the Personality that Hell can reach us. The earth is the symbol of the physical body, the moon that of the astral body, and the sun that of the Divine Spark. The first two are feminine while the sun is masculine. The moon waxes and wanes as if to show us that for a little while its role is to reflect all that is evil and infernal and, for another period of time, all that is good and heavenly.
>
> Sensitive and receptive beings are very vulnerable because they do not know how to protect themselves. This is why mediums are often at the mercy of all kinds of negative influences. Whereas solar beings are the Magi and with the Magi, it is the masculine side that predominates—the will, the need to give, to build, to influence, to act in all its forms. When a human being has integrated both his natures, the solar and the lunar, then he possesses true perfection— he is an androgynous being and knows how to give and how to receive.[8]

In the perspective of this central insight and philosophy, what is Armageddon and what are the nature and basic dynamics of the "last great Inner War?" Armageddon is the Biblical term which has become a key word for those who like to speculate upon and interpret the various symbolic meanings of Revelation. The first fundamental spiritual insight into the true nature and function of Armageddon is that this term cannot be interpreted literally but, rather, symbolically; thus, it does not designate a war in the outer, physical world but an inner clash and conflict in the

consciousness and Soul of a human being. The second is
that Armageddon, the Great Inner Conflict, takes place not
only once but many times, on different levels of consciousness. As such, it is a most important and significant process
that faces every human generation and, in particular, every
candidate for spiritual Initiation.

Technically speaking, every true Initiation, including
the four elemental ones and the three spiritual ones, directly involve some aspect or manifestation of Armageddon —
some major crisis, or test, involving a "death" and a
"resurrection." The first, the Earth Initiation, involves the
breaking of the physical body or some major aspect of one's
physical health which may have profound implications for
one's psychological health. The second, the Water Initiation, involves the breaking of the heart, or a major emotional
crisis. The third, the Air Initiation, deals with the breaking
of the mind, or a major mental crisis in which one's core
assumptions, ideas, and philosophy of life have to be given
up and changed. Finally, the fourth, the Fire Initiation,
generally deals with the breaking of the will and of the ego
during which one may go through an actual physical death,
or near-death experience as these are now called by the
newly emerging science of thanatology. And it involves a
genuine out-of-the-body experience where the focus of
one's identity and consciousness is transferred from the
physical to the astral body. But the most real and awesome
manifestation of Armageddon occurs during the fifth Initiation, which is the first truly spiritual Initiation, wherein the
center of gravity of one's consciousness and the control of
the personality passes from the lower self to the Higher
Self, from the personality to the Soul. For here, all the forces
of Light and darkness, all the vices and virtues, and all the
resources of the personality, developed in this incarnation,
and of the Soul, developed over many incarnations, are
weighed and pitted against each other for the final control

of the personality and of the human consciousness of the candidate. Here, all of one's energies, life force, and vitality, all of one's desires and emotions, all of one's thoughts and ideas, and all of one's yearnings and aspirations are shaken up, disorganized, and then reorganized in a different fashion.

At the age of twenty and a half, I went through my first great test and trial in this life, my Earth Initiation. At the age of eighteen, my physical and psychological health began to give me some serious problems with strange symptoms and with no organic cause that could be identified even by the best medical authorities and tests. I had pains and tensions in my head, especially around my eyes and forehead. My face would flush up and burn for long periods of time making me red like a tomato and for no apparent cause. I would have chronic fatigue and find it very difficult to muster the energy and motivation to do anything. Finally, my emotions would race up and down and I had the impression that I was in the process of losing control of my thoughts and emotions.

Needless to say, this created a great deal of anxiety and turmoil for my family and myself. After many vicissitudes and no fundamental solution for my situation, I finally met a woman in Paris, who was a Mystic and an Initiate, and who told me what I had, why I had developed this situation, and that it was a test and crisis I had to live through. She also gave me practical suggestions as to how I could help myself and gave me both meaning and hope for my situation. My health then improved quite a bit until the culmination of this test came with a motorcycle accident that injured my spine and left me semi-handicapped with, this time, very identifiable physical symptoms and causes. For another two and a half years I struggled with this condition to regain my health and to live a normal life in spite of the fact that, again, the best medical opinions and conclusions were that

I would remain physically semi-handicapped. This time, however, I had a mental framework in which to imbed and interpret what was happening to me and I had a source to whom I could turn for advice, guidance, and hope. After a great deal of work, a lot of suffering, and much anxiety and self-pity, I managed to pull myself together and to live a normal and productive life. Many times I went to the very edge of despair, lost my faith and my will to go on and seriously desired to put an end to my life. Yet I also realized that one is never given more than he can bear and cope with . . . provided he uses *all* of his resources and potentials, without holding anything back and giving it all he has got. And I pulled through being stronger and wiser, and having met some extraordinary human beings who understood what I was going through and who could give me directions, companionship, and a living example. In particular, upon the directions of the woman in Paris, I found a spiritual school in New York City, where I was studying that which provided me with all the materials, skills, and fellowship I needed at the time.

At that point, when I was in my early 20's, I wrote a very important paper on what was happening to me, on its meaning and larger implications, drawing at the same time from my direct lived experience and from the higher and intuitive stores of my Superconscious. The gist of this reflection is the following:

The evolution of all forms of life, from the unicellular organism to human nature and beyond, clearly shows discontinuities, mutational jumps, or metamorphoses. In human life, birth and death, illness and existential crises, an unforecasted "turn of fortune" positive or negative, the loss or separation of a dear one, meeting with a special person, changing jobs or residence, and matrimony or divorce are common examples of such discontinuities which involve both subjective and objective change.

In spiritual life, the expression, transformation, and expansion of human consciousness, the most important metamorphoses have traditionally been called Initiations. Initiation implies both inner and outer battles, struggles, sufferings, and a "death" or "crucifixion" and an extension and enlargement of consciousness, a discovery and "explosion" or one's inner energies and potentials, and a heightened capacity for knowing, loving, and creating. In short, it entails a major crisis and opportunity characterized by a "death" and a "rebirth." It is upon the outcome of this crisis, which is always composed of external events that are predetermined and unchangeable, and of one's perception, definition, and reaction to these events—of one's state of consciousness—which are fluidic and changeable, that Initiation or an awakening and functioning in a higher state of consciousness and life depends.

These crises and "tests," therefore, can rightly be viewed as one of the truly essential things we have come to accomplish here on earth—as an "examination" leading the candidate, when successfully passed, to a higher "class" in life. Their central features are always an expanded consciousness, a fuller capacity to love, and higher creative energies. These crises are called by many names (e.g. the Dark Night of the Soul, the Hall of Judgment, the meeting with the Guardian of the Threshold, etc.) and are symbolically represented by very vivid images and encounters with animals, dragons, giants, devils, etc. which are as different in character and infinite in variety as life itself. In every case, however, they are the final result and objectification of a long series of causes set in motion by the candidate himself and corresponding to parts of his own being and life. During these crises, the old dilemma, verbalized by Hamlet: "To be or not to be" becomes a living reality for the candidate which, like the riddle of the Sphinx, he must face, battle, and conquer—and thus live more abundantly—or fail and "die" only to begin all over again at a later time. The usual setting for this crisis, which I had to face and live through in my early 20's, is that the candidate finds himself utterly alone, misunderstood, and deserted by all on the physical plane and, seemingly, also by his Higher Self in his consciousness, thus being thrust in darkness.

At this point, it is a matter strictly between the forces of Light and Darkness at war within himself. And there, in the inner theater of his consciousness, he must meet them all and face them all, and set them one against the other: all his assets and liabilities, all his strengths, talents, and good deeds against all his weaknesses, vices, and bad deeds. For this memorable feud, which all human beings must eventually face and which none can escape, all his innermost energies and resources are gathered. Then, silently and often known only to himself, the battle begins.

All that he holds most dear and cherished, that he feels he "knows" and "trusts" is put at the stake and seems to go, as though sucked into a black hole. The candidate finds himself, perceives himself, and experiences himself as though sinking in the middle of a dark, cold, and unending quicksand. First his physical health and life, or that of his dear ones, then his emotional and mental health and theirs and, finally, his very essence and being—his capacity to know and understand, to feel and love, and to will and create are put at the stake and threatened with annihilation. It is at this point that the Soul of the candidate truly descends into Hades, into his conscious, into the midst of Hell itself, where all values, all points of reference, all anchorages: all that is true, noble, good, and beautiful dissolve and become, as it were, meaningless. All the basic ties and connections the disciple has with the world seem to loosen up, break and dissolve until he is left utterly alone and bereft of all external supports, having but his lower and Higher Self, and all his vices and virtues, that are brought into judgment and weighed one against the other.

There, in that inner state of being and through this great trial, the candidate learns firsthand, by direct "burning" personal experience what he might have read, heard, or been warned about on the path to human and spiritual growth and inner illumination: his own imperfections, limitations, and weaknesses, the conceit, foolishness, and distortions of his human self which are, at that point, revealed to him by Fire and experienced by him to the very core of his being and consciousness. There, too, he learns how God, the Divine Light, always comes to him, "knocks at the very door of his heart and Soul," and eternally tends to heal him, purify him, elevate him and resurrect him.

Finally, it is also there, in his darkest but most glorious hour of trial, in the lowest hell and depths of nothingness, self-centeredness, and slow death that the candidate finds, *at last*, the Great Pearl, the treasure of treasures—the breakthrough of the Light . . . and his personal resurrection on a higher level of being and consciousness. It is here, in other words, that he finds the living key to Salvation and his own personal meaning for it—which means to become more *alive* than before and to become more *whole* in his *being, consciousness, and life*. It is here that he will experientially rediscover the living meaning of the words: faith, wisdom, love, creativity, beauty, and self-expression. As Karlfried von Durckheim beautifully explains it, in terms of his own experience of this:

> Only to the extent that man exposes himself over and over again to annihilation, can that which is indestructible arise within him. In this lies the dignity of daring. Thus the aim of (spiritual) practice is not to develop an attitude which allows a man to acquire a state of harmony and peace wherein nothing can ever trouble him. On the contrary, practice should teach him to let himself be assaulted, perturbed, moved, insulted, broken and battered—that is to say, it should enable him to dare to let go his futile hankering after

harmony, surcease from pain, and a comfortable life in order that he may discover, in doing battle with the forces that oppose him, that which awaits him beyond the world of opposites. The first necessity is that we should have the *courage to face life*, and to encounter all that which is most perilous in the world. When this is possible, meditation itself becomes the means by which we accept and welcome the demons which arise from the unconscious—a process very different from the practice of concentration on some object as a protection against such forces. Only if we venture repeatedly through zones of annihilation can our contact with Divine Being, which is beyond annihilation, become firm and stable. The more a man learns whole-heartedly to confront the world that threatens him with isolation, the more are the depths of the Ground of Being revealed and the possibilities of new life and becoming opened.[9]

After a certain period of time, which may seem interminable and obstacles which may appear insurmountable, after having "died" many times and been "resurrected" as many times by the Spirit of God, the candidate is free, once again, to live a "normal" life, the ordeal being passed. Truly reality is infinitely better, greater, and more varied than fiction, and life is a glorious and peerless opportunity, God's greatest gift to man, to find Him, unite with Him and become like Him. The strong, fearless, and beautiful souls who love adventures and challenges delight in Life and sing songs of praise to the Creator, the Father of Lights, and the author of "every good and perfect thing," for what would life and man be without sufferings and crises?"

What I wrote then, more than twenty years ago, is still very true today and was almost prophetic of what I would have to face in my second great crisis, or initiation, in my midforties, which began at the crucial age of forty-two. It also prepared me, philosophically and existentially, for what I would have to face on another level of being and dimension of my consciousness. While the first great crisis, which I view as being my Earth Initiation, involved, basically, the "breaking of my body," but with mental and emotional as well as spiritual consequences, the second great crisis, which I see as being my Water Initiation, involved basically, the emotional dimension and the "breaking of my heart," but also having physical, mental, and spiritual consequences. And, in a sense, it went even further, involving several dimensions and aspects of the Air and Fire Initiations as well as it profoundly affected my mind and way of thinking, my will and order of priorities, and finally my ego and its slow death and transformation.

At the end of my forty-first year, I had really reached the peak and culmination of my present life, major objectives, and ambitions. In a sense, I had succeeded in getting exactly what I had dreamed and planned since my teens and what my human self, or ego, wanted. I had come to the United States and stayed here; I had found a living and growing answer, and source of knowledge, for the fundamental questions of life, and a way to consciously pursue my human and spiritual growth. I had met extraordinary and spiritually evolved human beings and become their friend and confidant. I had completed my studies, acquiring several degrees including the most advanced one, and built a substantial library. I had come in touch with and become involved in several spiritual organizations and had developed my own lectures, workshops, groups, and methods. I had reached the top of my career as a professor and had gotten my own house and plan for financial independence. Finally, I had also met and married the soulmate I had always looked and waited for; and I had been put in charge of a large sum of money to invest as I saw fit and had been knighted as a "Knight Commander of Malta" in Valletta, Malta on December 24, 1980. At this point, had I continued in a linear fashion, I would have worked for financial independence and retired from my present work as a university professor to lead the ideal life of a gentleman of leisure and a freelance philosopher-mystic. But God and my Higher

Self had other plans for me! As I was told on the island of Malta on the day of my investiture: "I would soon earn and live the decoration I had just been given"—the Maltese Cross symbolizing the opening of the Heart Center with the inner convergence of the eight Beatitudes. Sure enough, two and a half months later I had an appointment with destiny and was brought to face my Water Initiation.

While making plans to move to Montreal so that I could live with my wife on a day-to-day basis and achieve my final goal of doing spiritual work and psychotherapy on a full-time basis, I was told by her, on the telephone, that she wanted a divorce, that her mind was irrevocably made up, and that this was to be the final "proof" of my love for her; that if I really loved her, I should get a lawyer, file divorce papers, and not wait or try to argue her out of it!

At first, I could not believe my ears and refused to accept reality, but then when I did, my whole world crumbled and emotionally I went to pieces. This was the deepest and the most painful experience of my life which nearly cost me both my sanity and my life. Today, I am convinced that, had it not been for my spiritual philosophy of life and for my daily prayers (which at the time I quadrupled), I would not have made it through this ordeal. In a very brief period of time, I had a number of spiritual experiences which gave me both insight into what was happening and how I was to react, and the strength to go through this spiritual test, and to bear the pain and the loneliness it entailed. I literally saw myself "on the very edge of a precipice from which dark green tentacles were sprouting forth, seeking to wrap themselves around my body to draw me into the abyss whence they came. But, at the same time, I also saw Light coming down on my left, enveloping me and seeking to draw me up to its Source." Actually, nothing happened and I stood still, going neither up nor down, but being almost torn asunder by the two great contending forces. And, in a flash, I intuited that, should I be drawn into the abyss, I would probably become overwhelmed by the unconscious and lose my sanity while, should I be drawn into the Source of the Light, I would probably break through into my Superconscious and reach a form of enlightenment. But neither occurred and so I neither lost my mind nor reached enlightenment!

Then, over a period of a few days, in a very rapid succession, three major images or symbols appeared on the screen of my mind, both in my dreams and in my daydreams: I literally saw myself standing at Hiroshima after the explosion of the atomic bomb—an incredibly rich and vivid representation of the emotional devastation I was experiencing. This was followed by the image of a shipwrecked person who was holding onto a little piece of driftwood while observing his ship slowly sinking and then disappearing under water. This symbolized the end of my dreams and ideals as I had formulated them together with my wife. At the same time, I was unable to sleep for more than one and a half to three hours per day as the terrible inner agony and emotional torment would wake me up as soon as my exhausted body had recuperated the minimum amount of vitality to continue functioning. Then, I would wake up with a jolt and feel those terrible pains envelop me all over again while my heart was pounding wildly against my ribcage. Many times during that period I would dream of life continuing as before and then wake up to the reality of the radical change, and take my dreams for reality and reality for the nightmare . . . from which I very badly wanted to wake up. At that time, too, someone was sent into my life at the very moment when I felt that I had given all I had and that I would go to the hospital for basic therapy. This brought temporary respite to my basic anxiety and pains; it also showed me, once again, that when one truly reaches the outer limits of one's endurance and resources, one is never left without help from the Higher Powers as well as that one is never given more than one can truly bear ... if he gives all he has without reservations! But it very soon became also quite apparent that I was not going to regain what I had lost and that I still had to face solitude and aloneness.

It is at this point that I got my third and final image: that of a falling eagle who had lost his wings. This image was all the more significant as, when I was very young, I had a recurrent dream and picture of myself dying in a falling airplane. The probable meaning of this symbol was a representation of the end of my ideals and aspirations and the death of my ego as they had been fashioned up to that time. I desperately wanted to hang on and used all my resources: physical, emotional, mental, financial, social and spiritual to save my present ideals and my ego, and to remain alive as I was. But, I did not succeed, and inch by inch I *had to let go*, face the great void and take the final plunge!

Months went by, during which this great inner struggle continued relentlessly, but it was clear that the battle was being lost and that I would have to let go and change. At that time I complained bitterly, felt very sorry for myself, and fantasized taking my ex-wife and myself into death. I also took long walks in the night and looked at the sky and the stars ... feeling completely and utterly alone. At that point I truly felt lonely and unable to find a woman who would really understand me and love me, and I starved emotionally, moment by moment, not from the lack of food but from the lack of love energies and feelings. It is then that I truly experienced myself as a Faustian character and that I learned the deepest, most painful but important lesson of my life: that it is not *knowledge* or *power* (which I had assiduously sought until then), position or prestige, accomplishments or possessions, that the essence of one's being really longs for and searches for, consciously or unconsciously, but LOVE, genuine, high quality LOVE .... for it is only purified love that can bring true peace, life, and fulfillment.

Up to that point, I had spent the best part of my life seeking knowledge and understanding, pursuing my ideals and dreams, and acquiring power. These I had achieved to a certain extent, but I had not obtained *love* which I had assumed would naturally come by itself after I had obtained the former. It was also then that I began to lay the cognitive foundation for my "Love-Vitamin Theory" which, I feel, is one of the deepest and most practical contributions I have to make. And today, more than three years after the outbreak of the great crisis and transformation (which, like the Hopi Indians, I could call my personal *Great Purification*), I am still in purgatory wrestling with Light and darkness, suffering and the quest for meaning and purpose within myself. I am still moving up and down the ladder of my consciousness, having received, experientially, this time, from my Higher Self, the keys of Heaven and Hell, or the pathway into both my unconscious and my Superconscious. This implies the ability to see the *same external event* as both the *best* and the *worst* possible thing that could happen to me, or to any human being, the difference being the *level of consciousness* from which I would look at this event.

I am convinced that, for this lifetime, this great crisis, transformation, or purification, was, and still is, my own personal Armageddon, my true personal initiation, or the *death* of my old self and ego and the *resurrection* of my Soul and Higher Self. The process and events I had to face, and still have to face, are absolutely classical and fitting to a teeth the great archetype of initiation. Here, therefore, are my final conclusions on the subject of Armageddon; the last inner war: I was finally given to understand experientially rather than intellectually, by having to live through this rather than reading about it or discussing it, what are "death" and "resurrection" in the initiation process; what are the lower self and the Higher Self; what is "doing one's will" and "doing God's will;" what is true "egoism" and "altruism" and, finally, how the ascent of consciousness operates on the Tree of Life.

So long as one functions in the lower self, or the personality, and that one is "stuck" with the functioning of the three lower chakras, that one has not awakened and activated the *Heart Center* through a "death" and a "resurrection," it is impossible to do God's Will, to love others altruistically, and to really be a conscious and free "Temple for the Spirit of God"—for to do so would imply death . . . the death of the lower self: Moreover, as one is dying, either inch by inch or in a big crisis, the terrible agony and ultimate terror one has to face is the same: Facing *the Void* or *the Abyss*. As one lets go and "dies," what will wait for one on the "other side?" Will it be God, one's Higher Self, and a higher form of life and consciousness. Or, will it be annihilation and nothingness, or worse yet: A lower form of life where one has lost much of one's consciousness, energy, and capacity for self-expression. Until one goes through that death and is resurrected by God's spirit, there is no way of truly *knowing* or having the answer!

Schematically put, the lower self is rooted in the three lower chakras, while the Higher Self is grounded in the three higher ones, and the great turning point takes place in the fourth, in the Heart Center. It is here that "death" and "resurrection" occur, at least at the level of consciousness —thinking, feeling, and willing.

The first chakra deals essentially with the drive for *physical survival and security*, for satisfying the basic physical needs, and thus for money as a means to obtain that security. The second chakra deals basically with the drive for *emotional satisfaction and security*, for sex, affection, and being wanted at the sexual level. The third chakra is focused on the drive for *social position and status*, for esteem and respect: it is here that the sense of one's self-importance, position in the social hierarchy, and ability to get what one (the lower self!) wants come from.

The Higher Self, on the other hand, is rooted in the three higher chakras. The fifth chakra deals essentially with the drive to perceive and create *meaning and purpose in one's life*. It leads an individual to seek out and understand the laws of nature and God, the hidden principles of life. Because the basic drive here is to uncover what is hidden, it is here that an individual's consciousness becomes objectified, and this affects the speech center which then becomes a creative center in its own right. The sixth chakra involves basically *impersonal spiritual Love*, the point where personal goals and interests are replaced by goals and interests dealing, under the guidance and will of the Spiritual Self, with the unfoldment of human consciousness, the enhancement of Life, and the good of the whole. It is the true Christ consciousness center, through which one thinks, feels, wills, and acts as a Christ. When this chakra is fully opened, the personal gratification of the lower self is completely transmuted in order for that person to bring a particular higher principle of existence into manifestation, and one becomes an Avatar.

Finally, not much can be said intellectually about the activation of the seventh chakra, the highest mode of being possible for Life on Earth. Here striving or self-expression becomes so intense and aligned with the Will of God that it is the Will of God Itself and the individual becomes striving itself. Life and consciousness, here, are characterized by the individual becoming a point of expression between that which is finite and temporal and that which is infinite and eternal. As Aster Barnwell aptly puts it: "This person therefore (who has activated the seventh chakra) becomes a God-Man, since his existence is no longer a matter of a human being trying to improve upon himself, but rather a

Divine Principle trying to establish a permanent abode in an earthly body."[10]

The pivotal center, therefore, is the fourth or Heart Chakra whose basic striving is that for self-identity, self-acceptance, and belonging in the cosmic sense. It is the focal energy and consciousness point where "death" (of the ego or lower self) and "resurrection" (of the Higher Self) take place and, therefore, providing the arena and the fuel for Armageddon, the last great inner way and the turning point in one's personal evolution. As Barnwell explains:

> As this level, the consciousness is said to be liberated from the "lower forces," meaning the forces that promote individual strife and inhibit collective human advancement. When the consciousness reaches this level of development, the individual seeks to *act out of a sense of purpose rather than as a response to external stimuli*. Such a person may, however, spend too much time seeking approval from others. The principles of Life that are expressed here is that of inclusion or empathy.[11]

It is this great crisis, I feel, that I have been undergoing for the last three years and which constitutes my own personal Armageddon, the greatest opportunity of my life to make true human and spiritual progress, and the turning point in the orientation of my consciousness and will. It is still not fully completed and thus its final existential outcome is yet undetermined.

Practical Exercise

Preliminary: Find the right place and the right position. Then make an effort of Introversion, Supraversion, and Infraversion.

Actual work: Review and Meditation

Focus your attention upon the traditional process of Initiation: what does Initiation mean to you? How many Initiations are there and what do they involve? At this point in your life, have you gone through any of them *existentially* and *experientially*, or do you merely have an intellectual understanding of its nature and dynamics?

What is the chakra system and how do Initiations relate to the chakras?

Now meditate upon the nature and meaning of Armageddon and connect it to your own personal life and autobiography. Have you experienced any of its basic aspects and phases? Are you ready for them? Are you doing anything to prepare yourself to undergo Initiation? What could you do now, practically and concretely, to prepare yourself to that end?

Write down your own personal psychospiritual autobiography. How would you cope with the crises described in this chapter? What can you practically do to prepare yourself for them?

Do you understand and can you practically work with the nature of your Being (lower self and Higher

Self) and of your consciousness (its structure, functions, and processes)? Are you presently ready to become the artist and creator of your nature and to perfect yourself systematically?

When you have completed this meditation and self-examination, make the appropriate entries in your workbook, as to what you have discovered, what you have done, what has happened, and how you were able to cope.

Chapter Nine

RESURRECTION:
Personal Easter

Thus far in this work we have sketched out a cognitive map of what is now happening both in oneself and in the world, in terms of a larger and more holistic perspective suggested by the Spiritual Tradition which shows underlying meaning and purpose, and thus that something good and valuable can be derived from *every human situation*, even the most painful and horrifying one. Then, we outlined a theory and practice to work toward achieving emotional purification, mental clarification, and personal consecration which involve the understanding and training of the three fundamental functions of the psyche: *feeling, thinking,* and *willing*.

We continued by studying how the training of the imagination and the opening of the intuition culminate in the dawning of the Light in one's own consciousness to prepare and arm oneself for the great battles, trials, and challenges of Life. These will inevitably lead to the various aspects, phases, and degrees of the last great Inner War called Armageddon, or the Apocalypse, in the symbolic language of the Sages which all of us must face and undergo at various points in our human and spiritual development.

In this chapter, we will be looking at the various meanings, aspects, phases, and degrees of Resurrection, or the "Personal Easters," as I have called them which also inevitably follow the great trials, battles, and "deaths" of earthly life.

From the standpoint of the Spiritual Tradition, or of personally experienced states of consciousness, we pointed out that the real meaning and purpose of earthly life is not the evanescent pursuit of security, pleasure, or happiness, but, rather becoming more than what we were when we arrived here: personal and collective growth, the actualization of our potentials and faculties, and the realization of our destiny. Basically, this means: hard conscious work, intentional suffering, and various "deaths" leading to equally various Initiations and Resurrections. Having done some of the hard work on oneself, experienced trials and sufferings, and undergone some of the personal "deaths" and Initiations and, especially gone through at least some major aspects and phases of your personal Armageddon, here is what you can now expect in terms of Resurrection or your "personal Easters."

Easter, like Armageddon, and all religious symbols and basic events, has many meanings and applications on various levels of consciousness and being, and happens more than once to an individual; not only in several lifetimes but even in the present one! Fundamentally, Easter has two meanings: one for the personality which applies to the physical, astral, and mental bodies and levels, and one for the individuality which applies to the Soul and its vehicles and faculties. Let us now look first at the meaning, implications and applications it has for the personality and then for those that it has for the individuality.

Easter is the Christian spring festival, but in its core and true meaning it has profound implications and a practical message for all human beings of all races and religions. Easter is a cosmic and anthropological phenomenon as well as a religious one, and as such, it has exoteric as well as esoteric meanings which are relevant and applicable to all human beings regardless of their race, religion, or level of evolution. The central meaning of Easter for Nature and the natural man is Rebirth, while for the spiritual person on the spiritual level it is Resurrection—as the Resurrection of Jesus the Christ is the *archetypal resurrection* of every human being . . . who has reached that level of consciousness and being!

For the world, rebirth in the spring means, as we can readily observe when we study the greatest of all books, that in which God writes His story and that of creation—Nature—that a new wave of life is flowing through the earth, the grass, the trees, and the animal kingdom. The grass grows again, trees sprout leaves and burgeons, the sap flow is revitalized, and animals and birds reappear in nature. The whole of nature, in fact, seems to respond to a new cycle, or rhythm, the spring season, in which life reawakens and quickens in its outward expressions and manifestations. The psychic and spiritual atmosphere of the world, as well as the energies of the earth and of biological organisms, are suffused and bathed in new light, warmth, and life that vivify and bring to life all that which they come in contact with.

In a human being, therefore, the same process of rebirth takes place, analogically, on the basic dimensions and vehicles of his personality—the physical, the emotional, and the mental—but with one basic difference with respect to nature: man must participate in this process, he must consciously and deliberately involve all his mind, his heart, and will. He must, in other words, focus his attention, his thoughts, and his feelings concerning this process and how it affects him if he is to reap the maximum possible benefits. This is because man's evolution is now a *conscious evolution* requiring his active and deliberate participation, whereas in nature evolution is still unconscious, responding to external stimuli rather than inner decision and guidance. If we focus our attention upon rebirth on the three basic levels of the personality we find:

1. *Physical rebirth* implies that a human being focus his attention upon carrying out an inner "house cleaning" as well as the outer and literal house cleaning he might do at this time. It means that he must reawaken, balance, and strengthen his physical body and its vitality and proper functioning. The Spiritual Tradition tells us that this may be accomplished by doing three basic things:
   a. By getting more sleep (one to two hours per day for a period of 3-4 weeks).
   b. By doing more physical exercise (sports, walking, breathing, yoga).
   c. By changing one's diet (going, for example, from meat to pasta to more fruits and vegetables).

2. *Emotional rebirth* implies the deepening, heightening, and revitalization of a person's feelings and capacity to feel and to awaken new emotions. This, in turn, can be done by doing three things:
   a. By getting involved with art and beauty (nature, painting, music); that is, by looking at and responding to beautiful things.
   b. By getting involved with people or revitalizing one's social relationships. Here one can reaffirm and deepen existing relationships through visits, conversations and writing, as well as develop-

ing new relationships with other people.

c. By cultivating prayer on a regular basis: using concentration, meditation, devotion, visualization, and invocation-evocation with appropriate spiritual exercises can act as powerful forces to dynamize and deepen one's emotional life and to enable one to feel more intensely and passionately.

3. *Mental rebirth* requires the broadening and expansion of a person's mental perspectives and cognitive grasp of the world by broadening his existing ideas and views, and by unfolding new ideas and views. This can be accomplished by doing four things:

a. By reading new, good books.
b. By getting involved in serious and meaningful discussions with other persons.
c. By reflecting, meditating, and writing.
d. By prayer and other spiritual exercises.

The dimension to which the Christian Easter points to in particular is that of spiritual Rebirth, or Resurrection, as depicted, symbolically and archetypally, by the Resurrection of Christ. Spiritual rebirth or Resurrection, moreover, implies two basic things:

a. First and foremost, the Resurrection or reawakening of the Christ's Spirit within us, of the Divine Spark from its entombment in our consciousness and being.
b. The unfoldment and crystallization of new attitudes and of a new state of consciousness which makes us perceive ourselves, other human beings, good and evil, and our purpose and work here on earth in a completely new light (e.g., the realization that life is without beginning and without ending, that we are

immortal beings, that both Good and Evil are God's servants and perform useful tasks, and that *all human experiences* can be used for our growth and His glorification).

Spiritual Resurrection can be brought about only through a manifestation of *Spiritual Consciousness*, which is the product of a genuine Spiritual Initiation or "death and rebirth" following a diligent practice of living the life, prayer, and facing life's great tests and ordeals.

Resurrection or spiritual rebirth involves not only a new state of consciouisness and a higher level of being brought forth by the action of the Divine Spark in our Souls, it specifically involves a whole new perception and understanding of the meaning and purpose of one's life and of the events therein. As it affects all of our Psychospiritual Centers and chakras, it implies the unfoldment of new attitudes and responses to the challenges of daily life. Thus:

1. At the first chakra level, the fight for physical survival, the Darwinian survival of the fittest and all its accompanying *fears, anxieties, angers,* and *frustrations* are now transformed into basic **acceptance and gratitude for what is happening to us and the ordeal or situation we are called to face at this point.**

2. At the second chakra level, the confrontation with emotional gratification or lack thereof depending upon whether we can find and have a mate, and the primordial fear of dying if one is not loved, the existential anguish of loneliness, are now transformed into true *courage*, the courage of being and living alone and overcoming the fear and deprivation of not being loved at the romantic and sexual level or, perhaps, even of having to depend upon God's love alone.

3. At the third chakra level, the power complex, the need to feel important and being esteemed in the eyes of others, the drive to achieve tangible and socially accepted situations is now transformed into true *contentment* with what one is and has with full faith that this is all that we really need at the moment.

4. At the fourth chakra level, the need for social approval, and the inability to say "no" to others who ask various things of us, as well as selling our conscience for the need to be accepted and loved is now transformed into true *compassion*, the ability to see and feel through the eyes and heart of the other person without losing or betraying oneself.

5. At the fifth chakra level, the drive to find the basic principles of life and the discovery of the laws and Cause and Effect is now realized in authentic personal *responsibility* and the ability to understand and live by the great cosmic laws of God and life.

6. At the sixth chakra level, the drive for unconditional, spiritual love, for the total acceptance of the other—stemming from one's ability to experience reality from his viewpoint, by "stepping into his own consciousness," as it were, leads to unconditional *acceptance* and true *service* to the other person.

7. Finally, at the level of the seventh chakra, the drive to let God express in our own consciousness and life manifests now as true *humility* or not being afraid of living the "ordinary life of ordinary people," as Aster Barnwell would say, but bringing through and manifesting the Divine Light, Fire, and Life or Wisdom, Love, and Creative Self-Expression

in one's daily existence.

As one is Resurrected from his own personal Armageddon, he emerges with a new consciousness and a new being that enables him to accept and face all of himself and all of life without fearing or rejecting any aspect or facet of one's being and of human life. It is the point when a human being can truly say *"Nihil humanum alienum a me puto,"* that is, "nothing that is human will be foreign to me" which will truly be experienced as a rebirth and a new life for that person.

When faced with a truly crucial and important crisis as those of Armageddon, the candidate has three basic choices:

1. He can go mad, become sick, or die;

2. Or, he can harden himself and become cynical and skeptical of all higher, beautiful, and good things;

3. Or finally, he can *accept* it, be grateful for it, and begin to work on himself for his personal transformation—which is what happens to the person who successfully passes his Armageddon and who, therefore, experiences his own personal Resurrection, or Rebirth, where new meaning and purpose are revealed to him concerning his personal life and life in general.

The average person in his normal experience of life does not experience life consciously and fully as he is blocked and distorted, limited and constrained by his fears and desires, by his anxieties, traumas, and personal scares. The greatest miracle and achievement is, indeed, to be able to **experience life fully and consciously, without fear and without greed, and this is what spiritual resurrection makes possible.**

At the cognitive level, personal Easter at the Soul level implies discovering and engendering the Philosopher's

Stone: fashioning a personal philosophy of life that will stand up as true Gold to all the trials and tests of one's life and daily experience. It means creating room and space in one's being for the Divine Spark to come fill it, live in it, and manifest Itself through it. It means finally knowing *where and how one fits into this universe, what it is that one seeks from life, how one will seek it, and what one will be ready to give in exchange for it . . . and what one will do with it once one has achieved it!*

Resurrection means being able to consciously and meaningfully cope with the nature and origin of the world and of one's being, and of their purpose and destiny as well as with the nature, origin, and function of Evil and its consequences: sin, suffering, and death.

Until this point, the candidate has still been living in the world of duality and dichotomies: life and death, joy and sorrow, vice and virtue, being constantly confronted with Good and Evil as being separate and inimical to each other. This was the consequence of the Fall which affected all human beings who ate of the Tree of Good and Evil. This is why God, the Higher Self, told the archetypal Man and Woman: "The time will come when you will eat of this fruit (of the fruit of the Tree of Good and Evil which is the knowledge of these great dichotomies), but now you are still too weak and if you eat of it you will *die* (that is, change your state of consciousness and level of being). The Tree of Life, when it is completely awakened and activated represents the essential unity where polarization does not manifest and which, therefore, is above Good and Evil. By eating of this "fruit," human beings put on a body of flesh, descended into the world of matter which we call the earth, lost their body of Light, and thus became "naked," and had to confront and struggle with Good and Evil—with Sin. The Serpent of the Garden of Eden represents the Astral Light, the Magical Agent, which has two basic aspects, that of

Light and that of Darkness, and which can therefore be used for both Good and Evil. Symbolically, that force can be represented by two triangles, one pointing upward toward the Spirit and the other point downward toward matter. ◇ From that mythical time onward, human beings had to become aware of and face both these forces whose nature is *relative*. For here all depends on man's level of consciousness and being, the forces he works with and for what end, the region in which he operates, and how he uses these forces. As Mikhael Aivanhov explains:

> The revolt of the Angels involves luminous beings who, influenced by physical life, once there no longer wanted to go back to God to evolve and grow. This revolt occurred when they were *away from God* in the worlds of matter and not when they were in the higher regions. And God said to them: "Stay there, you will learn many things, and when you will have enough of living in darkness and limitation, then come back and I will receive you" . . . This is God's true love: He has given the possibility to return to Him even to the most debased creatures. As He is Absolute Love even demons can return to Him and become redeemed. But it is their Pride that prevents them from returning.
>
> The history of original Sin is the history of man's descent into matter. What religions call the Fall is nothing more than the choice made by the first humans to descend into matter to explore it. Paradise is *within* each human soul, because each was originally in Paradise. God's thinking at that point was: 'They will suffer a little—a few million years —then they will come back and they will be so happy that they will forget their sufferings. What is a few million years before eternity?' God is not mad at human beings for their Fall, He waits for their return for, sooner or later, they will all return.[1]

One of the most important and fundamental questions that any human being can and has ever asked is: *Why does evil exist and what function does it perform?* It is only from the standpoint of a higher state of consciousness and level of being that one can answer this question. An image here can be of great evocative help to understand this paradox.

Aivanhov suggests the following image: think of the wheel driven by oxen to draw water from a well. By standing still on the same plane as the wheel, an observer would see some oxen moving toward him and others moving away from him, thus going in opposite directions. But, if this wheel could be looked at from a higher standpoint, from above as it were, one would see them going in the same direction and working toward the same goal! From the level of the personality and earth-life, good and evil present themselves, and are seen as *opposed forces* while, seen from the level of the Soul, they reveal their true nature: they are harnessed to do the same work. It is only because we do not look at them from "above," from the spiritual perspective of the Soul, that we experience them as antagonistic forces. If this is true, as the experience of the person who has gone through spiritual Resurrection reveals, then the only viable solution to all the basic problems of human life: sin, suffering, evil, and injustice are to expand our consciousness and raise our level of being to give birth to *spiritual consciousness*. This will then unveil the true face of good and evil as a circle, as the wheel of life where good and evil are harnessed for exactly the same purpose: to fuel growth, evolution, and the actualization of latent potentials and faculties. Both are necessary and we must experience and cope adequately with both. No one can come into this world and not face, confront, and struggle with evil. Yet, if we were to "destroy" evil, we would also destroy good.

Thus, we must accept, work with, and experience both, for we have no choice but to confront them . . . yet without focusing upon and thus feeding evil! This is the essence of the new cognitive perspective that is revealed and lived by he who undergoes Resurrection. As Aivanhov again puts it in a nutshell: "If we lived in the Sun, we would not know darkness, but as we live on earth, we *must* know polarity and alternation: night and day, light and darkness, life and death, good and evil, but learn how to utilize them and to work constructively with them."[2]

The earth, which could be compared to a house, has its "cone of obscurity," its "shadow" just like a house has its sewers and its garbage disposals. This is the true nature and origin of evil: *it emerges from the residues of the materials and the energies used to build and to enliven the earth*, which end up as unconscious, unbalanced, and poorly utilized forces. And all residues always attract all kinds of undesirable insects: roaches, ants, flies, mosquitoes, etc. These are the kinds of creatures we can expect to meet with when we go exploring this region in the false hope of finding true pleasures and happiness there! This is the world of darkness and suffering which is called "hell" but which is really the "garbage can" of the earth where all kinds of impurities are stored.

It is only when one has truly understood good through personal experience that one can face evil in a realistic and wholesome way. As Aivanhov puts it: "To descend into Hell, one must first ascend into Heaven" (that is, one must first climb to the Superconscious and get personally acquainted with it before one can safely descend into the unconscious). God is *above* both good and evil and is the source whence both issue. But evil is an existential, temporal "residue" of good and does not have an independent existence from good: it depends on good, it is born from good, and it is good that created it. This is why so long as human beings will give evil an independent existence, they will never be able to transform it and they will "feed" evil with their own thoughts, feelings and life force. As Aivanhov explains:

> The manifestations of Evil are necessary, but they are neither eternal nor absolute, they depend on the forces of Good! To transcend them and lose our fear of them, we must *rise up to their Source, God*. This is the most glorious work of the disciple: *to give birth to his spiritual consciousness*, to bind himself to the Lord within who will solve all his problems

> and transmute evil into good . . . Naturally, it is much easier
> to do Evil than Good because here on earth conditions are
> much more favorable to Evil . . . not because Evil is more
> powerful than Good.[3]

In the lower states of consciousness and regions of
being, it is much easier to do evil than good, but in the
higher state of consciousness and regions of being, it is
much easier to do good than evil. Hence, the fundamental
key to resolve the paradox of good and evil is to *rise to the
higher regions by expanding our consciousness.* To dominate or
transform evil it is not enough to be a servant of good,
because good is limited in the lower worlds. One must
become a servant of God who is both good and evil. Good
and evil are like brothers and sisters: to reconcile them, one
must go to the Father who controls both. It is the Divine in
human nature that, alone, can organize and direct these two
great and opposed forces. Aivanhov says that:

> There are two great schools on earth: that of Good and
> that of Evil. In the first one is told to reject all that is evil to be
> saved. In the other one fights against good, thinking one will
> conquer it and destroy it. Yet there is a third school that is
> above both and which *works with both.* Here evil is used but
> in *homeopathic doses to bring about its transmutation.* This school
> does not reject anything and teaches that if Evil exists it is
> because He allows its existence for a while . . . Above all do
> not think that God cannot overcome Evil. Evil is a poison
> which can *kill the weak and the ignorant,* but for *the strong it is a
> medicine which heals and can do fantastic things.* Hence, true
> Wisdom consists in working with Evil, directing it, and
> utilizing it.[4]

If God does not come to help and heal us when we ask
him to and to lead us back to Him, it is because we have set
up many blocks and barriers between us and Him by expressing negative ideas, feelings, and attitudes. If we close
the windows and doors of a house, the Sun cannot get in. It
is up to us to open the doors and windows. Normally, we
experience evil as hostile forces that would destroy us, but
this is so only because we do not like the lessons it brings

and because we do not have the wisdom and the strength to face it in a constructive way. Once thunder, water, and wind were hostile forces to human beings who worshipped them and feared them. Now, however, we harness them and make them work for us! The same must be done with the inner psychospiritual forces. Evil represents very powerful forces with which we do not have very good relations because we do not know yet how to direct and express them properly. Our conceptions of Good and Evil, more-over, are very relative. For example, to put water in our stomach is necessary to live, but to put it into our lungs is evil. Thus, by changing our state of consciousness and rais-ing our level of being, our perceptions about good and evil also change. The evil that destroys others can make us stronger, nobler, and better human beings. The point is not to fight it but to become wiser and stronger to resist it and utilize it properly.

Through the light of understanding and wisdom, evil can immediately be transformed into good, but if one does not understand it and utilize it properly, it does remain evil! As Aivanhov concludes:

> Only God Himself can annihilate Evil or truly transform it, we cannot do that yet. Hence, the best thing we can do is to find God and let Him work through us . . . We must change the words: to *fight, kill, destroy*, with *transform, utilize*, and *har-ness*. Then, be it sexual energy, anger, jealousy, resentment, an enemy or an illness, we will be able to transform them and utilize them to do Good, to evolve, and grow . . . Thus, whatever happens, one should ask: is this truly an Evil or a hidden Good? Human beings do not really know what is Good and what is Evil for them. So many "successes" have led people to catastrophes and many obstacles and dif-ficulties have been the cause of true growth and strength-ening.[5]

Concerning Good and Evil, Jesus said in the Gospels:

> The Kingdom of Heaven is like a man who has sown good seed but while he slept the enemy came and sowed weeds. Both grew up. The servants came and asked the man

whether they should pull up the weeds but he told them not to do so because in pulling up the weeds they could also pull up the seeds. Let them grow up until the time of harvest, then the selection will occur: the weeds will be pulled up and burnt and the seeds put in the granary.[6]

This saying teaches us a very important law of life: let good and evil grow side by side until the harvest time, for in trying to exterminate certain vices, we can make even worse ones grow or undo a lot of good. Good and evil are inextricably intertwined so that one cannot destroy one without also destroying the other. The key is to take evil in homeopathic doses to strengthen ourselves and render our judgment keener. And, just as the forces of evil succeed in drawing energy from good to transform it and utilize it for evil ends, so good can also draw from evil forces and transform them and utilize them for good. As Aivanhov puts it:

Jesus lived with weak, ill and degraded beings to make exchanges with them: to give them His Light, Love, and Purity, and to transform their vices. Thus He took the Sins of the World, that is, He drew from them their raw energies which He transformed in leaves of His Being and which He redistributes in the form of Light and Love. He who refuses to have contacts and exchanges with ignorant and evil persons and who associates only with distinguished, evolved, and educated persons *cannot evolve and is not a good alchemist* for he is deprived of certain ingredients which are essential for his growth.[7]

Aivanhov also makes an analogy between a tree and the various planes of being on which function human beings on different levels of evolution and consciousness.

Properly articulated, this analogy looks as follows:[8]

Higher Spiritual Plane:	Truth	Fruits	Great Masters
Lower Spiritual Plane:	Love	Flowers	Saints
Higher Mental Plane:	Wisdom	Leaves	Geniuses
Lower Mental Plane:	Knowledge	Branches	Talented Beings
Higher & Lower Astral:	Feelings	Trunk	Ordinary Beings
Physical Plane:	Sensations	Roots	Brutes

And he explains:

> Brutes are working in the roots of life, under the earth. Ordinary men work in the trunk, they let the raw materials flow through them which others will work with and transform. Talented men represent the branches: they send these raw materials toward the leaves and then let them return to the roots. They take to give and regulate exchanges. Geniuses are the burgeons whence come the leaves. It is here the Great Work really begins: the transformation of the sap under the sun rays. Saints are the flowers of the Cosmic Tree. By their colors, beauty, and perfume, they draw butterflies, insects, and humans. They work to produce fruits and thanks to them life becomes more pure and beautiful. The Great Masters are the fruits of the Cosmic Tree, the celestial food, the manna from Heaven. Geniuses, Saints, and Masters come to visit the earth, to spread their blessings and then they leave. On earth, love, wisdom, and beauty do not have very favorable conditons to remain for long. The physical body is linked with the Spirit, the Heart with the Soul, and the intellect with the Causal Body. This is why there are close links between Brutes and Masters, Ordinary Men and Saints, and Talented People and Geniuses.[9]

The time will come when human beings will have raised their level of being and transformed their consciousness, that good and evil will work together in the same direction to accomplish the same basic work: *to be at the service of Heaven.* But, as long as man opposes good to evil, he will be at war with himself and destroy himself. A look at our human body will soon reveal this basic insight: whenever we walk around and do something, we always take with us our higher and lower nature; why then separate them and set them at war with each other? These two sides, the higher and the lower *work together to ensure our existence and the development of all our human faculties.* If they are pitted against each other, it is only because man, in his ignorance, has introduced division and disorder within himself. Good, therefore, is not enough and has not solved the problem of evil and evil cannot destroy good. God can have no real adversaries—all beings and powers obey him.

It is interesting to analyze the story of the three great temptations of Jesus in the desert for the insights it gives us concerning the flow of the life force in the three lower chakras and the nature of good and evil.

> And Jesus was led by the Spirit into the desert to be tempted by the Devil. After having fasted for forty days, He was hungry and the Devil told him: "If you are the Son of God, order that these stones become bread." But Jesus answered: "It is written, man will not live by bread alone but by the Word of God." And the Devil told Him: "If you are the Son of God, throw yourself from the Temple for it is written: 'He will give orders to His Angels to take You in their hands so that your foot will not be dashed upon a stone.'" But Jesus answered: "You will not tempt the Lord Thy God." And the Devil took Him to a high mountain and showed Him all the realms of this world and their glory and told Him: "I will give you all these things if you will bow down and worship me." But Jesus answered: "Get behind me Satan, for it is written: 'You will adore the Lord Thy God and you will serve Him only.'" Then the Devil left Him and Angels came to minister unto Him.[10]

This passage clearly tells us that it was the Spirit of God that led Jesus into the desert to be tempted by the Devil, and the same is true for all of us. Trials and tests are necessary for our growth and Satan is, thus, ultimately, a servant of God. He and his spirits come down to tempt, afflict, and test human beings: to give them lessons and exams that will enable them to grow and evolve. And it is not Heaven that needs to test us to see how we are going to respond, it is we who need to know our own judgment and strength, and thus become aware of the necessity to improve ourselves. Thus, it is *for ourselves that we are tempted and tested!*

These three basic tests are linked with the first three chakras: the need to satisfy our basic physical drives, the need for emotional gratification, and the need for power. Aivanhov links them with the stomach, the heart, and the head and he explains:

> When he is a child, man lives constantly at the level of the stomach: *eating*. Then, he is thrown into the heart, he lives with faith, love but is driven to throw himself into the violent passions of the heart, hoping that God will send His Angels to protect him from their consequences. He thinks that Heaven will make an exception for him because he is in the Temple of religion of love and of the veneration and adoration of an adorable creature . . . who is not God . . . Childhood is linked to the problem of food, adolescence to that of feelings, and adulthood to that of the head . . . to master the world.
>
> Every disciple (and human being) must face and conquer these three archetypal temptations. How many sell their gifts for money while others feel that they can get away with anything and that Heaven will bail them out . . . In His answers, Jesus has given the key of *white magic*. The Word of God is also a certain kind of food . . . Anything can be transformed into Light and Light can be transformed into Matter.[11]

No one is above God's laws . . . not even God Himself, but there are many laws and energies which are yet unknown even by our most advanced scientist. True freedom exists before an action has been accomplished in the outer or inner worlds, thereafter we are bound by its consequences. In the third temptation, the Devil sought to separate Jesus from God by awakening in Him the spirit of pride. Pride is the hardest thing to overcome which, in fact, can only be conquered by God's grace! Its best antidote, however, is to worship God and serve Him above all else.

According to Aivanhov, the three weapons by which one can face these temptations are *hope, faith*, and *love*. Hope is linked with the stomach in that it can change "stones into bread," that it possesses the power to transform matter.

matter. Faith is linked with the heart and the lungs for this is the true temple where God dwells. When Jesus told the Devil "You will not tempt the Lord Thy God," He was affirming His faith in the God within, refusing to put this faith to the test for which He had no need. The third temptation deals with the head and can be overcome only through love. To "climb on the mountain" means to achieve knowledge, authority, and power . . . . and this is precisely the point when one is tempted by pride! Here, only the love of God can save the disciple from this temptation. As Aivanhov summarizes it:

> Hope, Faith, and Love are the three great weapons that enable us to triumph over all tests. Hope is the magical weapon against the accidents of material life; Faith enables us to feel God's presence within us, without the need to tempt Him to reassure us that He protects us; and Love enables us to remain faithful to Him and thus to escape the sin of Pride.[12]

And he elucidates:

> The Devil is God's worker who is like a big dog that bites the cows that transgress laws to teach them lessons. Tests, sufferings, and misery come only because there have been transgressions. As soon as man becomes a true servant of God, the big dog is still there, but he does not bite any longer, now he serves him![13]

Vices are no more than "creatures" who have set up house in a human being to make him a slave. And he must feed them because he invited them and fed them. The three essential medicines to get rid of them are *purity* (because it lets them starve as in purity there is no food for the undesirables), *Light* (which scares them and drives them away), and *warmth* (the fire of love which burns them up). Thus, what human beings need the most at this particular historical juncture is not more houses, cars, and money, but rather, *a philosophy of life* capable of guiding them through the manifold tests, sufferings, and hardships of life on earth.

When a particularly hard test comes, one should say to oneself: "Heaven wants me to develop certain qualities which I do not yet possess—what are they?" And then, one should thank Heaven for this test by showing real acceptance and gratitude. There are only two basic reasons why these tests and hardships come: either to pay a debt or to learn something new, and actualize new faculties and potentialities. And here, the greatest hindrance to human growth and self-actualization is either to think that difficulties and sufferings are the result of an injustice or that they are meaningless. Most human beings think that they have come to earth to be happy, secure, and to realize their ambitions when, in fact, they have come here to *pay their debts, to learn,* and to grow and become more than what they were.

One cannot overcome evil with evil, lies with other lies, or violence with more violence for, in so doing, we are bringing ourselves down to their level, we are vibrating in unison with their vibrations, and we become very vulnerable. To become invulnerable, one must learn to climb very high, like the birds. For once one has raised one's level of consciousness and climbed to the level of the Superconscious, one is out of reach of one's enemies whose vibrations are very different, and then one is truly safe. For even greater and faster results, one should increase one's love and generosity and, through Light and love, transform one's former enemies into friends.

As Aivanhov beautifully concludes.

> Your enemies are a blessing for you because they can help you become *strong* and *great*, and full of *Light* (or the reverse!). One must fight in this world but only with Light and Love. One's enemies are both a temptation and a blessing sent by the Invisible Worlds . . . You will never succeed in conquering an enemy by humiliations, violence and blows —only by Love and Light which will transform him into a friend! . . . No matter what difficulties come, do not show your sadness and discouragement, on the contrary, light all

your lamps, and then you will get all the help you need from Heaven. Become strong enough and wise enough to transform your anger and your pain into Light.[14]

In going through our many rebirths on different levels, to balance and recharge our various bodies and their faculties and energies, we are, in fact, preparing ourselves, purifying and consecrating ourselves for our personal Armageddon and our eventual spiritual Resurrection wherein genuine spiritual consciousness will dawn in our awareness and the Christ Spirit will rule our being and our life. It is at that point, when Resurrection, our personal Easter, really occurs that we finally know who we are, where we come from, where we are going, and what we have come to Earth to accomplish that we find and are able to use the Philosopher's Stone, the *elixir vitae,* and the Panacea; that our Higher Self, the Lord, can truly "come into His Kingdom" and "inhabit His Temple;" and that the mystery and paradox of good and evil can be finally understood and resolved . . . and that man will, once again, become actually the potential God he is and, thereby, reacquire his immortality, bliss, and sinlessness. No more can usefully be said about this great event which must be personally lived and experienced to be truly understood and realized.

Practical Exercise

Preliminary: Find the right place and the right position. Then make an effort of Introversion, Supraversion, and Infraversion.

Actual work: Meditation and Exercises

Focus your attention upon the cognitive map and the set of exercises we have been developing to look at yourself, at the world, and at life in a larger perspective so as to discern the unfolding meaning and purpose in all the events of your life. This is your Philosopher's Stone by which to orient yourself in all the vicissitudes and experiences of your daily life, provided it is something that you have developed *organically* and *experientially* and not merely assimilated *intellectually*.

At this point, you should be ready to write down and articulate your Philosophy of Life in terms of the following basic criteria or dimensions:

a. *Facing yourself:* Giving your personal and individual answer to the riddle of the Sphinx: Who you are, where do you come from, where you are going, and what is your purpose on this earth?
b. *Facing the enigma of life:* What is life? Where does it come from? What is its purpose?
c. *Facing the mystery of the universe:* What is the universe? Where does it come from? Where is it going? What is its basic purpose?

d. *Facing your basic value and ethical system:* What are your core values and ethical principles? Where do they come from? How did you put them together? Are you able to live them and enflesh them?

e. *Facing your karma and dharma:* What work have you come to do in this world? What are the main lessons you are to learn? To what extent are you able to live the above?

f. *Facing your mate:* How did you choose, or would you choose, the person you live with (or would live with)? What are your criteria for choosing a life partner and the rules regulating your relationship?

g. *Facing good and evil:* What are your present conceptions of good and evil? Can you recognize them in yourself and in the world? How do you cope with the evil you have to confront in this life?

h. *Facing your fears and ideals:* What are the major fears and ideals at this point in your life and how do you deal with them?

i. *Facing life:* Are you able to accept and integrate all the parts of your consciousness and being and all the parts of the world? Can you experience life fully without fear or greed? How do you cope with the sexual and aggressive drives?

Then, meditate upon, articulate, and write down your personal conception and experience of Easter: personal rebirth, at the personality level, in terms of the threefold rebirth of your vitality, emotions, and thoughts, and personal Resurrection, at the Soul level ... if you have gone that far!

Can you respond adequately to the great archetypal "tests" of the sevenfold chakra system to the extent that you have activated them and unblocked the life force flowing through them (that is: acceptance, courage, contentment, and compassion at the personality level and understanding the laws of life and responsibility, unconditional love and true service, and humility at the Soul level).

The above constitute your personal Philosopher's Stone which should enable you to perceive yourself and all of life in a new Light leading you to a new Life and a new level of being. What aspect of your philosophy of life should you be working upon at this time? Are you able to translate this mental conception into an actual embodiment in your life?

Is the development and expression of your mind, heart, and will harmonious and properly integrated?

Are you able to "move up and down the elevator of your consciousness," to ascend into your Superconscious and to descend into your unconscious? In other words, have you found for yourself the "keys of Heaven and Hell" and are you effectively able to expand and transform your level of consciousness so as to acquire true integrity, autonomy, and be true to your Higher Self? For this is the very heart of the process of self-actualization and self-realization, personality and Soul Sculpture, we are outlining for you in this work.

When you have completed this meditation and self-examination, make the appropriate entries in your workbook, as to what you have discovered, what you have done, what has happened, and how you were able to cope.

Chapter Ten

CONCLUSION:
The End of the Rule of the Personality and The Beginning of the Rule of the Soul

---

We are, indeed, living in most interesting times filled with all kinds of challenges: dangers and opportunities. At this particular historical juncture, the second half of the 20th century and, particularly, the last two decades of the second millenium after the birth of Christ, the individual, nations, and humanity as a whole, face a major Initiation, embodying several minor Initiations; that is, we are faced with very intense and accelerating psychospiritual and sociocultural change, the essence of which is *personal transformation*, quantitative and qualitative growth, self-actualization and self-realization. The quintessence of the great challenge that is before us is very simple: it involves *regeneration* or *degeneration*, making a decisive step forward in the expansion of our level of consciousness and evolutionary level of being, or making a decisive step backwards. Life cannot stand still; it must either progress or regress. Collectively, we are now faced with either nuclear extinction through another World War or ecological extinction if we do not get the pollution problem under control . . . or with moving into another culture and historical era, that of the Global Village. Individually, we are faced with emotional and psychological problems that could completely disorganize our personality and lead us toward a full breakdown and loss of our autonomy and constructive activity . . . or we could expand and transform our consciousness to the point where Spiritual Consciousness would finally be born and rule our personality and lives. The stakes are enormous, both collectively and individually, and we are all, each and everyone of us, called to do our part, called to do the personal growth and transformation work which is unique to our being and which only each individual can carry out. Today, we are called to look *within* rather than *without*, to unfold and express *love* rather than *power* and to change and transform ourselves rather than to control the world to satisfy our desire and feed our ego.

We are called, in other words, to develop a new and more comprehensive and functional philosophy of life that will enable us to perceive deeper and more integral meaning and purpose in our lives, daily events, and being; that will affect and regenerate our minds, our hearts, and our wills and actions; that will transform our traditional ways of thinking, feeling, and willing, our relationships, lifestyles, and life's goals. The expansion and transformation of our consciousness, for which we have developed a cognitive map and a general topography in this work will then, in turn, affect our words, relationships, and actions, which will transform our very being. We are called, in other words, to become New Beings, to take our next qualitative step on the evolutionary scale, and to cooperate and collaborate consciously at the completion of our being and the fulfillment of our destiny.

If our traditional values, our basic social institutions,

and all forms of authority are crumbling around us and if the traditional solutions are no longer working for our personal and collective health and well-being, it is indeed a strong warning that the time has come for us to move our center of gravity from the lower self to the Higher Self or to pass from what I have called "the rule of the personality" to the "rule of the Soul." In Christian religious symbolism, we are living in the time of the Apocalypse (the revelation of hidden truth), of Armageddon (the great inner, psycho-spiritual war or conflict), and of the Second Coming of Christ (the birth of Spiritual Consciousness and the individual human Soul). Truly, there could hardly be a more exciting and interesting time to be living in . . . at least for those who love life and God and who can courageously face all of life, including some of its most difficult tests and its highest rewards. In this work, we have outlined and studied some of the most important characteristics and some of the major processes that are involved in this massive transformation. Very old and very new insights and intuitions are breaking through into our culture through scientific, religious, and literary instruments and media which are leading to basic paradigm shifts, to a true redefinition of reality, knowledge, human nature, and human destiny—which will eventually culminate in a new philosophy of life that will include a science of human nature, a science of consciousness, and an integral art of living. But, it is not enough to touch and transform the mind. In a genuine transformation and expansion of consciousness, it is vital that the *heart*, our feelings, values, motivations—what we love—and the *will*, our choices, self-mastery, and ability to realize our ideal and objectives—what we want—be also touched and transformed. For this is the only way that our lives, our relationships, and our being will be transformed. In this work, we have focused primarily upon the cognitive dimension, making explicit some of the major intuitions, assumptions, and ideas that will produce this new philosophy of life. It is up to the individual to then, having gotten a glimpse and a foretaste of a higher vision of what can and should be, ignite his or her heart and to train and energize his or her will to embody and incarnate that vision.

One of the most important prerequisites of personal growth and the transformation process is to have a minimum amount of self-knowledge which will then allow one to gradually acquire self-mastery and self-integration, and to further unfold itself. One of the pillars of self-knowledge is to know and understand both where one is and what is going on within oneself and within the sociocultural universe in which one lives. This is precisely where this work began. We characterized our present historical period as possessing five basic distinctive features, namely:

a. *The law of polarization:* that one is compelled to make choices and to become committed to one set of values, beliefs, and life goals.

b. *The law of intensification:* that as human consciousness grows and expands, so our energies, emotions, imagination intensify themselves.

c. *The law of acceleration:* that everything, both in our inner and outer lives, accelerates its rhythm so that things which used to take a much longer period of time to unfold now occur in a much shorter period of time.

d. *The law of etherealization:* that the thrust of our evolutionary forces and consciousness is moving away from the physical to non-physical dimensions; that major tests and trials are now taking place increasingly more within our field of consciousness rather than in the world.

e. *The law of the unfoldment of consciousness and energization:* that the thrust of human evolution leads to an ever-greater expansion of consciousness and increase in vitality or life energies so that our capacity for good and evil, for regeneration and degeneration, has been greatly increased.

Finally, we pointed out that we now find ourselves at a point in personal biography and world history where a major transformation, or Initiation, is in process; that we are moving from the Piscean to the Aquarian Age and are called to face the Apocalypse, Armageddon, the Antichrist, and the Second Coming of Christ or Spiritual Initiation, which we interpreted in the Light of the teachings of the Spiritual Tradition. This is the "macro" picture which leaves us with a fundamental question: how to be able to remain balanced, centered, and connected with the Light in the very eye of the oncoming storm? Or, how can we unfold a philosophy of life and an art of living which will enable us to face and cope with every possible test, experience, and situation that might come to us during this period of time?

At the "micro" level we delineated and analyzed various steps or aspects of the personal work of transformation that we are called to undergo, namely: *emotional purification, mental clarification, personal consecration, vision unfoldment,* and the *opening of the Intuition.* These steps involve becoming acquainted with, training, and learning to master five of the basic functions of the psyche with their associated processes, namely: feeling and devotion, thinking and meditation, willing and concentration, imagination and visualization, and intuition and invocation-evocation. These really constitute the psychological aspect of the Great Work, working upon the development of the personality, or self-actualization. Then, we briefly dealt with the nature and proper use of the last two functions of the psyche and their associated processes, namely: biopsychic drives and energy transformation, and sensation and outer and inner observations. At that point, we began to deal with and analyze the spiritual aspect of the Great Work—fusing the Soul level with the personality level, namely: *The Descent of the Light or* personal Christmas, Armageddon *or The Last Great Inner War,* and *Resurrection* or *personal Easter* wherein one becomes a New Being living in a New Heaven and Earth. This analysis completed our journey of creating a cognitive map or a philosophy of life and an art of living truly capable of standing up to the great challenges, dangers and opportunities of our times.

In "emotional purification," we argued that, as we now stand at the end of the Piscean Age, which is an emotional age that deals with the development, purification, and coordination of the astral body, the final "tests" or "exams" of this period will be emotional in nature—that the major battles and challenges we will be facing will be *pyschological* in nature affecting our "emotions" in particular. To achieve emotional purification and balance, we must learn to rise to the level of the mind and learn to act rationally rather than reacting emotionally, to find the right relationship with all the persons who are important to us, and especially with God, the Divine Light, Fire and Life. And we must learn to cultivate beauty, moral virtues and self-control. Finally, we must also understand the nature and function of emotions as powerful forces arising from the subconscious, the unconscious, and the Superconscious, and learn how to express devotion, or to open our hearts, and to transform negative emotions into positive emotions.

In "mental clarification," we showed the nature and power of thoughts in our inner and outer lives and the tremendous importance to hold positive thoughts and to perceive meaning and purpose in what happens to us in our daily experience. We argued that the same event can be perceived, defined, and reacted to in very different ways according to *our level of consciousness* and to the *mental framework we apply to it*. We can literally raise our level of consciousness to reach Heaven where every event does have a meaning and a purpose and can be integrated in God's plan for us, even if it is experienced as being very unpleasant or painful. Or, we can lower our level of consciousness to descend into Hell where nothing has any meaning or purpose anymore—where we stand in great mental confusions, emotional suffering, and feeling powerless to do anything about this as our will has become exhausted. Our basic conclusion was that it is not what happens to us that is crucial as to how we perceive, define and react to a particular experience. The world can be perceived and interpreted through a dualistic perspective pitting good against evil, or it can be perceived and interpreted through a monistic perspective which shows that evil is but unbalanced and unconscious good and that it is the perception and definition of something as evil which really makes it evil, but this at the mental rather than at the living experiential level . . . which can occur, in this fashion, only after Resurrection.

To understand and be able to consciously change our mental frameworks, we must understand the nature and dynamics of thinking and meditation, and to react to any human experience by asking: What is the meaning and purpose of this experience? What am I to learn from this? Why is God allowing this to happen to me and how can I respond with Light and Love to its basic challenge?

In "personal consecration" we showed the crucial importance of the will and of dedicating oneself to a worthy ideal to achieve true autonomy, integrity, and responsibility for one's actions, for unless one is able to give one's whole self with all one's heart, mind, and energies to a given task, one cannot become and operate as a fully "human" being. Personal consecration involves, basically, a strong, well-developed, and skillful will and a high, well-deliberated cause, or purpose, to focus one's attention, energies, and resources upon. It is the process that enables us to become free, conscious, and in control of our being and destiny rather than remaining a slave of external forces and destiny. The will is basically the "focused energies of the self" and the director and organizer of the many dimensions, energies of the Self" and the director and organizer of the many dimensions, energies, and resources of the personality; and it is the fundamental expression of personal autonomy and integrity—the capacity of a person to function freely according to his own intrinsic nature rather than under the compulsion of external forces or of inner unconscious forces.

In "visionary unfoldment," we focused upon the nature and role of the *imagination* and the power of *visualization* for our inner lives and the expansion of our consciousness. The imagination is the image-making function of the human psyche which has a reproductive and a creative aspect as well as a subjective and an objective aspect. Images, symbols, myths, and rituals have great evocative power and can reproduce and affect the materials of all the other functions of the psyche. The power of visualization is the ability to call forth images and symbols upon which to focus our attention. It is closely linked with the mind and thinking, with the difference that the latter translate into words and sentences their focus of awareness while the imagination and visualization transform into images and symbols the focus of their awareness. The first actually deals with the conscious, waking mind, while the latter deals with the unconscious, Deep Mind.

The imagination also allows our consciousness to soar above the physical world and the present to encompass all other dimensions and worlds as well as the past and the future.

Before we can create anything new or become something more than what we are, we must be able to grasp it with our minds and our imagination—we must be able to visualize it and identify with it. Thus, the imagination and the power of visualization can act as a bridge, or link, between the physical world and the psyche; between what is and what could be. As such, they open up the process of inner-observation and awareness and are one of the major "keys" or passports to enter into and explore the inner worlds. In our waking state, the conscious mind conceptualizes and thinks in abstract words and sentences, but, when we let go of our conscious mind and let the Deep Mind take over, words, concepts, and abstractions cease, giving way to images and symbols ... which are connected with the Collective Unconscious, with God and Nature, and, at this level, we spontaneously recover one of the great attributes of God: *creativity.*

To train the imagination and the power of visualization, we should learn to let go of the conscious mind and to allow ourselves to become captured and focused upon the mental imagery that will emerge, and learn how to practice regularly various guided daydreams or inner journeys. Then, we should train ourselves to learn how to interpret and unveil symbols on different levels of being and consciousness. Having achieved this preliminary training phase, we can then apply the imagination and its power of visualization to the true psychospiritual work, the use of the Seven Fundamentals, unfolding it further in the process. Thus will imagination and the power of visualization reveal to us the further steps of our becoming and self-realization and become the creative bridge between the inner and the outer worlds.

It is at this point that we are ready for the "Opening of the Intuition" which is closely connected with visionary unfoldment and with the convergent activation of feeling and thinking. This is the first real connection or bridging of the personality with the Soul or of the psychological work with true spiritual work. And it marks the great passage from being other-directed to being inner-directed or self-directed when a person can finally achieve true integrity, autonomy, and self-determination ... rather than being a creature of circumstances. For now the gates are open and the final expert, authority, and source of guidance and inspiration has been found *within oneself* and is ever-ready to be called upon to shed light and to provide true discernment upon all the complicated and paradoxical situations of earthly life.

The intuition and its twin processes of Invocation-Evocation imply, etymologically, the teachings from within or seeing from within and is the bridge that links up the conscious with the Superconscious and, eventually, the human with the spiritual Self. It is the pathway through which spiritual consciousness, illumination, Initiation, or divine revelation must necessarily travel. When the intuition is properly activated, it will enable a person to go from a question to the answer to that question without going through the in-between logical or empirical steps.

Invocation involves symbolically creating a "Pyramid" where each of its four corners includes Concentration (willing), Meditation (thinking), Devotion (feeling), and Visualization (imagination) converging upon a point, the top of the Pyramid which represents the image or symbol chosen for that exercise. This is what is known as human effort or aspiration, the psychological, human part of this work. *Evocation* will then answer Invocation with the downpouring of spiritual energies experienced as Light, Fire, Life, which transforms visualization into True Vision. This is the manifestation of intuition coming down, symbolically, into the center of the Pyramid from its top and which constitutes Grace or inspiration, the spiritual part of this work. Silence and ritual can be used together and sequentially to train and work with the intuitive process.

When the candidate has reached this point, he has

completed the first phase of the process known as self-actualization, the training and development of his personality as a coordinated and efficient tool. It is at this point that the descent of the spiritual Light, the birth of the spiritual consciousness or personal Christmas will occur in the Soul and consciousness of the candidate. This is his personal Spiritual Initiation which is so well described, symbolically, by the birth of Christ and the mandala of the manger. For this to happen, a healthy and properly functioning physical body is necessary, together with the proper training of the five basic psychospiritual muscles of our consciousness: willing, thinking, feeling, imagination, and intuition. Then, his conscious and Deep Mind can unite their joint efforts of concentration, meditation, devotion, visualization culminating in Invocation-Evocation to give birth to the Christ-child, the Divine Light, within the field of consciousness of the candidate.

The first major portion of the Great Work, self-actualization, is based essentially on the systematic study and training of the seven functions of the psyche and their basic processes on three basic levels:

a. *The psychological* which deals with the study and training of the personality.
b. *The psychic* which involves the exploration and harnessing of the latent energies of the mind, ESP and PSI phenomena, but only as a by-product of true spiritual work.
c. *The spiritual* which entails the exploration of the Superconscious and the discovery of the spiritual self to achieve a proper alignment with its life, will, and consciousness.

These are the basic "tools" or "muscles" that are used by the practical person, the scientist, and the artists, as well as the mystic, the occultist, and the magician, but on different levels and in different degrees.

The second major step in the Great Work is the descent of the Light in the personality or the dawning of true spiritual consciousness which is symbolically and archetypically represented by the Christmas story. This event, seen from the spiritual perspective, applies to all human beings, and is something that will happen in the future, requiring definite preparatory work and conditions for it to occur. All the basic persons and symbols here represent some aspect or phase of the process of having Christ—spiritual consciousness—be born, live, and rule our personality and lives. And the essence of this process involves training and directing "thinking, feeling, and willing," to bring all our minds, hearts, and souls, our human knowledge, love, and creative energies to worship the Divine within and to serve our fellow human beings in the world. This is the central objective of the Great Work of human growth and spiritual regeneration toward which all authentic psychological and spiritual systems aim as their final culminating goal. Thus, this story or legend should be used as the theme and object for serious concentration, meditation, contemplation, and theurgic work . . . to become co-creators with God in our becoming and further development as spiritual beings.

A final spiritual analysis, the crucial concept and reality of "Light" revealed that on the divine plane, it is the energy and manifestation of Divine Light, Fire, and Life, three in expression but one in essence. On the spiritual plane, Light is the source and essence of consciousness and wisdom, love and feeling, and will and creative energy. On this level, it is this Light that reveals the Self and enables the Self to express itself in consciousness, love and power. At the mental level, Light manifests itself as the "fuel of the mind:" consciousness, knowledge, awareness, and clarity. At the emotional level, Light manifests itself as the "emotional fuel:" love, warmth, feeling and courage to live fully. Finally, at the physical level, Light manifests itself as life, vitality, and energy that is used by the physical body to carry out its activities on the physical plane.

When it comes to Armageddon, the "last great inner war" is nothing more than the final conflict between the *personality*, or the lower self, and the *individuality*, the Higher Self, for the control of the field of consciousness, the state of mind, and the actions of a given person. When the candidate has discovered the Higher Self and has experienced the dawning of spiritual consciousness in his being, it is logical to assume that the old and the new self, the lower and the Higher Self, will have to face each other and struggle for the control of the personality and life of the candidate. Basically, the lower self includes the first three chakras (physical survival, emotional satisfaction, and power and recognition). It is basically materialistic, egoistical, and egocentric, wanting to take rather than to give. The Higher Self, on the other hand, includes the three highest chakras (understanding the laws of cause and effect: responsibility, true service, and humility), and it is idealistic, altruistic, and self-giving. The first fights and struggles for the survival, well-being, and self-affirmation of the personality; that is of the biological organism with its psychosocial identity and specific cultural strivings. And it does so with the help of the biopsychic drives and instincts, of the passions and lower emotions, of the lower mind, and the sociocultural ideals of a materialistic and egocentric civilization. The second fights and struggles, but with Love and Light, faith, self-sacrifice, and patience, for the good of the whole and for the working out of God's plan on Earth.

The basic objective here is not to fight or kill the personality but rather to train it, discipline it, and put it to work for the individuality! Both aspects and natures have their place and their function in God's plan which provided for both! The major work here which is the true beginning of the Great Work in its truly *spiritual* aspect is: *the transmutation or transformation of evil into good, of darkness into light, of hatred into love . . . of death into life!* One's greatest weapons in this inner struggle are: meditation, contemplation, and identification (seeking the Light and wisdom; awakening and fanning the inner fire of love; and binding oneself with God and the life force.

Actually, Armageddon is a symbol for a profound and archetypal human and spiritual crisis leading to a new state of consciousness and a new life. It is the great trial that always precedes a genuine Initiation. On the elemental levels, it involves the Earth Initiation or the "breaking of the physical body," the Water Initiation or the "breaking of the heart," the Air Initiation or the "breaking of the mind," and the Fire Initiation or the "breaking of the human will and the ego." But it is only during the fifth Initiation, the first truly *Spiritual* Initiation, that the center of gravity of one's consciousness and the control of the personality truly passes from the lower self to the Higher Self, and this is the most memorable and the purest expression of Armageddon. It is after this experience that one receives, experientially, the Keys of Heaven and Hell or the ability to ascend at will into the Superconscious or descend at will into the unconscious.

After the various great trials and crises, or Initiations, always come various rebirths and finally spiritual Resurrection. The great glyph and symbols representing those events are archetypally represented in the Easter story or legend and, as with the Christmas story, now the candidate undergoes a personal Easter. Rebirth essentially involves a renewed expression of life flowing through a certain aspect, dimension, or person. Thus, one can consciously cooperate and work in such a fashion as to bring about a physical, emotional, and mental rebirth. It is after many such rebirths, on different levels and in different degrees, that spiritual Resurrection will finally occur enabling the Divine Spark to come into His Kingdom and to truly rule the consciousness and life of the candidate. This process entails a true "death" and "rebirth" wherein life and reality will appear in a very different form and will be reacted to in a very different way than before.

For the first time, in our human growth and development, we will acquire a comprehensive and effective philosophy of life that will enable us to meet and pass successfully all the great tests and ordeals of life, and to be able to unblock, activate, and harmonize all of our chakras. Thus, we will progressively be able to first intellectually, then emotionally, and finally existentially accept and be grateful for whatever life brings us; to have the courage to be alone and to face life with its good and evil; to be contented with what we have and are, at this point; to have true compassion for all beings; to discover the laws of cause and effect and to achieve personal responsibility; to develop and manifest unconditional love and total acceptance for other human beings and thus be of true service to them; and, finally, to manifest genuine humility, "living the ordinary life of ordinary human beings" but being infused with and radiating divine Light, fire, and life.

Finally, and most important, in the light of the new spiritual consciousness we have acquired, to be able to solve the riddle of our own being, its nature and destiny, to resolve the paradox of good and evil, and to achieve the purpose for which we have come into the physical world— to live a truly *mature human life* wherein we have finally identified with the *Divine within* and developed and coordinated our "bodies" and their faculties and potentialities to function as "His Temple" on Earth.

It is at this point that we will have reconciled the human with the Divine, that we will be able to transmute evil into good (or, rather, the spirit in us will do that for us for only the Divine can really accomplish this), and that the "end of the rule of the personality, or lower self," will have been achieved leading to the beginning of the "rule of the Soul, or the Higher Self." This is the sublime and final goal prefigured and promised by all great world religions and the culmination of the Great Work of all genuine esoteric, philosophical, and Spiritual Traditions. Paradoxically, it is also only at *this point* that we finally truly become ourselves and are able to fully express ourselves, in our personality and in the world; and thus that we become mature human beings, spiritual adults, and children of God who know the will of their Father, with whom they are at-one, and thus able to manifest Him consciously on Earth, realizing His kingdom or plan at the microscopic and macroscopic levels. This is the profound truth adumbrated by the concepts of our "passing from the fourth to the fifth kingdom (from that of human beings to that of spiritual beings) and of our "becoming the 10th hierarchy" completing the great Chain of Being that goes from the spirit to matter and from matter back to Spirit.

After Resurrection has occurred *experientially* we have a new self and, indeed, live "under a new Heaven and upon a new Earth," the old self having "died" or "left space" for the new self to be born. In modern, empirical terms this means that we now identify our "self" not as we formerly did with our physical body, our emotions, our thoughts, ambitions and aspirations, and our social roles and position, but, rather, with our Divine Spark, with the spirit within us, and with life and consciousness flowing through all human beings and living beings. At this point, we know, experientially that "what we do unto others, we do unto ourselves" as spiritually and ontologically we are one, and thus we work for the long-range and effective good of the whole rather than for our short-range selfish personal interests. We also know that we are incarnate spirits or gods at-one with the universal God who is the very source and essence of life, love, and consciousness, who loves us with ineffable, incomprehensible, unconditional love, who is just and merciful, omniscient and omnipotent (in His own time-frame which is eternity), and thus we have returned home or found a new harmony and belongingness with life and the universe. Finally, we know our purpose and work in this world and are able to read the book of Nature and write our own unique and personal story in it. And it is at this point that we can truly be and express ourselves, and accomplish our purpose doing God's Will, for we have finally achieved human and spiritual adulthood and maturity which makes us conscious co-workers with the eternal. Thus is Christ born again and again, and a new star lights up the inner firmament as the world becomes transformed by the Spirit of God acting through a full human being!

After Resurrection has been experienced and realized, it is literally not us, the little human ego or self that lives, but the Spirit of God that lives and breathes, thinks, feels, desires, wills, speaks, and acts through our personality which has finally become completed as His temple and vehicle of expression, and that collectively as humanity we become the 10th hierarchy. At this point, all work, all strivings, all aspirations, sacrifices, ordeals and tests as we know them from our human standpoint and consciousness cease, as it is God that lives and acts through us. The Great Work has been accomplished, and the reign of the Holy Spirit has come in power and in truth. All books, conferences, courses, outer guidance and instructions, churches, spiritual schools, and esoteric organizations become obsolete as guidance and life now come from *within* rather than from *without*. Hence, the true insights and work proposed in this book which I originally called the "Challenges of our Times, Their Nature, Dangers, and Opportunities," pertain to what comes before, or precedes, Resurrection which is its final culmination. Go back to the cognitive framework, or philosophy and art of living, which is suggested in this work, pull up your shirt sleeves, open and give your heart, your mind, and your will and begin to *live* and *enflesh* what we have called here emotional purification, mental clarification, personal consecration, visionary unfoldment, the opening of the Intuition, the Descent of the Light, and personal Armageddon and, with God's help and the help of your brothers and sisters in the Light, *realize your own resurrection, become the unique god you are meant to be and already are!*

To meet the basic challenges of our times, to utilize their opportunities and avoid their dangers, one should bear in mind the following seven fundamental points that synthesize the essence of the present work:

I. One must want to change, to grow, to reach up to the next qualitative step in human evolution—to consciously *work* for one's *self-actualization* and *self-realization*. This not only at the cognitive but also at the affective, conative, and existential levels. This means not only to think about this great goal and to gather the necessary knowledge but also to feel it in one's heart and to will it so as to live it and thus to enflesh it, to incarnate it. This powerful ideal and goal can either be reached through suffering and by finding oneself in various existential and psychological crises, which will precipitate it or through Wisdom and the sheer love and desire for what is good, what is true, and what is beautiful—what is *really* worth achieving in this life and which has been called by the sages and the saints of all ages: the Great Work, the *Ars Magna*.

II. To achieve this Great Work of personal growth, self-transcendence, or self-actualization and self-realization, an integral philosophy of life, grounded in a science and art of man, of consciousness, of life, and of relationships, is absolutely necessary. These in turn, are based upon, according to the present convergence and synthesis of the Sacred Traditions of the past and the best of modern science, gaining systematic and progressive *self-knowledge, self-mastery,* and *self-integration.*

III. To acquire this systematic and progressive self-knowledge, self-mastery, and self-integration one must necessarily *understand* and *train* the seven functions of the psyche with their associated psychological processes, namely:

    a. *Willing:* Concentration, Affirmation.

    b. *Thinking:* Meditation.

    c. *Feeling:* Devotion.

    d. *Imagination:* Visualization.

    e. *Intuition:* Invocation-Evocation.

    f. *Biopsychic Drives,* or Impulses: Energy Transformation and Transmutation.

    g. *Sensation:* Outer and Inner Observation.

IV. Then, one must train and unfold, systematically and progressively, one's knowledge of and ability to work with the power of:

    a. Concentration

    b. Meditation

    c. Contemplation

    d. Doing Ritual Theurgic Work (see: *The Nature and Use of Ritual*)

V. This will lead to an authentic and lived transformation and expansion of one's level of Con-

sciousness and of one's level of being, and the
creation and unfoldment, or unveiling, of a new
reality and being—of an ongoing psychosynthesis.

VI. Though couched in many words, dogmas, or
formulae, the basic sequence is ever the same,
following the Path of the Tree of Life:
   Knowing, Feeling, Willing, Experiencing
   Living, Becoming, Being

VII. Then, and only then, will the candidate truly find
and be able to express his true Self to, love God,
his fellow human, and life with his whole Heart,
Mind, and Soul which are both the *means* and the
end. And to accomplish this Great Work, the
Candidate will benefit more than words can tell
by the guidance and presence of genuine Initiates or teachers and the fellowship of like-
minded brothers and sisters.

This is the great challenge of our times . . . and of all
times. We, who are living today in the second half of the
20th century, now have the greatest opportunity to finally
accomplish this . . . and the only true danger is to stop half
way, not to walk to the end because of lack of faith, courage,
or inner harmony.

Practical Exercise

Preliminary: Find the right place and the right position. Then make an effort of Introversion, Supraversion, and Infraversion.

Actual work: Meditation

Focus your attention upon the times we are living in, the crises and opportunities they entail and thus the challenges they present to all beings who are alive today. We are now facing a major collective and personal Initiation with several minor ones that lead to personal and collective Psycho-Socio-Spiritual Transformation. For we are now truly living in the times of the Apocalypse (the revelation of hidden truths), of Armageddon (the great inner psychospiritual conflict betwen the Higher and the Lower Self) and of the Second Coming of Christ (the birth of Spiritual Consciousness in the individual human Soul). This can lead to a powerful and rapid personal and collective degeneration culminating in death, or to an equally powerful and rapid personal and collective regeneration culminating in life and Spiritual Consciousness. One of the major tests and injunction of our times seems to be, indeed, how to remain balanced, centered, and connected with the Light in the eye of the oncoming storm, both personal and interpersonal. How do you perceive, define, and respond to your personal challenges at this point in time? What does

225

history and life, God and men, seem to be demanding of you now?

In this work, and others of the same series, we have outlined a philosophy of life and an art of living, a cognitive map and many tools and instruments, drawn both from the sacred traditions of the past and from the best of modern science, to enable you, the reader and candidate, to know yourself better, to acquire progressive mastery over your energies, dimensions, and faculties, and to integrate your being. Now that you have read this work, and most likely, others as well, and that you have begun at least some of the personal work, what are you going to do with your life, with your time, with your energies and faculties—How will you act in the world? What service will you render? What is your own, unique contribution and part in God's plan for yourself and for humanity? What role are you to play and how can you best play it with the resources you have available?

When you have completed this meditation and world-examination, make the appropriate entries in your workbook, as to what you have discovered, what you have done, what has happened, and *how you are prepared to live!*

Appendix A

THE "MUSCLES OF CONSCIOUSNESS"

It has now been over 25 years that I have been active in the Human Potential Movement, the Consciousness Circuit, the Aquarian Frontier, and various esoteric organizations and groups—as an observer, a participant, and a leader. I have attended and been a lecturer at a great number of New Age symposiums and lectures, and I have joined many psychological, esoteric, and spiritual groups dedicated to human growth and spiritual development. This I have done because the *leitmotiv* of my personal and professional life has always been the study of human nature and human behavior, and the expansion of human consciousness and the development of spiritual consciousness.

I used to have a great deal of enthusiasm and very high hopes and expectations for this kind of endeavor and for the people I would meet at these gatherings and who belonged to these groups. While my enthusiasm for and dedication to human development and spiritual awakening have remained and, in fact, grown and intensified over the years, my hopes and expectations for what people could actually achieve by attending these groups, symposiums, and lectures have greatly diminished. I noticed that, just as in the world where most people seek financial wealth and social status but few actually achieve it, so in the Consciousness Circuit and the New Age groups *great are the hopes and promises but few are the results!*

Most people attend symposium after symposium, lecture after lecture, taking various courses and applying different techniques and methods, or they join one or more esoteric or spiritual organizations, or yet they find and follow one or more Guru but soon settle down in a new routine with very little actual *change* in their lives and being. The only thing that really happened is that they found and accepted a few new ideas and beliefs to meditate upon and discuss with their friends; ideas and beliefs such as: reincarnation and karma, the subtle bodies, the psychospiritual centers, the various auras, the Masters or more evolved human beings. These ideas have, basically, remained in their head and have not really descended into their heart, nor have they been enfleshed in their lives. In other words, as they have heard, read, or discussed these ideas and beliefs but not really *lived* them and *incarnated* them, little has actually happened in their lives and beings and not much basic change really occurred.

Many of these people will, later, either fall into a given routine of mechanically reaffirming certain ideas and principles, with no actual connection with their real lives and selves, or they will become disillusioned and disappointed in the spiritual quest as many other people have become disillusioned, or burned out in the quest for money and status. A most interesting book to read, along these lines, is Robert de Ropp's *Warrior's Way*, which is his own personal spiritual biography and odyssey through many New Age groups and spiritual organizations. The basic question one can ask at this point (and which I did ask myself) is: *What has gone wrong? Why have so many high ideals and lofty objectives failed to deliver what they promised and aimed at?*

The answer to this fundamental question, which lead

and gave birth to what I call today the "muscles of consciousness," came to me, by analogy, when one day I was reflecting upon my diary and meditating on what happened to a dear friend of mine and myself in the summer of 1957. It came to me all at once, in a flash of intuition that provided the foundation for the most important aspect of our consciousness I call the "muscles of consciousness."

At that time, my friend and I were students at the University of Denver and had been invited by my parents to spend the summer in Europe. During that academic year, we had worked very hard on our course work and, being quite ambitious, in our quest to make the dean's list and to achieve academic distinction, we had completely neglected our physical bodies, doing little or no exercise and sport, eating and drinking too much, and leading a very sedentary intellectual life—a very unbalanced life!

My parents, who knew what was going on, at least in my case, were very eager that we use the summer to get back in good physical shape by involving ourselves with different sports. To this end, they provided us with the best available instructors for water-skiing and playing tennis on the Italian Riviera and for snow skiing in Switzerland. Our instructors were, indeed, excellent and very dedicated persons, but all their efforts availed naught! We could see what they were doing, we understood what they were telling us, and we could have written superb papers as the principles and techniques involved in all three sports, but our bodies were absolutely incapable of following through and of doing what our minds were telling them to do!

It was at this point that the Swiss ski instructor really got at the heart of the situation when he told us, in a flash of intuition and recognition: "Boys, you are in bad physical shape! Before you do anything else and waste your time and mine, go and build and coordinate your physical muscles!" This, of course, was the answer. For over a month, we did just that: we went to a gymnasium and learned and practiced all kinds of physical exercises designed to build and coordinate our physical muscles until they got back in shape. Then, we went back to our old instructors and were now able to carry out their instructions and to have our bodies do what they were told to do, thus learning at last good snow skiing, water-skiing, and tennis.

A breakthrough had occurred which broke the deadlock into which we had fallen and which opened the door of the "room" we wanted to get into. The same breakthrough happened to me much as I was considering the psychological and spiritual blocks or dead ends into which so many people had fallen, and provided me with the answer to the basic question I had raised before: *What went wrong with all these spiritual idealists and enthusiasts?*

The answer is, of course: Do we not also have consciousness or psychospiritual muscles? And should not these muscles also be trained and coordinated before we can expect any kind of genuine change and growth to occur in our consciousness and being? Naturally, we do have such "muscles" so that the basic question now becomes: what are these "muscles" and how can they be properly developed and coordinated so that they can be applied in human growth and spiritual awakening?

To answer these questions, in a disciplined and systematic way, we must first ask ourselves: what is human consciousness and what are its structure and functions? Just as if we wanted to develop and coordinate physical muscles we should first ask ourselves the question: What is our physical body and its anatomy and physiology? The most valuable model of the human psyche is, as far as I am concerned, that proposed by psychosynthesis developed by Roberto Assagioli. In formulating and then articulating the now famous "Egg of Psychosynthesis," describing the structure of the psyche, and the "Star or Flower of Psychosynthesis," describing the functions of the psyche, Assagioli put together the most comprehensive, up-to-date, and sophisticated model of the human psyche. In a nutshell, the structure of the psyche is composed of seven basic elements which are: The Human Self, the Spiritual Self, the Field of Consciousness, the Preconscious, the Subconscious, the Unconscious, and the Superconscious. The functions of the Psyche are also seven, namely: Willing, Thinking, Feeling, Intuition, Imagination, Biopsychic Drives or Impulses, and Sensations.

My central thesis and most important postulate are this: *The most important muscles of our consciousness are those associated with willing, thinking, feeling, imagination, and intuition. And that these muscles are just as important for mundane or physical endeavors as they are for psychological or cultural endeavors and for spiritual endeavors.* These, in other words, are the core psychospiritual tools for successful living and for the expansion of human consciousness and for spiritual awakening. Without a minimum amount of training and coordination of these muscles, no exercise, technique, or consciousness raising and spiritual development program can truly get underway, let alone succeed! For as the Spiritual Tradition has rightly put it in a nutshell: "First, we must *know* something, then we must *feel* it, and only at that point can we *live* it in order to *become* it." These "muscles of consciousness" are truly the ABC's, the foundation for all conscious change, personal growth, and psychospiritual transformation on *any* level. They are:

1. *Concentration* associated with *willing* or the focused energies of the Self, the ability to say "yes" and to say "no" to ourselves and to others, or, in other words: to know what we want and to know what we do not want. The will can be compared to a battery that can be charged as well as discharged and concentration is, in itself, a science and an art.

2. *Meditation* associated with *thinking* or thinking in a focused and disciplined way about any subject: mundane, human or spiritual. Meditation can also be considered a science and an art that have to be properly understood and mastered.

3. *Devotion* associated with *feeling* or directing one's emotions and opening one's heart and energizing whatever subject one is concerned with. The ability to express devotion or to put one's heart into a subject of one's choice is a profound science and an art that have to be cultivated and developed.

4. *Visualization* associated with *imagination* or the ability to create images or symbols to represent inwardly what one is concerned with, in a tangible and concrete way, and to allow these images and symbols to "come alive" and to unfold in one's field of consciousness. To visualize properly is, likewise, a science and an art which are now being rediscovered with the study and application of mental imagery.

5. *Invocation-Evocation* associated with *intuition* or the ability to focus all of one's attention or concentration, one's thinking or meditation, one's feeling or devotion, and one's imagination or visualization upon a given topic or subject and then to empty one's consciousness to receive the energies and impressions that might then flow into it at that point. The proper training of the intuition and the mastery of invocation-evocation are not only a science and an art but, perhaps, the most important psychospiritual work one can do to contact one's Higher Self and obtain guidance and conscience from within in these tur-

bulent times when all external authorities and experts are slowly crumbling!

Concentration, meditation, devotion, visualization, and invocation-evocation must be cultivated and developed first *individually* and then *concomitantly* when one reaches the stage of training the intuition which requires the previous mastery and coordination of the first four to enable one to work with invocation-evocation. What religion and the spiritual traditions call faith, and to which they give so much importance, is really a triangle of the focused and coordinated use of concentration-will, meditation-thinking, and devotion-feeling ("Thou shalt love the Lord Thy God with all thy heart, all thy mind, and all thy Soul") with visualization-imagination of the proper images and symbols at its base. The image of the pyramid can also be used wherein the four corners and angles of the pyramid represent, respectively: concentration-willing, meditation-thinking, devotion-feeling, and visualization-imagination, which thrust upward toward the top and point of the pyramid, forming a grand invocation, to be answered by evocation—the descent in the center of the pyramid of true inspiration or the intuitive insight and energy.

The final question I will address myself to in this Appendix is: how can we, concretely and practically, develop and apply, in our daily lives, these "muscles of our consciousness" or core psychospiritual tools, first individually and then together and simultaneously in the opening of our intuition? Obviously, each one could be the object of a long lecture or even a book and several practical exercises and techniques have already been discussed, so I shall be very brief and focus only upon some of the most important guidelines and exercises that bear some repetition, and that will enable each one of you to use your own personal experience of the reality and development of each of these

"Muscles" and "Tools."

1. *Training of the Will and Concentration:* The will is the key function of the psyche as it relates the energies of the Self to all the other functions. It is neither a great deal of raw energy nor a blind determination to do what one wants to do at all cost. Rather, like the director of a play, the will focuses, directs, and utilizes all the *energies* and *resources* of one's consciousness and of one's human environment to achieve the goals and objectives that are wanted and focused upon. More than a physical or a bio-psychic energy, the will is a *psychospiritual energy*, the energy of life, of the Self, working through the psyche and the biological organism, to accomplish and realize one's objectives. As such it is the key to one's *freedom* and *integrity* as a human being.

   a. Learn to focus upon, or concentrate upon, a physical object, then a feeling, a thought, an image, and finally, a symbol or a basic theme.

   b. Learn how to say "no" to others, to desires and longings in yourself, and to various inducements of circumstances, no matter what the attraction or the temptations are. For, whenever we resist ourselves or others, or deny ourselves, *we charge our will* and, conversely, whenever we give in to temptations and desires, and seek instant gratification, we weaken our will.

   c. Learn to reflect upon and determine what you really want and don't want, and then make sure that you pursue what you want and avoid what you don't want. Never abandon a plan, project, or undertaking you have carefully selected and in which you believe because of the difficulties or the time involved. If something is worth starting, it is worth completing!

2. *Training of Thinking and Meditation:* Thinking of getting a cognitive grasp of the outer and inner universe. It implies developing thoughts and ideas about what exists and is happening both outside and inside of our being so that we can become more conscious of outer and inner reality and make sense out of them. Here, it is vital to remember a most important psychological law: the psychospiritual energies of the psyche will follow and energize whatever we are thinking about or directing our thoughts toward. Indeed, we become what we think or contemplate!

Meditation is the process by which we think in a systematic and disciplined way and it involves three basic inner aspects: reflective, receptive, and contemplative meditation.

Reflective meditation involves organizing all our thoughts, ideas, and experiences—all that we know, have learned and experienced—about a given subject in a clear, coherent, and integrated way. It means bringing all the materials that pertain to our chosen topic from the Subconscious and the Preconscious into the field of consciousness so that we can behold them and become aware of them.

Receptive meditation involves clearing and emptying our minds of all our acquired knowledge and experience about our chosen subject so that new insights, associations, and information may be received. Here, the main process is to let go, to relax and become fully receptive, once our attention has been fixed upon a given subject.

Contemplative meditation is the spiritual

dimension of meditation. It follows the first two steps and involves expanding our state of consciousness through a chosen spiritual exercise so that we can now behold our chosen subject in an altered state of consciousness, become at-one with it, and let the materials pertaining to it now flow from the Superconscious into the field of consciousness. It is inspired and intuitive thinking about our given subject so that new aspects and insights may be gathered from the Superconscious and the Divine Spark.

The topics one can choose as a subject for meditation are as many and as wide as life itself: they can be qualities such as joy, courage, peace, love, wisdom; *the symbols of basic prayers* such as Heaven, Father, Kingdom, or a whole prayer; life goals and plans or the ideal model of a personality one would like to develop.

3. *Training of Feeling and Devotion:* While willing produces energy and life, thinking yields knowledge and understanding, feeling awakens love and the ability to have and to express deep emotions, or to feel deeply about whatever we focus our attention upon. Life, knowledge, and love are truly the food for our inner being and indispensable components for any person to be properly equilibrated, psychologically integrated, and humanly fulfilled—to be able to live as a full human being.

Feeling is the ability to evoke emotions, to feel deeply and passionately about something, to be truly moved from the heart by whatever we focus our attention upon.

Devotion is the process of expressing and focusing emotions and feelings about a given subject of our choice. To feel deeply and passionately about something we must involve our will, images, thoughts, and symbols that stir up something in our makeup and that will open the doors of the Deep Mind.

What we need here is a good meditation on our emotions: what does and does not move us. Then, we must discover and utilize the images, thoughts, symbols, and the particular situations and relationships that evoke profound and genuine feelings from us. Through *prayer* and *beauty* we can also energize and amplify the quality and intensity of our emotional responses. The name of a person, the image of someone we love or admire, the recall of a particularly emotionally charged event—all these can be powerful triggers to cultivate devotion.

4. *Training of Imagination and Visualization:* Just as the power of observation is crucial to gather knowledge about the physical world and to orient ourselves in that world, so the power of inner observation, or visualization, is crucial to gather knowledge of the inner worlds.

The imagination is the image-making faculty and visualization is the power to see things with the "eye of the mind." Imagination has both a "female," or reproductive nature, and a "male," or creative nature (the ability to reproduce on the screen of the mind anything one has seen or experienced and the ability to create new things, events, or stories). The imagination and the power of visualization have an immense evocative and awakening power for our emotions, thoughts, and even for our intuition, by resonating with an opening up of the various regions of the psyche (the subconscious, unconscious, and Superconscious) with their related energies, vibrations, and states of consciousness. The essence of visualization is full concentration and absorption in the fantasy one is living which acts as the key to unlock the doors of the unconscious and of the Superconscious.

The basic exercise to develop the imagination and the power of visualization is guided imagery or the inward journey; for, just as we can take journeys in the outer, physical world, so we can also take inward journeys in the psychological and spiritual worlds of the psyche. The most important inward journeys involve:

a. Taking a trip to the sea and exploring its depths; taking a trip to a mountain to find the Temple of Silence or the Temple of the Sun, or a Guardian of the Mysteries; and taking a trip under the Earth to explore its caverns and depths.
b. Encounters with other beings during the trip—human, animal, or angelic, and dialoguing with them, giving them something and receiving a present from them.
c. One can take these beings with oneself in moving through the psychological space going up or down, and watching for transformations that are likely to occur in them or in oneself.

While one is taking an inward journey, it is very important to study oneself, using the Consciousness Checklist, to observe any changes that may occur in one's state of consciousness, and to be able to describe them. One should also bear in mind that every being and event encountered represents, analogically, *a part of* one's being and of one's life.

5. *Training of Intuition and Invocation-Evocation:* Con-

centration, meditation, devotion, and visualization are the central psychological "muscles" or "tools" which form the base from which the fifth, *intuition*, with its twin processes of *invocation-evocation*, is to emerge to crown the whole edifice.

Intuition means seeing from within or the teachings from within. It is the bridge or channel that links up the field of consciousness with the Superconscious, and the human with the spiritual Self. This is why it is the only faculty that is half psychological and half spiritual in nature and that links up the psychological with the spiritual dimension of our being like a true "ladder of Jacob." Genuine spiritual illumination, true spiritual initiation, or Divine Revelation, must *All* come through the channel of the intuition which must be open for such purpose. Once the channel of intuition is open and the spiritual energies (the Light, Fire, and Life of the Spiritual Self) can flow through it, they will enliven, quicken, and bring to life all the other functions and literally transform one's consciousness, translating it from the realm of nature to the Kingdom of God. Then, and only then, will a person be guided from *within* and receive all the answers to the most basic questions and problems of life from his own Higher Self rather than from the various external experts and authorities!

To activate and open up the intuition a sequential process known as invocation-evocation is used. In Invocation, the first four functions of the psyche—willing, thinking, feeling, and imagination—are used in a synchronous fashion so as to concentrate all of one's attention upon the Spiritual Self residing in one's Head Center, direct all of one's thoughts and meditations to Him, send Him all of one's love and feelings, and visualize Him in one's favorite image or symbol. This creates an upward-thrusting triangle with concentration and meditation at the outer two triangles, devotion at the center, and visualization at the base. Another basic image or model that can be used is that of the pyramid where concentration, meditation, devotion, and visualization form the four angles meeting at the top from which evocation, or the intuitive energies, flow down the center of the pyramid. When this is done to the best of our present abilities, invocation will be answered by evocation, which is a down-pouring of spiritual energies into our field of consciousness wherein spiritual Life energizes our human will and concentration, spiritual Light illuminates our meditation and thinking, spiritual fire warms and expands our feelings and devotion, and spiritual vision opens up and crowns our visualization. Ultimately, however, it is important to remember that intuition, with its accompanying inspiration and revelation are *spiritual gifts* and not human or psychological achievements.

As such, a life of devoted prayer, selfless service to others, wholesome leisure and recreation, and a proper perspective and balance in all the things one does is, perhaps, the best way to obtain the gift of true initiation which only the Spiritual Self can bestow. It is also vital to learn how to listen to and recognize the "voice of the Intuition" when it does manifest itself and how to cultivate peace, or systematic relaxation, and life, or systematic stimulation, in our whole personality.

Appendix B

CONSCIOUSNESS CHECKLIST

The Consciousness Checklist described below is a practical instrument we have derived from Roberto Assagioli's Egg of Psychosynthesis which represents, diagrammatically, and describes the *structure* of the human psyche. Its seven basic categories, or questions, are drawn directly from the Field of Consciouness and its seven functions: Willing, Thinking, Feeling, Intuition, Imagination, Biopsychic Drives, and Sensations. It is a most important *psychological tool* designed to enable the candidate to develop his/her capacity for inner observation and to monitor what is really happening in his/her consciousness, to note and evaluate the qualitative and quantitative changes and psychospiritual transformations that might occur as the result of the particular work that is being done, using ritual or practicing other psychospiritual exercises.

It is the primary tool, operationalized from psychosynthesis theory, for self-observation and consciousness-examination we are offering the reader and candidate. As such, it should be properly memorized and understood in its sequential order, and then used before, during, and at the end of doing the entire range of individual meditations, exercises, and rituals we are suggesting in this work. Its proper use will enable the ccndidate to systematically become aware of his/her inner state, of the processes and materials at work in his/her field of consciousness, and of possible *transformations* that will occur therein. These should then be noted mentally and/or entered in his/her workbook.

This is a tool that I have used not only for esoteric/spiritual work but also for psychological, human growth, and psychotherapeutic purposes, and which has yielded excellent results. Its merit is to be, at the same time, simple and practical as well as systematic and exhaustive, tapping not only quantitative but also qualitative materials and possible changes.

The Consciousness Checklist

1. What *Sensations* are you presently aware of in your Field of Consciousness?
   a. Seeing
   b. Hearing
   c. Tasting
   d. Smelling
   e. Touching
   What sensations are particularly strong, and which are weak?
   Where do these sensations come from?
   Realize that you are *not* these sensations, but that they are tools for you to contact the physical world.

2. What *Biopsychic Drives* or *Impulses* are you presently aware of in your Field of Consciousness?
   a. Hunger
   b. Thirst
   c. Fatigue
   d. Sexual arousal

e. Anger or Aggressiveness
What biopsychic drives are particularly strong, and which are weak?
Where do these biopsychic drives originate?
Realize that you are *not* these biopsychic drives or impulses, but that they are tools for you to use and that you control them.

3. What *Emotions* and *Feelings* are you presently aware of in your Field of Consciousness?
   a. Joy
   b. Sorrow
   c. Love
   d. Fear
   e. Excitement
   f. Depression
   g. Other
   What emotions and feelings are particularly strong, and which are weak?
   Where do these emotions and feelings come from?
   Realize that you are *not* these emotions and feelings, but that they are tools, that *you* control them, that they are not really a part of your true being, but that they act as a source of great energy and drive, joy or sorrow.

4. What *Images* or *Symbols* are presently activated in your Imagination?
   a. Natural
   b. Human
   c. Spiritual
   What images and symbols are particularly strong, and which are weak?
   Where do these images and symbols come from?
   Realize that you are *not* these images and symbols, but that they are tools for you to reproduce the other

functions of the psyche and experiences you have had or could live.

Presently, is your image-making function and power of visualization strong or weak?

5. What *Thoughts* or *Ideas* are presently going through your mind?
   a. Of the Past
   b. Of the Present
   c. Of the Future

   What thoughts or ideas are particularly strong, and which are weak?

   Where do these thoughts and ideas come from?

   Realize that you are *not* these thoughts and ideas, but that they are tools for you to express yourself on the mental level, and that you can control them.

6. Is your *Intuition* presently active in your Field of Consciousness?
   a. Spiritually
   b. Mentally
   c. Emotionally
   d. Physically

   If it is active, what is it telling you?

   Does any part of your being oppose or thwart your intuition?

   Can you distinguish between your intuition, emotions, imagination, and biopsychic drives?

   Realize that you are *not* your Intuitions but that these are tools for you to contact the deeper and higher parts of your being and of life.

7. What are you presently *Willing*, or to what do you direct your *Attention*?
   a. Physical objects

b. Emotional objects
c. Mental objects
d. Spiritual objects

How well can you presently use your will and ability to concentrate upon the above objects? In your outer and inner work, are you able to do what you want and not to do what you do not want?

What is preventing you, if anything, from using your will efficiently?

What can you do to *consciously* develop your will further?

Notes

Chapter 2: **Emotional Purification**

    1: Sedir; *Quelques Amis de Dieu;* Amities Spirituelles, p. 105. Translated by Peter Roche de Coppens.

    2: *Ibid.,* p. 104.

    3: *Ibid.,* p. 105.

Chapter 3: **Mental Clarification**

    1: Ferrucci, Piero; *What We May Be: Techniques for Psychological and Spiritual Growth;* Tarcher, 1982, p. 103.

    2: *Ibid.,* pp. 103-104.

    3. Vivier, Robert; *Delivrez-nous du Mal: Antoine le Guerisseur;* Bernard Grasset, 1936, pp. 225-226. Translated by Peter Roche de Coppens.

    4: *Ibid.,* p. 169.

    5: *Ibid.,* pp. 317-318.

    6: *Ibid.,* pp. 300-301.

    7. *Ibid.,* p. 315.

    8: *What We May Be; op. cit.,* pp. 107-108.

    9: *Ibid.,* pp. 109-110.

Chapter 4: **Personal Consecration**

    1: de Ropp, Robert; *Warrior's Way;* Delta, 1979, p. 2.

    2: *Ibid.,* p. 1.

    3: de Ropp, Robert; *The Master Game;* Delta Books, 1968, pp. 11-12.

    4: Nightingale, Earl; Tapes.

    5: *What We May Be; op. cit.,* p. 73.

    6: *Ibid.,* p. 74.

    7: *Ibid.,* p. 75.

8: *Ibid.,* p. 77.

9: *Ibid.,* p. 77.

10: Assagioli, Roberto; *Psicosintesi: Armonia della Vita;* Edizioni Mediterranee, 1966, p. 17. Translated by Peter Roche de Coppens.

11: *Ibid.,* p. 42-43.

12: *Ibid.,* pp. 43-44.

13: *Ibid.,* pp. 59-60.

14: *Ibid.,* pp. 77.

15: *Ibid.,* p. 78.

16: *Ibid.,* p. 79.

17: *Ibid.,* p. 80.

18: *Ibid.,* p. 83.

Chapter 5: **Visionary Unfoldment**

1: Assagioli, Roberto; *Psychosynthesis: A Manual of Principles and Techniques;* Viking Press, 1971, p. 144.

2: Assagioli, Roberto; "Transpersonal Inspiration and Psychological Mountain Climbing;" Psychosynthesis Research Foundation, 1973, p. 3.

3: *Ibid.,* p. 6.

4: *Ibid.,* p. 8.

5: "Symbols of Transpersonal Experiences;" Psychosynthesis Research Foundation, 1969, pp. 5-14.

6: Roszak, Theodore; *Unfinished Animal;* Harper & Row, 1975, pp. 19-20.

7: *Ibid.,* p. 87.

8: *Ibid.,* p. 89.

9: *Ibid.,* p. 93.

Chapter 6: **The Opening of the Intuition**

1: *What We May Be; op. cit.,* pp. 221-222.

2: *Ibid.,* pp. 223-224.

3: "Transpersonal Inspiration and Psychological Mountain Climbing;" *op. cit.,* pp. 6-7.

4: *Ibid.*, p. 7.

5: *Ibid.*, pp. 7-8.

6: *What We May Be; op. cit.*, p. 225.

7: *Ibid.*, pp. 225-226.

8: *Ibid.*, p. 224.

9: *Ibid.*, p. 224.

10: Unpublished Essays and Articles, MGMA, first year set V, pp. 7-8.

11: *Ibid.*, pp. 11-12.

12: *Ibid.*, pp. 12-13.

Chapter 7: **The Descent of the Light: Personal Christmas**

1: *What We May Be; op. cit.*, p. 86.

2: *Ibid.*, p. 91.

Chapter 8: **Armageddon: The Last Great Inner War**

1: Aivanhov, Omraam Mikhael; *La Clef Essentielle pour Resourdre les Problemes de l'Existence;* p. I. Translated by Peter Roche de Coppens.

2: *Ibid.*, p. VII.

3: *Ibid.*, pp. 18-20.

4: *Ibid.*, pp. 31-34.

5: *Ibid.*, pp. 37, 48-51.

6: *Ibid.*, p. 41.

7: *Ibid.*, pp. 42-45.

8: *Ibid.*, pp. 57, 65, 74.

9: von Durckheim, Karlfried Graf; *Daily Life as Spiritual Exercise;* Harper and Row, 1972, p. 14.

10: Barnwell, F. Aster; Unpublished Works.

11: *Ibid.*

Chapter 9: **Resurrection: Personal Easter**

1: Aivanhov, Omraam Mikhael; *L'Arbre de la Connaissance due Bien et du Mal;* Collection Izvor 210, p. 21. Translated by Peter Roche de Coppens.

2: *Ibid.*, p. 35.
3: *Ibid.*, p. 40.
4: *Ibid.*, p. 49.
5: *Ibid.*, pp. 61-62.
6: *Ibid.*, p. 67.
7: *Ibid.*, p. 74.
8: *Ibid.*, p. 76.
9: *Ibid.*, pp. 77-80.
10: *Ibid.*, p. 97.
11: *Ibid.*, pp. 103-106.
12: *Ibid.*, pp. 111-112.
13: *Ibid.*, p. 113.
14: *Ibid.*, pp. 159, 165.

Bibliography

Assagioli, Roberto. *Psicosintesi: Armonia della Vita.* Roma: Edizioni Mediterranee, 1966.

—————*Psychosynthesis: A Manual of Principles and Techniques.* New York: Viking Press, 1971.

—————*The Act of Will.* New York: Viking Press, 1973.

—————*Le Vie dello Spirito.* Roma: Guiseppe Filipponio, 1974. Under Nom de Plume "Considerator."

"Symbols of Transpersonal Experiences." New York: Psychosynthesis Research Foundation, 1969.

"Transpersonal Inspiration and Psychological Mountain Climbing." New York: Psychosynthesis Research Foundation, 1973.

"Psychosynthesis: Height Psychology." New York: Psychosynthesis Research Foundation, 1974.

Unpublished Essays and Articles. Peter Roche de Coppens Library

Aivanhov, Omraam Mikhael. *Oeuvres Completes.* Vols. I-XXVIII. Frejus, France: Editions Prosveta, 1980-84.

—————*La Clef Essentielle pour Resourdre les Problemes de l'Existence.* Vol. XI.

—————*Vers une Civilization Solaire.* Collection Izvor 201, Frejus, France: Editions Prosveta, 1980.

—————*L'Homme a la Conquete de sa Destinee.* Collection Izvor 202.

—————*Noel et Paques dans la Tradition Initiatique.* Collection Isvor 209

—————*L'Arbre de la Connaissance du Bien et du Mal.* Collection Izvor 210.

—————*La Liberte, Victoire de l'Espirit.* Collection Izvor 211.

——————*La Lumiere, Esprit Vivant.* Collection Izvor 212.

——————*Nature Humaine et Nature Divine.* Collection Izvor 213.

——————*Les Secrets de Livre de la Nature.* Collection Izvor 216.

Barnwell, F. Aster. *The Meaning of Christ for Our Age.* St. Paul, Minn.: Llewellyn Publications, 1984.

——————*The Two Wings of an Eagle.* To be published.

——————*The Path of Process.* To be published.

Denning, Melita and Philips, Osborne. *The Magical Philosophy.* St. Paul, Minn.: Llewellyn Publications, 1974-79 (Vols I-V).

von Durckheim, Karlfried Graf. *Daily Life as Spiritual Exercise.* New York: Harper and Row Perennial Library, 1972.

——————*Hara, Centre Vital de l'Homme.* Paris: Le Courrier du Livre, 1968.

——————*Exercises Initiatiques dans la Psychotherapie.* Paris: Le Courrier du Livre, 1968.

——————*Le Maitre Interieur.* Paris: Le Courrier du Livre, 1970.

Emmanuel, R. *Les Cents Visages de l'Amour.* Paris: Editions R. Andre.

——————*L'Homme Face au Fantastique.* Paris: Dervy-Livres, 1971.

——————*Reconciliation avec la Vie.* Paris: Dervy-Livres, 1971.

——————*Pleins Feux sur la Grece Antique: La Mythologie vue par ses Ecoles de Mysteres.* Paris: Dervy-Livres, 1973.

——————*Les Floralies de l'Esprit.* Paris: Dervy-Livres, 1976.

Ferrucci, Piero. *What We May Be: Techniques for Psychological and Spiritual Growth.* Los Angeles: Tarcher, 1982.

Fortune, Dion. *The Esoteric Orders and Their Work.* London: The Aquarian Press, 1955.

Grey, William G. *The Ladder of Lights.* London: Helios Books, 1968.

—————*Inner Traditions of Magic.* New York: Weiser, 1970.

—————*A Self Made by Magic.* New York: Weiser, 1976.

—————*An Outlook on our Inner Western Way.* New York: Weiser, 1980.

—————*The Tree of Evil.* New York: Weiser, 1984.

Halevi, Shimon ben Z'ev. *Tree of Life.* New York: Weiser, 1971.

—————*Adam and the Kabbalistic Tree.* New York: Weiser, 1974.

—————*A Kabbalistic Universe.* New York: Weiser, 1977.

Keutzer, Carolin S. "Transpersonal Psychotherapy: Reflections on the Genre." *Professional Psychology: Research and Practice.* 1984. Vol. 15, No. 6, 868-883.

Nightingale, Earl. *Tapes.* Collection held by Peter Roche de Coppens.

Regardie, Israel. *Twelve Steps to Spiritual Enlightenment.* Dallas, Tex.: Sangreal Foundation, 1969.

—————*The Philosopher's Stone.* St. Paul, Minn.: Llewellyn Publications, 1970.

—————*The Middle Pillar.* St. Paul, Minn.: Llewellyn Publications, 1970.

de Coppens, Peter Roche. *Spiritual Man in the Modern World.* Washington, D.C.: University Press of America, 1976.

—————*The Nature and Use of Ritual.* Washington, D.C.: University Press of America, 1976 and 1979.

—————*Spiritual Perspective.* Washington, D.C.: University Press of America, 1970.

—————*Spiritual Perspective II: The Spiritual Dimension and Implications of Love, Sex, and Marriage.* Washington, D.C.: University Press of America, 1980.

—————*The Nature and Use of Ritual for Spiritual Attainment.* St. Paul, Minn.: Llewellyn Publications, 1985.

—————*Practical and Living Christianity.* To be published.

—————*The Invisible Temple.* St. Paul, Minn.: Llewellyn Publications, 1987.

de Ropp, Robert. *Warrior's Way: The Challenging Life Games.* New York: Delta, 1979.

—————*The Master Game.* New York: Delta, 1968.

Rossner, John. *The Psychospiritual Roots of Christian Gnosis.* St. Paul, Minn.: Llewellyn Publications, to be published.

—————*From Ancient Magic to Modern Science: Recovering the Primordial Tradition.* St. Paul, Minn.: Llewellyn Publications, to be published.

—————*The Primordial Tradition and Contemporary Spiritual Experience.* St. Paul, Minn.: Llewellyn Publications, to be published.

Roszak, Theodore. *Unfinished Animal.* New York: Harper & Row, 1975.

Sedir. *Quelques Amis de Dieu.* Paris: Amities Spirituelles, 1954.

—————*Les Forces Mystiques et la Conduite de la Vie.* Paris: Amities Spirituelles, 1956.

—————*Les Guerisons du Christ.* Paris: Amities Spirituelles, 1956.

de Souzenelle, Annick. *Le Symbolisme du Corps Humain.* Paris: Editions Dangles, 1984.

Vivier, Robert. *Delivrez-nous du Mal: Antoine le Guerisseur.* Paris: Bernard Grasset, 1936.

STAY IN TOUCH

On the following pages you will find listed, with their current prices, some of the books and tapes now available on related subjects. Your book dealer stocks most of these, and will stock new titles in the Llewellyn series as they become available. We urge your patronage.

However, to obtain our full catalog, to keep informed of new titles as they are released and to benefit from informative articles and helpful news, you are invited to write for our bi-monthly news magazine/catalog. A sample copy is free, and it will continue coming to you at no cost as long as you are an active mail customer. Or you may keep it coming for a full year with a donation of just $2.00 in U.S.A. ($7.00 for Canada & Mexico, $20.00 overseas, first class mail). Many bookstores also have *The Llewellyn New Times* available to their customers. Ask for it.

Stay in touch! In *The Llewellyn New Times'* pages you will find news and reviews of new books, tapes and services, announcements of meetings and seminars, articles helpful to our readers, news of authors, advertising of products and services, special money-making opportunities, and much more.

The Llewellyn New Times
P.O. Box 64383-Dept. 677, St. Paul, MN 55164-0383, U.S.A.

•   •   •

TO ORDER BOOKS AND TAPES

If your book dealer does not have the books and tapes described on the following pages readily available, you may order them direct from the publisher by sending full price in U.S. funds, plus $1.00 for handling and 50¢ each book or item for postage within the United States; outside USA surface mail add $1.50 per item postage and $1.00 per order for handling. Outside USA air mail add $7.00 per item postage and $1.00 per order for handling. MN residents add 6% sales tax.

FOR GROUP STUDY AND PURCHASE

Because there is a great deal of interest in group discussion and study of the subject matter of this book, we feel that we should encourage the adoption and use of this particular book by such groups by offering a special "quantity" price to group leaders or "agents".

Our Special Quantity Price for a minimum order of five copies of APOCALYPSE NOW is $29.85 Cash-With-Order. This price includes postage and handling within the United States. Minnesota residents must add 6% sales tax. For additional quantities, please order in multiples of five. For Canadian and foreign orders, add postage and handling charges as above. Credit Card (VISA, MasterCard, American Express, Diners' Club) Orders are accepted. Charge Card Orders only may be phoned free ($15.00 minimum order) within the U.S.A. by dialing 1-800-THE MOON (in Canada call: 1-800-FOR-SELF). Customer Service calls dial 1-612-291-1970. Mail Orders to:

LLEWELLYN PUBLICATIONS
P.O. Box 64383-Dept. 677 / St. Paul, MN 55164-0383, U.S.A.

THE NATURE AND USE OF RITUAL
by Dr. Peter Roche de Coppens

The New Age is not a time or place, but a *new state of consciousness*. To bring about this new consciousness, we need a viable source of revelation and teaching that gets to the heart of our Being and Reality: a way of living and seeing that leads to a gradual, organic and holistic (or 'holy') transformation of the present consciousness and being.

The basic aim of this book is to render explicit the essence of this process of *bio-psycho-spiritual* transformation in terms of our own indigenous Spiritual Tradition, which we can find in the very basic Christian Prayers and Documents.

Perhaps at no time in history has the need for new consciousness been greater — if indeed we are to survive and fulfill our destiny and the Divine potential that is seeded within each person.

At no time has the opportunity been greater, for access to the highest esoteric knowledge, the most refined spiritual technology, is now available to bring about the transformation of consciousness on a massive scale—only if each of us accepts this goal as our personal responsibility.
0-87542-675-1, 229 pages, softcover, illus.   **$9.95**

THE INVISIBLE TEMPLE
By Peter Roche de Coppens

The Invisible Temple is not a building or location. It is not a particular congregation of people. It *is* wherever there is a focal point for spiritual energy. It is located where that energy is generated, amplified and transformed for whatever purpose is needed. In other words, The Invisible Temple exists for us when we become a spiritual light generator.

In the tradition of Regardie's *The Middle Pillar*, this book shows how you can generate, transform and amplify spiritual energy. But it goes further by showing how this can be done with a group of people, making a spiritual light generator that is almost beyond comprehension!

Filled with illustrations and exercises, this book gives occult techniques for spiritual attainment within a largely mystic Christian framework (but with constant reference to other traditions to show the universality of the techniques themselves). It can easily be used by Christians, Jews, Pagans and any others on a spiritual path. The structure of the book is also Qabalistic, and the symbols and rituals were actually drawn from a Qabalistic Tradition. Here is a book that can truly help you to live magically!
0-87542-676-X, 300 pages, illustrated, 5¼" x 8," softcover.   **$9.95**

THE INNER WORLD OF FITNESS
Melita Denning

Because the artificialities and the daily hassles of routine living tend to turn our attention from the real values, *The Inner World of Fitness* leads us back by means of those natural factors in life which remain to us: air, water, sunlight, the food we eat, the world of nature, meditation, sexual love and the power of our own wishes—so that through these things we can re-link ourselves in awareness to the great non-material forces of life and of being which underlie them.

The unity and interaction of inner and outer, keeping body and psyche open to the great currents of life and of the natural forces, is seen as the essential secret of *youthfulness* and hence of radiant fitness. Regardless of our physical age, so long as we are within the flow of these great currents, we have the vital quality of youthfulness: but if we begin to close off or turn away from those contacts, in the same measure we begin to lose youthfulness.

0-87542-165-2, 240 pgs., 5¼ x 8, softcover. $7.95

THE ART OF SPIRITUAL HEALING
by Keith Sherwood

Each of you has the potential to be a healer; to heal yourself and to become a channel for healing others. Healing energy is always flowing through you. Learn how to recognize and tap this incredible energy source. You do not need to be a victim of disease or poor health. Rid yourself of negativity and become a channel for positive healing.

Become acquainted with your three auras and learn how to recognize problems and heal them on a higher level before they become manifested in the physical body as disease.

Special techniques make this book a "breakthrough" to healing power, but you are also given a concise, easy-to-follow regimen of good health to follow in order to maintain a superior state of being.

0-87542-720-0, 209 pages, softcover, illus. $7.95